THE

PRINCIPLES AND PRACTICAL OPERATION

OF

SIR ROBERT PEEL'S ACT OF 1844

EXPLAINED AND DEFENDED:

Second Edition.

WITH ADDITIONAL CHAPTERS ON MONEY,
THE GOLD DISCOVERIES, AND INTERNATIONAL EXCHANGE;

AND

A CRITICAL EXAMINATION OF THE CHAPTER
"ON THE REGULATION OF A CONVERTIBLE PAPER CURRENCY"
IN MR. J. S. MILL'S

Principles of Political Economy.

BY

R. TORRENS, Esq., F.R.S.

LONDON:
LONGMAN, BROWN, GREEN, LONGMANS, AND ROBERTS.
1857.

PREFACE TO THE SECOND EDITION.

To the First Edition of my Tract on the Principles and Practical Operation of Sir Robert Peel's Act of 1844, the following additions have been made:—

I. A preliminary chapter on the question, whether Bank-notes, immediately convertible into coin, should be placed, in common with coin, in the category of money; or, in common with cheques and bills of Exchange, in the category of credit?

II. A critical examination of the chapter on "The Regulation of a Convertible Paper Currency," in Mr. J. S. Mill's "Principles of Political Economy."

III. On the effect of the new supplies of gold upon the Australian currencies.

The length to which the reply to Mr. Mill has been carried demands some explanation.

As the mechanical divisions of employment com-

pel us to receive the greater part of our physical
enjoyments from the hands of others, so the intel-
lectual divisions of employment constrain us to
receive the greater portion of our opinions from the
minds of others. The chemist adopts the Newtonian
theory on the authority of the mathematician; the
mathematician receives the discoveries of Davy and
Faraday without repeating the experiments by
which they were realized. On intricate questions,
requiring long and patient investigation, the opinions
even of the most enlightened class will have their
origin, in a majority of cases, not in knowledge but
in faith. Hence, principles are received upon trust,
doctrines become creeds, authority is implicitly followed, and blind leaders are enabled to assume the
guidance of the blind. Now the high and deserved
reputation, as a profound and original thinker, which
Mr. Mill has hitherto maintained, and the influence
which his authority might be calculated to exert on
public opinion, render it essential, at the present
juncture, to inquire how far he may be qualified to
decide upon the merits of the Act of 1844.

Mr. Mill has chosen to place himself on the same
platform with Mr. Tooke; and he cannot fairly
expect from the audience whose suffrages he seeks, a
reception more favourable than that which is given
to his co-candidate for a seat in the Parliament of
Fame. Having identified himself with Mr. Tooke,
his authority upon questions of monetary science

cannot be greater than the authority of Mr. Tooke. In estimating either, we estimate both.

What, then, is the authority of Mr. Tooke in monetary science? One of his admirers—Mr. Lawson, the author of "Money and Morals"—has raised him to the level of Adam Smith, has hailed him as the "Second Father of English Political Economy," and has boldly affirmed that his discoveries are " the immoveable pillars upon which a true science of money must be built." But what is the authority of Mr. Lawson? Mr. Lawson himself informs us that his first lessons in monetary science were derived from those "brilliant pamphlets in which the experience of the banker put on the scientific precision and polish of the schools." Nevertheless, through some unaccountable perversion of taste, after having drank at the pure well of science undefiled, he sought the muddy waters of a surface drainage, and turned from Overstone to Tooke. It is difficult to conceive how the pupil of Lord Overstone could have become the disciple of Mr. Tooke. But his conduct in embracing the " immoveable pillars," and in regarding Mr. Tooke as " the Second Father of Political Economy," although unaccountable, was not without an example. Mr. Mill had previously pronounced Mr. Tooke to be the highest authority in monetary science; and had erected his theory of currency on the basis of the "immoveable pillars." The stability

of the structure must depend upon the strength of
the foundation. The weight of Mr. Mill's authority
must be measured by the solidity of the basis on
which it is supported.

Now, the discoveries which in the estimation of
Mr. Mill have placed Mr. Tooke at the head of
monetary science, are as follows:—

I. That a rise of prices is not preceded, but followed, by an increase in the amount of the circulation.

II. That an increase in the amount of the circulation is the effect, and not the cause, of a rise of
prices.

It will be seen upon a close examination, that
these vaunted discoveries, instead of being "immoveable pillars" on which a true science of money must
be built, are but mirage-formations which a ray of
analysis dissolves. · In a country not possessing
mines of the precious metals, and having its currency
regulated on the principle of metallic variation, as,
under the provisions of the Act of 1844, the currency of this country is actually regulated, the only
way in which the circulation can be increased is, by
the action of a favourable foreign exchange. But
a favourable exchange cannot be preceded by a rise
of prices, for the obvious reason that a rise of prices
above the ordinary level causes an adverse exchange,
an exportation of bullion, and a contraction of the
circulation. Neither is it possible that an increase
in the amount of the circulation should be the effect

and not the cause of an increase of prices, for the obvious reason, that an increase in the amount of the circulation is the effect of a fall of prices below the par of exchange level. An abundant harvest renders the proportion of commodities greater in this than in other countries, lowers prices, and causes a favourable exchange, an influx of bullion, and an expansion of the circulation. On the other hand, a deficient harvest renders the proportion of commodities to money less in this than in other countries, raises prices, and causes adverse exchange, export of bullion, and contraction of circulation. So long as the currency shall be regulated, as it now is, on the principle of metallic variation, so long will its amount be governed by the state of the foreign exchanges; and so long as the amount of the currency shall be regulated by the exchanges, so long will a fall of prices be the antecedent of an expansion of the circulation, and a rise of prices the antecedent, not of an increase, but of a diminution of the circulation. Mr. Tooke's vaunted discoveries are nothing more than gratuitous assumptions contrary to fact.

There is, however, a conceivable, I will not say a possible, process under the operation of which an increase in the amount of the circulation may become the effect of a rise of prices, and the theory of Mr. Tooke and Mr. Mill be verified by fact. This process I will endeavour to explain.

A certain school of physiologists account for the existence of mites and maggots by the assumption that they make themselves. Now, in order to account for the existence of an extension of the circulation under a rise of prices and adverse exchanges, we have only to generalize the reasoning of these physiologists, and to assume that sovereigns and bank-notes possess the property of spontaneous generation. According to this physiological theory, when a rise of prices occurred in England, dust and nuggets in California and Australia would dig themselves out of the earth, and crush themselves out of quartz, navigate themselves across the ocean, and, entering the Royal Mint, stamp themselves into standard coin. At the same time, paper would begin to manufacture itself, to write upon itself promises to pay, and to glide noiselessly and ghostlike into the till of the Bank.

Let no one attempt to dispose of this theory of currency self-creation by an incredulous smile. It should be regarded as a sound and legitimate theory. The hypothesis upon which it rests is the only conceivable hypothesis by which it can be made apparent that an extension of the circulation is the effect of a rise of prices. If the theory of currency self-creation be inconsistent with fact, Mr. Tooke's discoveries must be false. But the discoveries of the highest authority in monetary science—discoveries which have placed their author on a level with Adam

Smith, and the correctness of which, as affirmed by
Mr. Mill, has been established by elaborate research
"on the mere ground of history," cannot be false.
The discoveries cannot be controverted. The
"pillars" are "immoveable." An hypothesis which
accounts for phenomena which no other conceivable
hypothesis can account for, must be received as legitimate. Will any disciple of Mr. Tooke venture to
overthrow the authority of his master by denying
that coin and bank-notes possess the property of self-
creation?

That a brilliant but superficial writer—a dealer
not in the science, but in the poetry of money—like
the author of "Money and Morals," should have
become a disciple of Tooke after having been a pupil
of Overstone, is a fact which it is sufficiently difficult
to account for. How then can we comprehend the
melancholy fact, that the author of "Unsettled
Questions in Political Economy" should have de-
scended to the rank of those who receive as an established truth a pretended discovery which cannot be
explained or defended, except upon the absurd
assumption that currency creates itself? The solution of the problem may perhaps be found in the
following passage, borrowed from a letter breath-
ing the true spirit of advanced and enlightened
science, addressed by Mr. Norman to Sir Charles
Wood.

"The expansion of the various sciences, which has

taken place within a few years, cannot fail to give rise to serious reflection. Life is now not long enough to enable even the most studious man to obtain a reputation for encyclopædical knowledge; and the time is rapidly approaching, when renown in the ranks of learning and philosophy will be reserved for him who has mastered one of the many branches into which each separate science will then have divided itself. This tendency to expansion, though more peculiarly remarkable in physics, is also very conspicuous in the moral sciences. Adam Smith probably thought that he had left but little of the domain of Political Economy unexplored; the public attention, however, is now engrossed by questions connected with one single branch of the science, viz., the currency, so refined and intricate as to have eluded his observation."*

These views are at once original and instructive. Although we have some splendid specimens—a Bacon, a Franklin, and a Brougham—of omni-scientific genius, yet it is nevertheless true, that " renown in the ranks of learning and philosophy will be reserved for him who has mastered one of the many branches of science." Life is not now long enough to permit a single mind to produce both a Novum Organum and a Wealth of Nations. A gifted grasper after fame, who might have been a Bacon, or who might have been an Adam Smith, essaying to be

* Letter to Sir Charles Wood, p. 7.

both, is neither. The deepest waters shallow as they spread.

In the volume which I now offer to the public nothing has been added to my former animadversions on the doctrines advanced by Mr. James Wilson. This has not arisen from any want of consideration for that able—and on questions not connected with the regulations of the currency—enlightened economist. I have hitherto regarded him as being, from his superior abilities, his access to official records, and his influential position, as the most formidable opponent of the Act of 1844; and I should have continued so to regard him, had not the errors into which, as I conceive, he has fallen, received an elaborate refutation from an authority whose access to the sources of official information is equal to his own, and who has investigated them with greater diligence, accuracy, and success. Mr. Arbuthnot, who had been private secretary to Sir Robert Peel during the passing of the Act of 1844, and to Sir Charles Wood during the discussions on the Act in 1847, has met Mr. Wilson on his own ground, and vanquished him with his own weapons. He has refuted the statistical arguments against the Act of 1844 as effectually as similar arguments against the resumption of cash payments were refuted forty years ago by Ricardo's reply to Bosanquet. In disposing of the statistical arguments against the Act, Mr. Arbuthnot has rendered invaluable service. As he has justly stated in his recent publication, " without doubt statistical returns are invaluable to those who carefully study them.   But the information they afford consists only of a great accumulation of facts; and as zealous controversialists have ever been prone to seize the first fact that suits their argument, so with the growth of statistics has sprung up the disposition to misapply them. Few have the opportunity of threading their way through the mass of details which it is necessary to investigate in order to detect a single error; and some service may be rendered to truth and science by a patient inquiry into assertions and arguments which, though lightly adopted, are often specious and captivating. The object I have in view is to unravel the tangled web of fallacious reasoning, which is the consequence, if not the cause, of a careless and confident reference to facts, and to prove that candid investigation will confirm the principles on which the Act of 1844 is founded."*

In relation to the principles which I have attempted in this volume to explain and to defend, I have many obligations to acknowledge. First, and mainly, to Lord Overstone. His Lordship, in one of his lucid expositions at the Political Economy Club, propounded the doctrine, that the separate functions of issue and of discount should be intrusted to separate departments. The importance of such a separation flashed upon me. My mind dwelt upon it, and

* Sir Robert Peel's Act of 1844 Vindicated, p. 7.

the further explanations and suggestions of his Lordship convinced me that the principle of the separation of departments supplied the requisite complement to the theory of currency, as established by Adam Smith and Ricardo ; and that the practical application of that principle to the Bank of England was the only. means by which the convertibility of the circulation could be permanently secured.

In common with all who have taken an interest, whether commercial or scientific, in the state of the currency, I am largely indebted to Mr. M'Culloch. His Treatise upon Money, appended as a note to his edition of " The Wealth of Nations," is the most complete and correct which has hitherto been given to the public. The " Commercial Dictionary " has brought the results of science into every counting-house in the kingdom. His latest labour—that of collecting and editing the tracts and letters of Lord Overstone—has rendered an invaluable service to the cause of truth and science. The volume, comprising these admirable productions, will be preserved in the libraries of science, in juxtaposition with the " Report of the Bullion Committee," and with the congenial productions of Horner, Huskisson, and Ricardo, on the maintenance of our metallic standard.

To Mr. Pennington—one of the deepest and most original thinkers of our day—I was early indebted for valuable communications on subjects connected with banking, and with the regulation of the currency, on the principle of metallic variation.

To the very able and instructive "Letter on the Monetary Pressure of 1847," addressed to Sir Charles Wood by Mr. Hubbard, I am indebted for the explanation I have given of the process by which the vast foreign debt incurred at that period was liquidated, without endangering the convertibility of the currency.

To the chapters on money, and the regulation of convertible paper currency, now presented to the public, I have appended a reprint of a tract entitled "The Economists Refuted," which I published in 1808. It has been out of print for many years; and I may be expected to assign some reason for its present reappearance.

It is now very generally admitted that Adam Smith's explanation of the manner in which foreign trade enriches a nation was at once incomplete and erroneous. His theory of the benefit conferred by commerce was, that it afforded an outlet for the surplus produce of a country, and enabled the capital employed in effecting international exchanges to replace itself with a profit; and in accordance with this theory, he contended that the home trade is more advantageous than the foreign, because two capitals are replaced with a profit in the home trade, and only one in the foreign. Assuming the truth of this very imperfect and erroneous theory,

Mr. Spence contended, in a very ingenious publication entitled "Britain Independent of Commerce," that the decrees of the first Napoleon, excluding this country from commercial intercourse with continental Europe, could have no effect in diminishing the wealth of the nation, inasmuch as the capital disengaged from the foreign trade might be employed, with equal advantage, in extending the home trade. This doctrine was zealously expounded by Mr. Cobbett, and became very popular. Under these circumstances, I published "The Economists Refuted;" and explained, I believe, for the first time, the nature and extent of the advantages derived from trade. The principles which I propounded in "The Economists Refuted," Mr. Ricardo subsequently adopted in his great work on Political Economy and Taxation; and as my previous publication had been long out of print and forgotten, it was generally believed that it was reserved for Mr. Ricardo to correct the erroneous theory of Adam Smith, and to show that the benefit resulting from foreign trade consists of the increased production created by international divisions of employment.

I had shown that the increased production thus created was divided, in variable proportions, between the countries exchanging their respective productions. In the view of the question presented by Mr. Ricardo, the advantages derived from foreign trade were confined to only one of these countries. Mr.

Ricardo's error was corrected by Mr. Pennington; and the correction, if I rightly remember, was adopted by Mr. James Mill in the third edition of his " Principles of Political Economy."

Such are the circumstances which have induced me to reprint, without alteration, my long-forgotten tract. My object in doing so is, to claim my right to be regarded as the original propounder of so much of the corrected theory of the nature and extent of the advantages derived from foreign trade as may be comprised in the view which I ventured to present to the public forty-nine years ago.

ROBERT TORRENS.

February, 1857.

CONTENTS.

CHAPTER I.

B

SIR ROBERT PEEL'S ACT OF 1844.

CHAPTER I.

ON THE PRELIMINARY QUESTION, WHAT IS MONEY?

THE select committee of the House of Commons on Banks of Issue, which was appointed in 1840, and over which Sir Charles Wood presided with such pre-eminent ability, devoted no inconsiderable portion of its time and attention to the inquiry, "what consti-tutes money?" On this elementary question the most opposite opinions were maintained. While Lord Overstone and Mr. Norman maintained, in accordance with the principles established by Adam Smith and Ricardo, that the money or currency of the country consists of coin and of bank-notes immediately conver-tible into coin, Mr. Tooke and his followers advanced the novel doctrine, that bank-notes immediately con-vertible into coin do not possess the properties of money; that they are, in common with cheques and bills of exchange, mere forms of credit; and that to subject them to any legislative restrictions different

from those which are equally applicable to the other
forms of credit with which they coincide, is erroneous
in theory, and mischievous in practice.   As the main
arguments of the opponents of the Act of 1844 are based
upon the doctrine thus advanced by Mr. Tooke, a preliminary inquiry into its validity seems desirable before
proceeding to an explanation of the principles and
practical operation of the Act.

Before we can frame a correct definition of the
term money, we must have a distinct perception of
the several uses to which money is applied, and of
the specific attributes with which it is invested. Now,
money is employed as a measure of value, as a
medium of exchange, and as an ultimate equivalent,
by the tender and acceptance of which obligations are
legally discharged and transactions finally closed; and
the attributes with which it is invested are derived from
the laws and usages of the civilised world.   Hence it
is apparent that any object which is appropriated either
by positive law, or by usage having the force of law;
to these several uses, comes under the denomination
of money; and that no objects or things save those
which have been so appropriated can be included
under that denomination.   Money may therefore be
defined as consisting of those tangible objects which
can be passed from hand to hand, which law, or usage
having the effect of law, has established as measures
of value, as media of exchange, and as equivalents,
by the tender and acceptance of which payments are
made and transactions finally closed.

It is universally admitted that the several functions
comprised in this definition are fulfilled by coin of
legal weight and fineness. A pound sterling, which

is nothing more than 123,274 grains of standard gold manufactured into coin, is both by law and usage the standard unit by which, in this country, the value of property is measured. In the transactions of the market, coin of standard weight and fineness will at all times and under all circumstances be accepted as a medium of exchange and transfer. A payment in coin releases the debtor or purchaser from all further claim; and an acceptance of payment in coin, while it deprives the creditor of all further claim, places in the hands of the vendor the full equivalent for which he had contracted. Whether regarded as the measure of value, as the medium of exchange, or as the ultimate equivalent by which transactions are finally closed, coin is money under its most perfect form. But coin, eminently qualified as it is to perform the functions, does not possess exclusively the character of money. That character is derived, not from intrinsic qualities, but from imparted qualities; and the law and usage which impart it to the precious metals, may equally impart it to other objects.

Are Bank-Notes Money?

Is a bank-note, convertible into coin upon demand, money? A brief consideration of this question will convince us that it must be answered in the affirmative. A Bank of England note, while convertible into coin, is a legal tender; is equivalent to coin, can be directly passed from hand to hand, and performs, in all the transactions of the market, functions identical with those which are performed by the coin it represents. If coin is a measure of value, bank-notes immediately convertible into coin, and conse-

c

quently equivalent to coin, must also be a measure of value. The measurement is performed with equal accuracy, whether we employ the metallic standard itself in the form of coin, or a perfect equivalent of that standard in the form of convertible notes. Again, as regards a medium of exchange, the convertible note is in some respects superior even to coin. In all the larger transactions of the market, bank-notes are employed, to the entire exclusion of coin, as the medium or instrument by which property is transferred. The same may be said with respect to the third essential characteristic of money—the power of effecting payments, discharging engagements, and finally closing transactions. In point of fact and experience, this essential function of money is in all transactions of magnitude performed more conveniently and more extensively by bank-notes than by coin. They have been made legal tender—they have been monetised by Act of Parliament. They measure value, they effect exchanges, and they finally close transactions, as perfectly as coin. That merchants and bankers should have deliberately denied to them the character of money, would have been altogether incredible, had not the marvellous fact been proclaimed and recorded by themselves.

Having ascertained that our bank-note circulation, while convertible into coin, is invested by law and usage with the attributes of money, we proceed to consider whether these attributes are possessed by paper currencies not convertible into coin. Mr. Tooke, while affirming that convertible notes are not money, contends that inconvertible notes issued by Government are money. According to this doctrine, convertibility demonetises, while inconvertibility monetises paper currencies. Previous to the suspension of cash payments, the notes of the Bank of England were not money, because they were convertible into coin ; after the suspension they became money, because they were not convertible into coin ; and on the resumption of cash payments, the power of converting them into coin again divested them of the character of money.

Although the advocates of the Tookean principle involve themselves in a *reductio ad absurdum* with regard to convertible currency, they are perfectly correct in attributing to inconvertible currencies the character of money. To contend that an inconvertible currency does not possess the essential attributes of money, would be tantamount to maintaining that, during the suspension of cash payments, England was destitute of a measure of value, of a medium of exchange, and of an equivalent by which transactions could be closed. Numerous and strange as are the fallacies into which, in dealing with the currency, superficial thinkers are liable to fall, yet this ultra-absurdity no one could be found to uphold. During the suspension of cash payments, the bank-note was employed to measure values, to effect exchanges, and to close transactions ; and therefore, during the suspension of cash payments, the inconvertible bank-note possessed the essential attributes of money.

It has been a prevalent opinion, that money consists exclusively of the precious metals ; and that a paper circulation, whether issued by Government or by banks, whether convertible or inconvertible into coin, so far from possessing the essential attributes of

c 2

money, is nothing more than a convenient form of
credit by which the employment of actual money is
economised. This opinion is altogether erroneous.
The precious metals are money, not on account of any
essential properties inhering in themselves, but because the laws and usages of the civilised world have
invested them with the functions of measuring value,
of facilitating exchanges, of adjusting balances, and of
finally fulfilling contracts. But the same law and
usage which confers on the precious metals the character of money, might equally confer that character
on any other object. In point of fact, various other
objects, corn, cattle, bars of iron, nails, and shells,
have in different ages, and in different countries, been
invested by law or by usage with the attributes of
money.

Are Cheques Money?

When a portion of the money of the community
is transferred from the desks of its owners to
banks, a new instrument of exchange is called into
existence, namely, cheques drawn against deposits.
Are then cheques money? The question must be
answered in the negative. Cheques do not increase
the quantity of money; they merely transfer from
one individual to another a portion of the money
already in existence. The person who draws a
cheque upon his banker for one hundred pounds, will
have, as soon as the cheque is honoured, less money
by one hundred pounds, while the receiver of the
cheque will have more money by one hundred pounds
than before. The drawer cannot have less until the
instant upon which the receiver shall have more; the

receiver cannot have more until the instant upon which the drawer shall have less. The act of transfer cannot by possibility increase the quantity transferred.

The first recipient of a cheque, instead of himself presenting it at the bank for payment, may pass it as a medium of exchange and purchase to a third party, the third to a fourth, the fourth to a fifth, and so on indefinitely. It may, therefore, be asked, does not the cheque during this process supersede the use of coin and bank-notes, and thus increase the quantity and become a component part of the money of the community?

The question must be answered in the negative. Although cheques dispense with the passing of money from hand to hand, they do not constitute any portion of its actual amount. They perform no function save that of ordering a payment. The drawer of a cheque for one hundred pounds must have a deposit or a credit for one hundred pounds with the bank on which he draws; and it is the deposit or the credit, and not the cheque, which effects the payment. Without the deposit, the cheque would be worthless; without the cheque, the deposit would possess the same purchasing and paying power as before. The only function which can be performed by the cheque is that of relieving the owner of the deposit from the inconvenience and loss of time he might suffer by going to the bank and drawing out his money in person.

It is quite true that when the owner of a deposit pays a cheque to A., A. may pay it to B., B. to C., and so on indefinitely; and that on each successive transfer of the instrument, a purchase may be effected. But then it is equally true that the owner of the

deposit might have drawn out bank-notes of equal
amount, that he might have paid the notes to A., that
A. might have paid them to B., and B. to C.; and that
on each successive transfer of the cash, a purchase
might have been effected. So far the two series of
transactions exactly coincide. But there is, nevertheless, an important and a characteristic difference
between them. The successive purchases effected by
the bank-notes are final purchases; each successive
transaction between the buyers and the sellers is
closed, not to be reopened, on the instant on which
the notes are paid. On the other hand, the series of
purchases effected by the cheque are not final purchases. Until the cheque is honoured, the whole of
the transactions of which it was the medium remain
unsettled; and should it be dishonoured, each successive vendor would have a claim upon his purchaser
for its amount. Cheques possess a purchasing, but
not a paying power. The paying power resides in
the deposits, the order for the payment or transfer of
which the cheques convey; and should this order not
be carried out by an actual payment or transfer, the
transactions, of which they were the medium, cannot
be finally closed until the amount of the dishonoured
instrument shall be paid in coin, or bank-notes.

It may be objected that, in the great majority of
cases, cheques are not dishonoured, and that, with
the exception of rare and unimportant cases, the
transactions of which they are the medium, are finally
closed, and the essential functions of money effectually
performed. To this objection the conclusive answer
is, that so long as the honouring of a cheque is not
an accomplished fact, but a future probability, so

long do the transactions, of which it was the medium, remain unsettled, and the essential function of money unperformed. And further, when a purchase has been made by a cheque drawn against an actual deposit, in a solvent bank, the closing of the transaction is effected, not by the transfer of the cheque from the purchaser to the vendor, and from the vendor to the bank, but by the transfer of a deposit in the books of the bank, or by a payment in coin or notes over the counter.

It is of the essence of money, that it closes transactions between payer and payee. It is the ultimate paying power; and it is self-evident that nothing can be an ultimate paying power which must itself be ultimately paid—that no transaction can be finally closed by the acceptance of a medium which must itself become the subject of a future transaction. Bank of England notes would not be money if the transactions, of which they are the medium, remained open until they were converted into coin. Coin would not be money if it could not be a final payment until it had been exchanged for bullion. *A fortiori*, cheques cannot be money so long as it is necessary to the final closing of the transactions into which they enter that they should themselves be paid by the banks upon which they are drawn.

Are Bills of Exchange Money?

Bills of exchange are extensively employed in commercial transactions, both domestic and foreign. Although these instruments possess, in common with cheques, the property of facilitating exchanges, yet in other respects there is a marked distinction between them. A cheque represents money in deposit, available on demand; a bill of exchange represents money in expectation, available at some future period. No public trader, no private individual, could make a purchase by a cheque unless he had a deposit or bank credit to the amount of the purchase; but a trader, although not possessing any command of money, or even any property whatever, might effect purchases to an indefinite extent, trusting for the ·means of ultimate payment to resales, it might be of the very goods for which his acceptances had been given.

Again, the drawer of a cheque was the possessor of a deposit, with which, had he chosen to draw it out, he might have made a direct money payment. The receiver of a cheque on a solvent bank, becomes entitled to draw out coin or notes, and acquires the option of making a direct and immediate money payment. The same may be said with respect to the successive parties through whose hands the cheque may pass. It is obvious, therefore, that the intervention of the cheque cannot, by possibility effect a greater number of payments than those which might have been equally effected by drawing out in coin or notes the deposit against which it was drawn, and by passing the cash from hand to hand in direct payments. It is altogether different with respect to bills of exchange. These deferred credit instruments may effect an indefinite number of purchases, which, without their intervention, could not be effected at all. For example, A., a wholesale merchant in London, wishes to purchase goods to the amount of one thousand pounds, from B., a manufacturer in Manchester. C., a retail dealer in London, desires to replenish his stock by purchasing such goods from A. To effect these transactions by the intervention of money, A. must have one thousand pounds to hand to B., and C. one thousand pounds to hand to A. But neither A. nor C. has one thousand pounds either in hand or in deposit, and consequently, these several purchases and transfers cannot be effected by coin, or by bank-notes, or by cheques drawn against deposits. But they may be effected by the instrumentality of bills of exchange, A. may give to B. a bill for one thousand pounds, payable at ninety days after date, while C. may give to A. a bill for a like sum, at eighty days, and may effect, in the course of the period it has to run, retail and ready-money sales to the amount of one thousand pounds. At the expiration of the eighty days, he passes the cash in discharge of his bill to A., who passes it in discharge of his acceptance to B., and thus, goods to the amount of one thousand pounds are transferred from the producer to the merchant, from the merchant to the retailer, and from the retailer to consumers, although neither producer, merchant, nor retailer had, at the commencement of their sales and resales, the command of any money capital whatever. It will be apparent from this example, that through the instrumentality of bills of exchange, an indefinite number of sales and resales of the same identical goods may be effected between producers, merchants, and retailers, without any payment in coin, or notes, or transfer of deposits, until the retailer has finally disposed of them for cash to the consumer; and it will be equally apparent that, until the retailer should have been paid for the goods, in cash, by the consumers, none of their successive transactions could be finally closed.

The fact that bills of exchange effect an indefinite number of purchases, without requiring the intervention of coin, or bank-notes, or transfers, until the bills are finally paid by their acceptors, is urged by a certain school of economists as a practical proof that they perform, equally with bank-notes, the functions of money, and that if bank-notes are to be placed in the category of money, bills of exchange must also be so placed. But these reasoners exclude from their consideration the all-important fact that when purchases are effected by bank-notes the transactions are final, and require no subsequent adjustment. This establishes the essential difference between purchases effected by bank-notes, and purchases effected by bills of exchange. The former are final the instant the bank-notes have been accepted; the latter are not final until the bills of exchange have arrived at maturity, and are paid by their acceptors.

When it is asked, Are bills of exchange money? it must be answered, that one of the essential properties of money they unquestionably possess in a pre-eminent degree. They are, next to the precious metals, the most extensive media of exchange. By the universal concurrence of the commercial world, they are the levers by which all the larger masses of property are moved. But do they possess the other attributes which are also essential to the character of money?

Are they measures of value? Are they ultimate equivalents? These questions must be answered in the negative. The measurement of value and the final fulfilment of engagements are functions of money which bills of exchange do not, and which, under our existing laws and usages, they cannot perform. A bill of exchange cannot be employed to measure the relative value of other things, because it possesses the peculiar property of varying in value in relation to itself. A bank-note for one hundred pounds payable to bearer on demand, while variable in value in relation to commodities, is invariable in relation to itself: it represents one hundred of our monetary units on the day of its issue, and one hundred of these monetary units it continues to represent throughout the whole period during which it may remain in circulation. A bill of exchange for one hundred pounds, on the contrary, does not represent one hundred units of our money until the day on which it falls due ; and during the whole of the period it has to run, its value, in relation to one hundred monetary units or pounds sterling, varies from day to day, and with every variation in the rate at which it can be discounted. In estimating the value of any species of goods, I may say that they are worth a hundred sovereigns, or a hundred pound bank-note; but I cannot say that they are worth a bill of exchange for one hundred pounds, because I cannot know what number of pounds sterling or monetary units the bill may be actually worth until I shall have first ascertained the period which it has to run, and the rate of discount at which it can be turned into cash. Before

it can be employed as a measure of value, it must
itself be measured.   It is obvious that bills of exchange perform no species of measurement whatso-
ever. They are not measures, but subjects of measurement.   Their value cannot be brought into
comparison with that of commodities, because their
worth in relation to commodities remains utterly
unknown, and can be only vaguely guessed at until
the value both of themselves and of the commodities
for which they are offered have been previously estimated in coin or in bank-notes. And further still,
they cannot become even the medium of transfer
until the value both of themselves and of the property
to be transferred has been previously estimated and
expressed in coin or in bank-notes. ·   ,

While a bill of exchange is not, and from its very
nature cannot be, employed as a measure of value, it
records upon its face that it is not an ultimate equivalent. It does not effect an actual payment; it merely
promises that an actual payment shall be made at a
future day; and the transactions in which it is concerned cannot be closed until that promise is fulfilled.
A bill of exchange is a purchasing, but not a paying
power. A purchase effected by coin or by bank-
notes, or by the transfer of a deposit, is a ready-
money purchase, while a purchase effected by bills of
exchange is a credit purchase.   The person who
buys goods with coin, or bank-notes, effects at one
and the same time both a purchase and a payment:
a person who buys with bills of exchange makes a
purchase, and at the same time incurs a debt.

Mr. Tooke and his followers have avoided the error

of classing bills of exchange in the category of money ;
but they fall into another error not less opposed to
philosophical arrangement and to the methods of
science, that of classifying bills of exchange and notes
payable upon demand under the common denomina·
tion of "forms of credit;" and of jumping to the
inference that the common denomination denotes common properties. While contending that bills of exchange do not perform the functions of money, they at
the same time maintain that bank-notes payable in
coin being, like bills of exchange, mere forms of
credit, perform no functions other than those which
are equally performed by bills of exchange.

In science as well as in religion, fanatics are to be
found who refuse to receive the evidence of their
senses. A person so wedded to a currency theory, or
so deficient in analytical power as to be unable to
perceive a distinction between the bill of exchange
which he offers for discount and the bank-notes advanced to him by the discounter, is not, in relation to
his espoused opinions, within the pale of ratiocination.
But the logical errors analogous to those which he
regards as legitimate, when in accordance with his
preconceived notions, may possibly be seen in their
native absurdity when exemplified in relation to other
objects. Were a mathematical student, after classing
triangles and quadrangles under the common denomination of right-lined figures, to assume as his premise
that the common denomination expressed common properties, and to conclude that the number of angles was
the same in each, the most implicit believer in the
Tookean faith could not fail to perceive the palpable
fallacy of the reasoning and the palpable absurdity of

the conclusion.   Yet not less palpably fallacious is the logic, and not less obviously absurd is the conclusion of the currency fanatic who places bank-notes in the same category with bills of exchange, and infers that the former possess no properties other than those possessed by the latter.

We have already remarked that bills of exchange possess a purchasing but not a paying power, while convertible notes possess both.   But this distinction, however striking and important, is not the only distinguishing difference between the attributes and the operations of the two instruments.   When an additional amount of bills of exchange is brought into the discount market, the *demand* for money capital is increased; and when an additional amount of bank-notes is brought into the discount market, the *supply* of money capital is increased.   In the former case the rate of interest is raised, in the latter it is lowered. Again, an increased supply of bills of exchange creates, while an increase in the supply of bank-notes relieves, a pressure on the money market.   That theoretical inquirers substituting generalisation for analysis, and mistaking partial similitude for complete identity, should fall into the error of placing bank-notes in the same category with bills of exchange, may admit of explanation ; but how merchants and bankers, practically acquainted with the actual operation of the money market, should fall into such a misconception, passes comprehension.

Objections answered.

Two distinguished economists, M. Michel Chevalier and Mr. J. S. Mill, controvert the views presented in the preceding pages, and contend that bank-notes, convertible into coin, instead of belonging, in common with coin, to the category of money, belong, in common with cheques and bills of exchange, to the category of credit. The high authority of these eminent and influential teachers of the science demands from a candid searcher after truth, that the doctrine which they inculcate upon this elementary and important question should be either admitted or refuted. I accept the alternative, and venture on the refutation.

M. Chevalier, in a course of lectures on political economy, delivered in his capacity of professor at the College of France, denies that the bank-note should be included in the definition of money. He says, "Those persons who insist that the bank-note should be held to be money, have never been able to trace a line of demarcation, which should be clear and distinct, between a bank-note and a bill of exchange."

We submit to the candid consideration of this eminent economist, that the daily phenomena of the money market establish between bank-notes and bills of exchange a line of demarcation so clear and so distinct, that we cannot, without a departure from the most obvious rules of scientific classification, place them in the common category of credit. The line of demarcation may be traced through examples innumerable.

First. In a period of commercial pressure, one merchant has one thousand pounds in Bank of England notes, another has one thousand pounds in bills of exchange, and both have immediate payments to make to the amount of nine hundred pounds. Does not the simple statement of this case bring out into prominent relief the broad line of demarcation between notes and bills? Can it be doubted, either on commercial or on logical grounds, that the owner of the notes has the immediate command of a thousand pounds in money, and that the owner of the bills has not? Is it not a fact that the former can make an immediate and final payment to the amount say of nine hundred pounds, and that the latter, before he can effect such a payment, must discount his bills in order to obtain the requisite amount in notes? and is not the existence of this fact a practical demonstration that in the actual transaction of the market, banknotes are held to be money, and that bills of exchange are not?

Second. A merchant, with a slender amount of original capital, engages in extensive transactions upon credit. He has accepted bills falling due to the amount of twenty thousand pounds, and he holds bills not yet arrived at maturity to the amount of twenty-two thousand pounds. Were there no distinction between bills of exchange and bank-notes—did they possess in common the power of effecting final payments—this merchant could meet his engagement, and realise ample profit on his credit transactions. But the line of demarcation between these instruments is so marked, their properties are so dissimilar, that if the merchant cannot sell his bills for notes, he goes into the 'Gazette' instead of continuing a profitable trade.

Third. Let us pass from individual example to the general discount market. What is it that gives existence to that market? nothing on earth save the broad line of demarcation between bank-notes and bills of exchange. Did the two classes of instruments equally possess the power of satisfying engagements, · the holder of immature bills would tender them to his creditors in liquidation of his debts, and receive a final discharge. Wherefore is this course not adopted? Why does the merchant go into the discount market and sell his bills for notes in order to hand them over in discharge of his engagements? Simply because bank-notes have the property not possessed by bills of exchange, of finally closing transactions; in other words, because bank-notes are held to be money both legally and commercially, while bills of exchange are not held to be money either commercially or legally.

Fourth. What are the circumstances which constitute ease, and what the circumstances which constitute pressure in the money market? What are the specific causes which at one period render money superabundant, and what the opposite causes which at another period intensify pressure into panic? The true answers to these questions place in the clearest light the line of separation between bank-notes and bills of exchange. There is ease in the money market when the amount of bills seeking discount bears the ordinary proportion to the amount of bank-notes at the command of the discount houses; and there is pressure when the proportion of bills to notes exceeds the ordinary proportion. Money is a drug in the market when the amount of bills offered to the discount houses

D

in exchange for bank-notes is less than the amount of
bank-notes which the discount houses have to invest
in mercantile securities. Pressure is intensified into
panic when the supply of bills seeking discount exceeds the amount of loanable bank-notes in the hands
of discounters to such an extent that advances cannot
be obtained upon mercantile securities of the first
class. To analyse the phenomena of the discount
market, is to trace out the broadest possible line of
demarcation between bank-notes and bills of exchange.

Fifth. Bills of exchange are discounted in bank-
notes. To discount a bill of exchange is to advance
a loan for the period during which the bill has to run.
Bank-notes constitute the loan; the bill of exchange
constitutes the security on which the loan is lent. To
maintain that there is no line of demarcation between
bank-notes and bills of exchange is the same thing as
to assert that there is no difference between loans and
securities. Surely this is a proposition which M. Chevalier will not, on reconsideration, reaffirm.

This accomplished economist objects to the characteristic difference as regards paying power which I
have sought to establish between bank-notes and bills
of exchange, upon the legal ground that when a bill
of exchange is not indorsed by the buyer, the seller
must hold himself to be paid, although the bill should
not be discharged when due. He says, "One of the
" writers who has taken the most prominent part in
" maintaining the opinion I am here combating, is
" Colonel Torrens, who seems to have thought that
" he had discovered a characteristic difference between

" the bank-note and the bill of exchange in saying
" that a payment was made .once for all from the
" moment the seller had received bank-notes from the
" buyer ; but that if the buyer made the payment by
" a bill of exchange emanating from himself or a third
" party, he would nevertheless not be absolved from
" the debt until the bill of exchange having become
" due, should have been paid ; in other words, the
" bank-note would possess for the discharge of a debt
" a special power which would be wanting to this bill
" of exchange. The distinction which Colonel Tor-
" rens thus draws is not admissible.

" It might at once be objected that if the bill of
" exchange has been remitted in blank, that is, with-
" out the indorsement of the buyer, the seller must
" hold himself to be paid, although the bill should
" not be discharged when due. But we will set aside
" this observation, however strongly it serves to
" prove the assimilation of the bank-note to the blank
" indorsed bill of exchange."

Now the fact here stated does not even in the
slightest degree invalidate the position that bank-
notes do, and that bills of exchange do not, possess
the power of final payment. Neither does it even in
the slightest degree prove the assimilation of the two
instruments. According to the law of England, and,
as I believe, according to the usage of the whole mercantile world, it is most rare that the bill of exchange
is so received by a seller, as to preclude him, either by
means of the buyer's endorsement, or otherwise, from
recovering from the buyer, if the bill be not paid by
the acceptor, or person primarily liable.

M. Chevalier's assumption that a bill of exchange blank indorsed is assimilated to a bank-note, because a payment effected by it has the same effect as a payment by a bank-note, in absolving the buyer from further liability, is altogether erroneous. Instead of similarity, there is the widest dissimilarity between the two transactions. A payment by a bank-note is a full and final payment, not only as respects the buyer, but also as respects the seller, the former being absolved from all further liability, and the latter receiving the full equivalent for which he had contracted. Even were it true that a payment made by a bill of exchange not indorsed by the buyer, and ultimately dishonoured, should be held to be a final payment as regards the buyer, it would as regards the seller be no payment at all. He would not have received the equivalent for which he had contracted. He would have thrown his goods away. From an inadvertent, perhaps from a fraudulent, failure on the part of the purchaser to comply with the requirements of the law in regard to the circulation of bills, the vendor would have parted with his property for nothing. The transaction would have been the subject of a transfer but not of a *bonâ fide* purchase; and should the purchaser who obtained property in ex- -change for an instrument made valueless by his own neglect to fulfil the requirement of law, be an honest man, he would indemnify the vendor by a *bonâ fide* payment in coin or in bank-notes.

In seeking to prove the assimilation of the bank-note to the blank indorsed bill of exchange, M. Chevalier has failed to recognise the facts that Bank

of England notes are by Act of Parliament legal
tender; that they constitute exclusively the note
circulation of the London money market; that
London is the central money market, not only of
the United Kingdom, but to no inconsiderable extent of the continent of Europe and of the commercial world; and that all bills of exchange,
whether domestic or foreign, drawn upon or accepted by London houses, are finally paid in Bank
of England notes, or by transfers of deposits, representing, indifferently, Bank of England notes and
coin.

The line of demarcation between provincial bank-
notes and bills of exchange is not so broad as between
Bank of England notes and bills of exchange, inasmuch as provincial notes are not legal tender. Nevertheless, there is no assimilation between provincial
notes and bills of exchange blank indorsed. The
vendor who accepts payment in the notes of a provincial bank, while that bank is solvent, receives
an actual and full equivalent which he cannot lose
unless he should, through his own neglect, have delayed to demand payment until after the bank had
become insolvent. The receivers of the notes of a
provincial bank which does not stop payment until
after they have had reasonable time to present the
notes for payment, obtain, as far as the payers of the
notes are concerned, the fulfilment of their contract,
and cannot suffer loss except through their own subsequent and wilful neglect. M. Chevalier will not fail
to perceive, that in so far as regards the practical
operations of the two instruments, under the law and

usage of the English money market, there can be no
assimilation between provincial bank-notes and bills
of exchange blank endorsed.

Mr. J. S. Mill concurs with M. Chevalier in denying to bank-notes the character of money, and in
placing them with bills of exchange in the common
category of credit.   It would have been scarcely
reasonable to expect, that the eminent French economist should have attained a perfect mastery of the
usages and laws of the English money market.   It is
otherwise with respect to our own distinguished logician.   Those who had hailed with deserved admira-
tion his earlier publication " On Unsettled Questions
in Political Economy " will have read, with a species
of melancholy disappointment, the chapter on the
Regulations of Currencies in his more recent publication " On the Principles of Political Economy."

Mr. Mill, while failing with M. Chevalier to recognise the fact, that Bank of England notes have been
made legal tenders, and monetised by Act of Parliament, concurs with him in denying to bank-notes
the properties of money; and in classing them in
common with bills of exchange in the category of
credit.   He adopts this classification, not upon the
ground that bills of exchange possess, equally with
bank-notes, the power of closing transactions, but
upon the ground that they possess, equally with bank-
notes, the power of influencing prices.   He says:—

" Some high authorities have claimed for bank-
" notes, as compared with other modes of credit, a
" great distinction in respect to influence on price than
" we have seen reason to allow :—a difference, not in

" degree but in kind. They ground this distinction
" on the fact, that bank-notes have the property in
" common with metallic money, of finally closing the
" transactions in which they are employed; while no
" other mode of paying one debt by transferring
" another has that privilege."

In this passage Mr. Mill does not controvert, but,
on the contrary, appears fully to admit the facts, that
bank-notes do, and that bills of exchange do not
possess the power of finally closing engagements.
Neither does he controvert the position, that the
power of finally closing engagements is an essential
attribute of money. He does not touch—he does not
even approach—the argument he undertakes to refute.
That argument, expressed in the syllogistic form
he so zealously defends, runs thus : all instruments of
exchange which law or usage has invested with the
power of finally closing engagements are money : bank-
notes are both by law and by usage invested with
this power : therefore bank-notes are money. The
eminent logician will scarcely hesitate to admit, that
in dealing with this argument, it was incumbent upon
him to show, either that the power of finally closing
engagements is not an attribute of money, or that
bank-notes have not been by law and usage invested
with that power. He does neither. He passes to
propositions, which, whether true or false, have no
bearing upon the question at issue. He says, the
authorities to whom he is opposed, " claim for bank-
" notes, as compared with other modes of credit, a
" greater distinction as regards influence on price than
" we have seen reason to allow." But distinction as

regards influence on price is not that for which his
opponents contend. What they contend for is, distinction as regards power of finally closing engagements, and this essential distinction Mr. Mill has seen
no reason to disallow. On the contrary, he appears
to regard it as an admitted fact.

CHAPTER II.

ON THE ORIGIN, OBJECT, AND OPERATION OF THE ACT OF 1844.

THE question regarding the renewal or repeal of the Bank Charter Act of 1844 will be brought under the consideration of Parliament, for final decision, in the course of the present session. It is therefore of the highest importance, that the public should have a clear and distinct perception of the objects which that Act was intended to accomplish ; of the results which it has actually produced ; and of the consequences which its abolition would involve. The acquisition of accurate knowledge on these several points becomes the more indispensably necessary, because there has existed, even amongst intelligent and well-educated persons, an extraordinary contrariety, a perfect chaos of opinion, regarding the measures which ought to be adopted, for the future regulation of the currency. The merchants, bankers, and traders, who signed the London petition, pray for a relaxing power and a double standard. The Glasgow Chamber of Com-

E

merce require an expansion of the circulation by the
issue of one-pound notes by the Bank of England.
Mr. Tooke and his followers, while denouncing the
existing law without suggesting any definite substitute, repudiate the double standard and the one-pound
note.   Mr. Wilson, the able and indefatigable editor
of the ' Economist,' while regarding Mr. Tooke as
the first philosopher of the age, and denouncing the
principles of the Act of 1844, scandalises his master
by proposing that these same principles shall be so
extended as to embrace a one-pound note circulation, to the amount of 30,000,000l.   The accomplished and eloquent author of the ' History of the
French Revolution,' and his admirers, would furnish
us with paper money, of which the standard should
be, not a definite quantity of gold, but the indefinite
quantity of the paper money itself, which might constitute the market price of a definite quantity of gold.
The economists of the Birmingham school recommend
the more intelligible course of altogether dispensing
with the incumbrance of a standard; while Lord
Ashburton, whose opinions must ever be received
with respectful consideration, would have escaped
from the periodical revulsions resulting from an ill-
regulated paper currency, by causing the whole of our
bank-note circulation to be issued against bullion held
in deposit, as in the case of the Bank of Hamburgh.—
The principles of monetary science, as they were propounded by Adam Smith and Mr. Ricardo, and as
they have been extended and applied by Lord Overstone and Mr. Norman, present a clue by the guidance
of which we may hope to wind our way through the
mazes of this otherwise bewildering labyrinth.

Origin of the Act of 1844.

The Act of 1819 declared that the notes of the Bank of England should be once more convertible into gold, upon demand, at the rate of 3*l*. 17*s*. 10½*d*. per ounce. But although the law imposed upon the directors of the Bank the liability of payment in gold, upon demand, it did not give to the public any adequate security that the Bank should have the means of discharging that liability. The furnishing of these means was left to the discretion of the directors; and it was expected that their practical knowledge of the causes of the fluctuations in the money market would enable them to provide against all emergencies, by maintaining a sufficient reserve of bullion. The result has proved that, in intrusting the convertibility of the currency to the discretion of the Bank directors, Parliament committed a mistake.

In 1824 and 1825, a speculative phrenzy pervaded the country, which resulted in the contraction of foreign loans to the amount of 55,000,000*l.*, and in the formation of 626 joint-stock companies, whose projects would have required a capital of more than 372,000,000*l*. As the inevitable reaction approached, the directors of the Bank adopted no timely precaution for the protection of their coffers. Although the drain from their reserve of gold commenced in October 1824, yet it was not until the autumn of the following year that the continued abstraction of their treasure induced them to contract their issues. The contraction had been delayed to so late a period, and was now so sudden, particularly amongst the country.

issuers, that while it arrested the exhaustion caused by an adverse exchange, it created a new and more unmanageable drain from domestic panic. Credit was prostrated; seventy banking establishments were swept away in less than six weeks; the gold in the Bank was drained out to within a very few thousand pounds; and the country was brought "within a few" "hours of a state of barter."

Well might the late Lord Liverpool declare, in reference to the conduct of the Bank in 1825, " that " a system was wanted, which would exclude the " possibility of discredit and bankruptcy, by pre- " venting every individual, or association, from " issuing notes without an adequate guarantee.". Every variation in the seasons, and every adverse turn of the foreign exchanges, from whatever cause arising, furnished additional proof that the Legislature had committed a mistake in delegating to the directors of the Bank of England the important function of providing the means of securing the convertibility of the currency. The proof of their utter incapacity for the performance of this function reached the culminating point in 1839. The scarcely-credible extent of their mismanagement is well described by Mr. Tooke, in the third volume of his 'History of Prices.'

From February 1838, to January 1839, the average amount of bullion in the Bank was little less than 10,000,000*l.*, the highest amount being 10,126,000*l.*, and the lowest 9,336,000*l.*; while the average amount of liabilities, including circulation and deposits, was about 30,000,000*l.* This was a safe position as regarded the public interest, and it ought to have been a satisfactory position as regarded the peculiar interests of the Bank proprietary. When their stock of bullion, yielding no interest, was at the highest amount of 10,126,000*l.*, the portion of their circulation, which they had invested in securities, bearing interest, amounted to 22,838,000*l.* But the interest upon 22,838,000*l.* of securities was regarded as an inadequate compensation for the loss of interest upon 10,126,000*l.* of bullion; and the directors decided upon diminishing this loss, by reducing their reserve of specie. After lowering the rate of discount from 5 to 4 per cent., they resorted to the anomalous proceeding of shipping gold to the United States of America. Mr. Tooke might well remark that the adoption of this extraordinary course " forms an " additional instance of the impatience which, as " exhibited on former occasions, the Bank seems to " have felt, whenever there has been an accumulation " of treasure in its coffers, and of its resort to some " unusual effort to get rid of it." While the directors sought to reduce their reserve of treasure below the safe proportion to their liabilities, causes were manifesting themselves in combined operation, which presented signals not to be mistaken of an impending drain upon their coffers, requiring strong precautionary measures of counteraction. Large importations of foreign corn; the combination entered into by the banks and planters of the United States, for withholding the supplies of cotton from the manufacturers of this country; and the derangement of commercial credit on the continent of Europe, requiring importations of the precious metals into France, Belgium, the interior of Germany, and Russia;—these several causes, acting in combination, required on the part of the Bank directors vigilance to perceive the indications of danger, and promptness and firmness of purpose to apply timely and effectual precautionary measures. And what were the preparations which the Bank directors adopted for meeting the coming storm? They are narrated, not by an adverse witness, but by the very advocate who has pleaded most strenuously for intrusting the management of the circulation to the discretion of the Bank.

" Notwithstanding the increase of securities; not-
" withstanding the steady advance in the market rate
" of interest; notwithstanding the increasing mani-
" festation of the progress of circumstances requiring
" counteraction by a reduction, which could now be
" effected only by means more forcible and incon-
" venient than would have been requisite a few
" months sooner; and above all, notwithstanding that
" there had been a diminution of upwards of two
" millions of treasure, the Bank, instead of taking
" warning, and retracing its steps by a forcible
" reduction of its securities, actually, on the 28th of
" February 1839, issued a notice offering advances
" to the 23rd of April, on similar securities, at the
" same low rate (3½ per cent.), as by the notice of
" November preceding. And notwithstanding an
" advance was still in progress in the market rate of
" interest, with a declining state of our foreign
" exchanges, and a consequent increasing drain upon
" its treasure, such was the apparent utter uncon-
" sciousness on the part of the Bank of approaching
" disturbance in the circulation, and still more of
" circumstances threatening its stability, that not a
" single step appears to have been taken which had

" even the semblance of an attempt at precaution,
" until the 16th of May following, when a notice was
" issued raising the rate of interest to 5 per cent."*

As it could not have been the intention of the
directors of the Bank of England to create a necessity
for a suspension of cash payments, their management
of the currency during the year 1839 appears altogether unintelligible. In May their securities were
increased from 20,700,000l., their amount in the
previous December, to 23,500,000l., while their
treasure was reduced from 9,300,000l. to 5,100,000l.
In September, the securities had increased to
25,900,000l., while the bullion had sunk to 2,800,000l.
A loan of 2,000,000l., obtained from the banks of
France, averted a suspension of cash payments.

The exhaustion of the treasure of the Bank of
England to within a few thousand pounds in 1825,
the imminent peril to which it was exposed in 1839,
and its escape from insolvency through the discreditable expedient of a loan from France, had now made
it manifest that, if the convertibility of the bank-note
was to be maintained, the management of the circulation must be committed to other hands than those of
the directors of that establishment. A Select Committee of the House of Commons upon Banks of Issue,
over which Sir Charles Wood presided with eminent
ability, was appointed in 1840. The witnesses
examined before this Committee comprised individuals
who combined the most extensive practical knowledge of the money market, with a perfect acquaint-
ance with the principles of monetary science. Upon
the main object of inquiry—the means of averting the

* History of Prices, vol. iii. p. 64.

danger of a suspension of cash payments — the evidence of Lord Overstone and of Mr. Norman was an appropriate supplement to Mr. Ricardo's evidence before the Bullion Committee on the resumption of cash payments; and the Act of 1844 was introduced by Sir Robert Peel, as the complement of his Act of 1819.

Objects and Provisions of the Act of 1844.

The objects of the complementary Act of 1844 were to secure the convertibility of the bank-note, to impart to the circulation a greater degree of steadiness than that which it possessed under the former law, and to cause our mixed circulation of coin and bank-notes to expand and contract, as it would have expanded and contracted under similar circumstances had it consisted exclusively of coin. In order to effect the accomplishment of these objects, the Act provided that the Bank of England should be divided into two separate departments, the one exclusively confined to the issue, circulation, and payment of notes, and the other to the ordinary business of a bank of deposit and discount; that the amount of notes payable to bearer on demand, uttered by the issue department of the Bank of England, unrepresented by bullion in deposit, should be limited to 14,000,000*l.*; that the amount of such notes uttered by the provincial banks throughout England and Wales should be limited to 8,000,000*l.*; and that the excess of the bank-note circulation, over and above these fixed amounts, should be issued against coin and bullion held in deposit.

These provisions of the Act of 1844 were framed

in conformity with the following principles:—1st, That the amount of a strictly convertible currency, which it is practicable to maintain, is determined, not by legislative enactments or by banking regulations, but by the natural law of equilibrium by which the precious metals are distributed throughout the commercial countries of the world: 2nd. That when from any temporary cause the amount of a mixed currency of coin and convertible notes exceeds the amount determined by the law of equilibrium, the level is restored by the return of a portion of the note circulation upon the issuers, in exchange for specie : 3rd. That when from any temporary cause the amount of a mixed currency of coin and convertible paper falls short of the amount determined by the law of equilibrium, the ordinary level is restored by an influx of the precious metals. From these principles it follows, as a necessary corollary, that when that portion of the note circulation which may be issued upon securities, is fixed below the amount to which, under the law of equilibrium, the currency must conform, that portion of the bank-note circulation will not be returned upon the issuers in exchange for treasure ; and that, except in cases of drain from domestic panic, there will always be retained in the coffers of the issuing body, a reserve of gold equal to the difference between the fixed amount of the circulation unrepresented by bullion, and the actual amount determined by the law of equilibrium.

Such being the principles upon which the Act was founded, it became incumbent upon those who were concerned in framing it, to ascertain, by a careful reference to past experience, the minimum amount below which, in recent times, the circulation of the Bank of England had never been reduced. Now, it appears by the Report of the Select Committee upon Banks of Issue (1840, App. 12), that in December 1839, the notes of the Bank of England were reduced to 15,532,000*l.* But this return included the Bank Post Bills, amounting to about 800,000*l.*, which are not included in the returns upon which the Act is founded. Therefore, making the proper reduction of this amount, the bank-notes in circulation in December 1839 (Bank Post Bills not included), must have been 14,732,000*l.* To this amount, however, must be added the amount of notes which, had the separation of functions then existed, the banking department would have been obliged to keep in its till to meet the demands of its depositors. This amount we know has been reduced on a recent occasion to 2,000,000*l.* Therefore, putting the two sums together, we shall have—

Bank-notes in circulation, December 1839 . . . . £14,732,000

Amount of notes required, as banking reserve 2,000,000

Total notes which would have been out of the issue department in December 1839 . . £16,732,000

Upon these grounds the framers of the Act assumed that, under a separation of functions, the minimum amount below which the notes out of the issue department could not be reduced under the action of the foreign exchanges, was 16,732,000*l.*: that if

14,000,000*l.* were permitted, under the provisions of
the Act, to be issued without a corresponding reserve
of bullion, the minimum amount which would be
required to be issued against bullion held in deposit
would be 2,732,000*l.*; and that as the reserve of
bullion could not, under such circumstances, be ever
reduced below 2,732,000*l.*, the convertibility of the
circulation would be secured.

The correctness of these views have been fully
borne out by experience. Theory has been verified
by fact. In so far as regards the perfect convertibility of the circulation, the anticipations of the
framers of the Act have been realised. From the
period at which its provisions came into operation up
to the present time, the reserve of bullion in the issue
department of the Bank has never been reduced below
8,000,000*l.*

*The Operation of the Act has been to impart to the Circulation
a greater degree of steadiness than that which it possessed
under the former law.*

While the prime object of the Act—the maintenance of sufficient reserve of bullion in deposit to
secure the certain convertibility of the bank-note—
has been thus completely accomplished, there has
been no undue contraction of the currency below the
amount at which it is practicable that an immediately
convertible currency should be maintained. The
limitation of the issues of the Bank upon securities to
14,000,000*l.*, so far from unduly contracting the
circulation below the level determined by the law of
metallic equilibrium, has prevented those temporary
depressions below that level which were of periodical

occurrence under the former system. We have seen, that when the Bank possessed the power of unlimited issue, it was in the habit of exercising that power in the face of an adverse exchange, until the exhaustion of its treasure compelled it to provide for its own safety by forcing down the circulation below the level of equilibrium, until the influx of bullion under a favourable exchange replenished its coffers. Under the existing law, the reflux and efflux of treasure has been automatic, obeying the natural law of equilibrium; and all forced and artificial elevations and depressions, above and below the level common to the commercial world, have been obviated. It will be seen, by a reference to the 'Gazette' returns, that during the year 1847—a year of unexampled difficulty —the highest amount of the gross circulation out of the issue department was 27,500,000*l*., and the lowest 22,500,000*l*.; and that the highest amount of the circulation out of the banking department was 20,800,000*l*., and the lowest 17,900,000*l*. But in 1836 —a year of greatly-mitigated pressure—the highest amount of the Bank circulation was 19,100,000*l*., and the lowest 16,700,000*l*.; while, during the monetary pressure of 1839, the highest amount was 19,300,000*l*., and the lowest 15,800,000*l*. The difference between the highest and lowest amount of the circulation in 1839 was 3,500,000*l*., while in the far more disastrous year of 1847, the difference between the highest and the lowest amount of the circulation out of the banking department and in the hands of the public has been only 2,900,000*l*.

But the difference in the extent of the fluctuation which occurred during the periods under review, does not tell the whole of the story in favour of the Act of 1844. In October 1839, the period of greatest contraction during that year of comparatively mitigated pressure, when the circulation, seven days' bills included, was reduced to 16,800,000*l.*, the reserve of bullion which was then applicable to the payment, both of the circulation and of the deposits, amounted to only 2,500,000*l.* ; while in June 1847, the period of greatest contraction during that year of greatly-aggravated pressure, when the circulation, also including seven days' bills, out of the banking department, amounted to 18,740,000*l.*, there was in the banking department a reserve in coin and notes of 5,600,000*l.* applicable to the payment of the deposits, and in the issue department a reserve in bullion of 9,600,000*l.* applicable to the payment of the circulation.

These figures are most important. They prove, beyond the possibility of doubt or question, not only that the Act of 1844 has secured the convertibility of the note circulation, but that the limitation of the issues of the Bank upon securities to 14,000,000*l.*, while imparting to the circulation a degree of steadiness greater than it before possessed, has had the effect of maintaining the circulation at a higher average level than that which was maintainable under the alternate expansions and contractions of the former law.

Under the operation of the Act the Circulation has expanded, as it would have expanded had it been purely Metallic.

While the primary object of the Act of 1844 was to secure the convertibility of the bank-note circulation, its secondary object was to provide that our mixed currency of coin and notes should at all times be equal in amount, and in value to what would have been under the like circumstances the amount and the value of a purely metallic currency. This secondary object has been fulfilled to the uttermost letter. A reference to the weekly returns published in the 'London Gazette' will show that, from September 1844 (the period at which the Act came into operation) up to the present time, the notes uttered by the issue department, over and above the fixed amount of 14,000,000*l.* uttered upon securities, have been increased or diminished in exact proportion to the increase or diminution in the amount of bullion in its coffers. So far as the amount of the circulation out of the issue department is concerned, the intention of the legislature has been fully accomplished.

It will also be found, upon a reference to the 'Gazette' returns, that the amount of the circulation out of the walls of the banking department has been increased and diminished, exactly as it would have been increased and diminished (other circumstances being the same) had the currency been purely metallic. This will be at once apparent on a consideration of the results which would have followed had the Act, instead of authorising the issue of 14,000,000*l.* upon securities, provided that the whole of the issues of the Bank of England should be represented by bullion in deposit. This provision would have rendered it necessary that the Government debt of 11,015,100*l.* should have been paid to the Bank, and that the directors should have appropriated that sum, with other securities to the amount of 2,984,900*l.*, to the purchase of 14,000,000*l.* of gold in the markets of the world. Under these arrangements the Bank of England would have been assimilated, as suggested by Lord Ashburton, to the Bank of Hamburgh. The bank-note would have been a bullion-note—a certificate for a given amount of gold, not only payable upon demand, but actually in deposit, and would have circulated as bank-money, as is now the case in Hamburgh, and was formerly the case in Holland. The issue department of the Bank would have been converted into a bank of deposit, and nothing more; while the functions and the operation of the banking department would have been left, to all intents and purposes, in the same state, and under the same influences, in which they have actually been left under the existing law.

It is obvious that had the issue department been assimilated to the Bank of Hamburgh, no change in the status of the Bank, or in its action on the money-market, could have been thereby effected, beyond that of causing the 14,000,000*l.* now issued upon securities to be issued against bullion. The aggregate amount of the note circulation, when issued wholly upon bullion, would have expanded and contracted with the influx and efflux of treasure, as the aggregate amount issued upon securities and bullion actually has done. The amount of deposits in the banking department would have increased and diminished under the action of the selfsame causes by which they have increased and diminished under the existing law ; the amount of the reserve of notes, retained to meet the demands of depositors, would have been regulated, as it is now regulated, by the discretion of the Bank directors, and, as a necessary consequence, the proportion of the gross circulation in the hands of the public at large, would have been the same as it hitherto has been.   Let us exemplify these results by a reference to the figures presented in the ' Gazette ' returns.

Had the whole circulation of the Bank of England consisted of bullion notes, represented by gold in actual deposit, the status of the Bank for the week ending on the 7th September 1844, when the said Act came into operation, would have been, with the single exception of the increased amount of bullion, identical with that published in the ' London Gazette ' for that period.   The bullion in the issue department would have been increased from 14,300,000*l.* to 28,300,000*l.* ; the gross amount of the circulation represented by bullion would have been what the gross circulation represented partly by. bullion and partly by securities actually was, namely, 28,300,000*l.* ; while the circulation in the hands of the public would have continued at 20,110,000*l.*, the deposits in the banking department at 12,200,000*l.*, the seven days' bills at 1,030,000*l.*, and the reserve of notes and coin at 9,000,000*l.*

The harvest of 1844 was the largest ever produced in this country ; the season was also favourable throughout Europe and America ; there was a large quantity of old wheat on hand ; and, as the natural consequence of these abundant supplies, the price of wheat in England, from September 1844, to the end of June 1845, averaged about 46*s.* per quarter. While agricultural produce was thus abundant, the state of trade was prosperous in the highest degree. The year 1845 was an unusually busy and profitable one, alike to the capitalist and the labourer, in every branch of production. The quantity of raw cotton imported and retained for consumption in that year was the largest on record. The same may be said of wool. The quantities of cotton, sugar, and tea imported and consumed in the country were also larger than in any other year. The declared value of the principal articles of British produce exported also exceeded that of any previous year; and the aggregate tonnage entered and cleared out from the United Kingdom showed a similar increase. From the conjoint operation of these several causes, from this extraordinary increase in the quantity of vendible commodities, money in this country no longer bore the same proportion to the transactions to be adjusted which it bore in other countries. The necessary consequence was, that a portion of the specie previously retained in other countries passed into this country, until by such new distribution of the metals the proportion of currency to transactions was rendered the same in this as in other countries. The bullion in the issue department rose from 14,300,000*l.*—its amount in April 1844—to 15,800,000*l.* in July 1845; the gross circulation from 28,300,000*l.* to 29,800,000*l.*; the circulation in the hands of the public from 20,100,000*l.* to 20,600,000*l.*; the reserve of coin and notes in the banking department from 9,000,000*l.* to 9,800,000*l.*; the deposits, representing the available capital placed by the public at the disposal of the Bank, from 12,274,000*l.* to 17,371,000*l.*; while the amount of private securities, indicating the extent of the banking

F

facilities afforded to commerce rose from 7,800,000*l.*, their amount in April 1844, to 12,600,000*l.* in June 1845, and to 12,900,000*l.* in the following July. Now it may be regarded as self-evident that the same identical results would have taken place had the circulation consisted of notes wholly represented by bullion in deposit, instead of consisting of notes partly represented by bullion and partly by securities. In one case, as well as in the other, the extraordinary increase in the quantities of vendible commodities must have caused the currency in this country to bear a less proportion to the amount of transactions than in other countries, and have led to an influx of bullion, and to an increase of issues, until the ratio between the amount of currency and the quantity of commodities had been equalized; and in either case the Bank directors would have been influenced by the same identical considerations in determining the respective amounts of their advances, of their securities, and of their reserve. During the increase of productive power which occurred in 1844 and 1845, the status of the Bank, and the incidents of the money market under the existing law, were exactly what they would have been had the whole circulation consisted of bullion-notes represented by an equal amount of gold deposited in the coffers of the issue department.

The exuberant harvest of 1844, and the extraordinary prosperity of manufactures and trade in 1845, caused a large increase in the quantity of vendible commodities, and, as a necessary consequence, in the quantity of that portion of them which constitutes loanable capital; while the general increase of wealth throughout the productive classes diminished the number of necessitous borrowers. The circulation expanded under the continuous influx of bullion, while, from the high state of commercial confidence, a less amount of currency was required to adjust the same amount of transactions as before. These concurrent causes reduced the rate of interest, increased the value of securities, and rendered it more difficult to effect investments at once safe and advantageous for the overflowing amount of available and loanable capital. This excited, as analogous conditions of the money market had too frequently done, a spirit of extravagant and reckless adventure; and the railway mania was the result. Between March and September 1845, joint-stock speculations for the immediate investment of capital were set on foot, involving a larger aggregate amount than had ever before been so invested in this country. The amount, to raise which for railways alone the sanction of Parliament was actually applied for in the following session, exceeded 340,000,000l. And if we include all the other schemes in which scrip, or letters of allotment, were actually selling in the market at a premium in July, August, and September 1845, the amount cannot be estimated at less than 500,000,000l. Now, during the whole of this period of extraordinary excitement, when everybody was buying or selling shares, and while the current rate of interest was only 2½ per cent., the state of the currency with respect to amount and to value, was the same as it would have been had the whole paper circulation been represented by bullion in deposit. The issue of 14,000,000l. upon securities did not reduce the value of the circulation

F 2

below that of the gold into which it was immediately convertible ; neither could the issue of the whole circulation against bullion in deposit have rendered it of higher value than the gold which it represented. All the causes which contributed to excite a spirit of extravagant and reckless speculation and adventure in 1845—the rapid increase in available and loanable capital—the influx of treasure—the consequent expansion of the currency—the increased disposition to lend —the diminished necessity to borrow, incident to a high state of commercial credit—the fall in the rate of interest—the increased value of securities, and the difficulty of effecting investments at once advantageous and secure : all these concurring causes, which have led to excessive speculation under the existing law, would have operated with undiminished force had the Act of 1844 required that the whole circulation should have been issued upon bullion. Under the existing law the spirit of speculation has been neither greater nor less than it would have been under a purely metallic currrency.

Under the operation of the Act the Circulation has contracted, as it would have contracted had it been purely Metallic.

Having traced the operation of the Act of 1844 during a period of prosperity, let us consider its effects under a period of disaster. If the season in 1844 was the most abundant which the country has seen, that of 1846 was the most disastrous which has occurred in modern times. The staple food of one-third of the population perished. Capital to the amount of 25,000,000*l.* was exported in payment for foreign provisions. Other causes of unusual potency concurred in diminishing the national wealth. The failure of the cotton crop in America reduced the supply and enhanced the price of the raw material of our most extensive manufacture. Floating capital to the amount of 1,000,000*l.* a-week was diverted from the production of commodities to the construction of railroads. The history of the commercial world presents no previous example of so great and so sudden a diminution of national wealth as that which occurred in England between June 1845 and December 1847. Let us consider whether this great and sudden diminution of the national resources acted upon the money market, under the provisions of the Act of 1844, as it would have acted had the currency been purely metallic, or had the whole circulation consisted of bullion-notes represented by gold in actual deposit.

In September 1846, the circulation out of the walls of the issue department was 29,800,000*l.*, represented by 14,000,000*l.* of securities, and by 15,800,000*l.* of bullion in deposit; and in January 1847, the circulation was 26,100,000*l.*, represented by 14,000,000*l.* securities and 12,100,000*l.* bullion. Now it is self-evident that had the whole circulation during these two periods been advanced upon bullion, the effect, as far as regards the issue department, would have been identical with that which actually occurred. The bullion-notes, like the existing notes, would have been reduced from 29,800,000*l.* to 26,100,000*l.*; and it is equally evident that, as regards the banking department, the reduction of the circulation from 29,800,000*l.* to 26,100,000*l.* would

have been followed by the same identical results,
whether the circulation had been issued wholly upon
bullion, or partly upon bullion in deposit, and partly
on securities. The substitution in the issue department of 14,000,000*l.* of bullion for 14,000,000*l.* of
securities could not have relieved the directors from
the necessity of keeping in the banking department a
reserve of notes to meet the demands of their depositors; and would have left in undiminished force
the considerations and the influences under which
they adjusted the proportion between the respective
amounts of their reserve and of their liabilities. Had
the substitution been effected—had the whole currency
been metallic in January 1847, when the abstraction
of bullion had reduced the circulation out of the
walls of the issue department from 29,800,000*l.* to
26,100,000*l.*, the directors would have retained, as
they did retain, 5,700,000*l.* of notes in the banking
department to meet the demands of depositors; and,
consequently, the circulation in the hands of the
public have been what it was—20,400,000*l.* Whether
the circulation had consisted of bullion-notes, as at
Hamburgh, or of credit-notes only partially represented
by bullion, as under the existing law, the drain of
treasure which reduced the circulation out of the
issue department from 29,800,000*l.*, its amount on
the 12th September 1846, to 26,100,000*l.*, its amount
on the 30th January 1847, would have equally
allowed the circulation in the hands of the public to
be increased from 20,000,000*l.* to 20,400,000*l.*; and
for the plain and obvious reason, that whether the
circulation had been wholly metallic or only partially
represented by bullion, the Bank directors would

have been at equal liberty to have diminished the reserve of notes in the banking department from 9,800,000*l.* to 5,700,000*l.*

On the 10th April 1847, the bullion in the issue department had diminished from 15,800,000*l.* to 9,200,000*l.*, and the circulation out of that department from 29,800,000*l.* to 23,200,000*l.*; while, in consequence of the diminution of the reserve of notes in the banking department to 2,800,000*l.*, the circulation in the hands of the public continued to be 20,400,000*l.*, being still an excess of 400,000*l.* above the amount of the circulation in the hands of the public in the previous September, when the bullion was 15,800,000*l.*, and the gross circulation 29,800,000*l.* The conduct of the Bank directors in thus reducing their reserve will be considered in the next Section. In this place it is sufficient to remark, that whatever their motives may have been, they would have led to the same identical course of action had the currency been purely metallic, which they actually led to under the existing law. As it is self-evident that the gross circulation, whether wholly or partly represented by bullion in deposit, would equally expand and contract as treasure should flow into or out of the coffers of the issue department, so it is equally self-evident, that under any given amount of the gross circulation, whether wholly or partially represented by bullion, the amount of the circulation in the hands of the public must increase or diminish as the Bank directors diminish or increase the amount of their reserve of notes.

The preceding review of the practical working of the Act of 1844 has, as I venture to believe, established the following conclusions upon evidence which cannot be overthrown :—

1st. That the primary object of the Act, namely, that of securing the convertibility of the bank-note circulation, has been fully attained.

2nd. That while this most important object has been attained, the average amount of the circulation and the extent of the accommodation afforded to commerce, instead of having been diminished under the operation of the Act, have been maintained at a higher amount than during any of the periods of monetary pressure which occurred under the former law.

3rd. That the amount of the circulation out of the issue department has expanded and contracted as bullion flowed into and out of the coffers of that department, as a purely metallic currency would have done.

4th. That the proportion between the amount of the circulation in the hands of the public, and the amount of the circulation retained as the reserve of the banking department, has fluctuated under the degree of discretion exercised by the Bank directors, exactly as it would have fluctuated under that same degree of discretion had the whole circulation been represented by bullion actually deposited in the coffers of the issue department.

5th. That inasmuch as it has maintained a sufficient amount of bullion to secure the convertibility of the bank-note, and has preserved the currency from any fluctuations, whether in amount or in value, greater than those to which a purely metallic currency would have been liable, the Act of 1844 has realized all the advantages which could result from the adoption of the suggestion thrown out by Lord Ashburton for assimilating the Bank of England to that of Hamburgh, and making the whole circulation to consist of bullion-notes represented by gold in actual deposit.

6th. That the system adopted for the regulation of the issue department of the Bank of England possesses an important advantage over that which is applied to the Bank of Hamburgh, inasmuch as the provision which authorizes the issue of 14,000,000*l.* of notes unrepresented by bullion, liberates 14,000,000*l.* of treasure which would otherwise lie as dead stock in the coffers of the Bank, and adds it to the reproductive capital of the country.

The Act of 1819 for the resumption of cash payments was strenuously opposed by a numerous and not uninfluential section of the commercial community. Petitions, numerously signed by the merchants, bankers, and traders of London, were presented to the two Houses of Parliament, praying for the continuance of the restriction on cash payments, and setting forth that the return to such payments would " tend " to a forced, precipitate, and highly injurious con- " traction of the circulating medium of the country, " to lower the value of all landed and commercial " property, seriously to affect both public and private " credit, to embarrass and reduce all the operations of " agriculture, manufactures, and commerce, and to " throw out of employment a great proportion of the " industrious and labouring classes of the community." The directors of the Bank of England laid before the Chancellor of the Exchequer a representation, in which they declared that they could not, " by a

" seeming acquiescence, invest themselves with the
" responsibility of countenancing a measure calculated
" to compromise the universal interests of the empire
" in all the relations of agriculture, commerce, and
" revenue."   After these specimens of the small
degree of wisdom which serves to govern the opinions
of the commercial world, we need not be surprised
that an opposition, analogous to that which was
directed against the Act for the restoration of cash
payments, should now be directed against the complementary Act for providing the means by which
metallic payments may be permanently secured.
The account given by Mr. Fullarton of the popular
clamour which arose against the Act of 1819 may be
regarded as a sufficiently accurate description of the
character of the popular clamour which he has himself
contributed to excite against the Act of 1844 :—

" We all remember the popular hostility which, for
" many years, was directed against the measure of
" 1819 for the restoration of cash payments ; a hos-
" tility by no means confined to the unreasoning
" herd, but conscientiously entertained by many well-
" meaning people of education, and even by men of
" some considerable talent.   Whatever went amiss,
" whether prices fell or trade became stagnant, or
" speculation failed, the blame was invariably laid to
" the unhappy Peel's Bill.   To this origin were
" traced the great commercial revulsions of 1825 ; and
" every man who chanced to impair his fortune by
" absurd and hazardous adventures found a salve for
" his self-reproaches in attributing to the Bill the con-
" sequences of his own folly and improvidence.   This
" hostility continued to be maintained long, long after

" it had been demonstrated, by the most clear and
" convincing evidence, that the utmost practical
" change in the value of the currency which the
" Bill could have effected was infinitely short of
" that affirmed by its opponents, and after all their
" sinister predictions as to consequences had been
" falsified by its triumphant and easy success. Nor
" have the popular prejudices on the subject entirely
" subsided even at the present day. No one, indeed,
" except a small knot of deaf and incurable fanatics
" raises any longer a cry for a return to inconvertible
" paper."

We may, perhaps, be enabled to show that Mr.
Fullarton is not himself so entirely without sin as to
be entitled to cast a stone at the " deaf and incurable
" fanatics " who advocate a return to inconvertible
paper. But before proceeding to lay bare the misconceptions and inconsistencies into which Mr. Fullarton has fallen regarding the operation of the Act
of 1844, it will be proper to enter upon a preliminary
inquiry into the manner in which the directors of the
Bank of England have conducted the business of the
banking department under its provisions.

*On the manner in which the business of the Banking Depart-
ment of the Bank of England has been conducted from the
passing of the Act of 1844 to the close of the year 1847.*

By the provisions of the Act of 1844, the banking
department of the Bank of England was placed upon
the footing of an ordinary bank of deposit and discount. The directors of that establishment were as
completely divested of all control and responsibility,
regarding the amount of the notes put out by the

issue department, as if the Act had assimilated that department to the Bank of Hamburgh, and had required that the whole of its issues should be represented by bullion in actual deposit. The functions of the banking department were strictly confined to the operation of banking, properly so called; and the conduct of the directors, in the exercise of these functions, must be estimated by their adherence to, or by their departure from, the same identical rules to which private bankers find it necessary to conform in order to maintain the credit of their establishments.

The primary rule of legitimate banking, without a strict and constant adherence to which no ordinary bank of deposit and discount can be secured against insolvency, is the maintenance of a due proportion between liabilities and reserve. Now there is nothing, either in the composition or in the circumstances of the banking department of the Bank of England, to exempt it from the necessity of a strict adherence to the primary rule, the cardinal principle, upon which alone the business of an ordinary bank of deposit and discount can be safely conducted. It differs from ordinary banks of deposit and discount in the following particulars :—1st. It exercises a greater influence over the money market in proportion to the greater amount of the capital at its command. 2nd. It receives, as the bank of the Government, the growing produce of the revenue, and advances what may be temporarily deficient in the actual resources of Government towards the payment of the quarterly dividends on the national debt. 3rd. It holds some considerable portion of the reserves of the other metropolitan banks. Now the slightest consideration will render it apparent, that each of these several circumstances by which the banking department of the Bank of England is distinguished from ordinary banks, so far from constituting an exceptional case, justifying a departure from the ordinary rules of legitimate banking, renders the observance of these rules more indispensably necessary, and invests their violation with more serious consequences, and therefore with a graver responsibility.

An ordinary bank of deposit and discount may inflict serious injury throughout the district over which its operations extend,* in two several ways. 1st. By unduly extending its accommodation to its customers, during a period of excitement, it may cause its reserve to bear so low a proportion to its liabilities as to render it necessary, under a change of circumstances, such as the commencement of a drain of bullion, to provide for its own safety by suddenly withholding the usual advances upon which the trading community with which it was immediately connected had been accustomed to depend.   Through this unsteadiness in its operations, this oscillation between over-trading and under-trading, an ordinary bank commanding a moderate amount of capital may create a monetary pressure in its own locality more or less severe.

2nd. Serious as the consequences of over-banking in this form and to this extent would be, the mischief would be greatly aggravated were the bank, under any miscalculation or oblivion of consequences, to attempt to support the trade of the neighbourhood by continuing its increased advances until its immediately available capital became inadequate to meet immediate demands. The stoppage of the bank would convert the local pressure into a local panic, inflicting serious loss upon many, and on not a few inevitable ruin. The loss and the ruin would be in proportion to the extent of the operations in which the bank might have been engaged. Now, those whose attention may have been directed to the embarrassment and distress resulting from the irregularity in the advances, and from the over-trading of ordinary banks of deposit commanding an available capital to the extent of a few hundred thousand pounds, will be able to form some estimate of the extent of the mischief which must be inflicted on the whole commercial interests of the country by irregularity in the advances and by the over-trading of a bank of deposit and discount, which has under its control a fund exceeding twenty or thirty millions. The force of the obligations under which the directors of the Bank of England are placed, to conform to the rules of legitimate banking, must be measured by the magnitude of the banking capital placed at their disposal, and the consequent magnitude of the evil consequences which must arise from any mismanagement of that large capital.

II. As the bankers of the State, charged with the important duty of receiving the produce of the public revenue, and of paying the quarterly dividends upon the public debt, the directors are especially called on to adhere, with unswerving constancy, to the primary rule of maintaining an adequate reserve. Nor can the fulfilment of this obligation, in so far as concerns the payment of the dividends, be regarded as an

arduous task. This will be immediately seen by a
reference to the 'Gazette' returns. In the first weeks
of January, April, July, and October, in each year,
the Government deposits in the Bank are at their
maximum, the receipts on account of the revenue
having, during the immediately preceding three
months, exceeded the ordinary expenditure of the
Government by the amount of the quarterly dividends; and on the third and fourth weeks of these
months the Government deposits are at their minimum, as the advances on account of the dividends
and of the ordinary Government expenditure exceed,
while the dividends are in course of payment, the
receipts on account of the revenue. While from this
cause the Government deposits fall to their minimum,
there is an increase of the private deposits; inasmuch
as a portion of the public creditors keep their cash
with the Bank of England, and on the receipt of their
dividends pay back into that establishment with one
hand the amount which they receive with the other.
Now, as these fluctuations occur periodically at fixed
periods, and as their amount and duration may be
calculated upon with a considerable approximation to
certainty, they present no peculiar difficulty, no exceptional anomaly, taking them out of the sphere of
ordinary banking operations. By adhering to the
rules of legitimate banking, by advancing in each
successive quarter in safe proportions (say two-thirds)
the growing amount of the Government deposits,
upon loans returnable upon the two first weeks of the
next ensuing quarter, the directors may conduct the
Government business with perfect safety to their
own establishment, and without any sensible con-

traction in the amount of the circulation in the hands of the public. And even if the state of the revenue should render it necessary, that, on the falling due of the dividends, the Bank should make an advance to Government on deficiency bills, such advance might be made in conformity with the strictest rules of legitimate banking, and without an inconvenient limitation of the private securities representing the accommodation afforded to trade, by a sale of, or by a borrowing upon, Exchequer bills, so timed that the amount withdrawn from the circulation in the hands of the public should be immediately returned to it through the payment of the dividends. While the magnitude of the pecuniary transactions of the Government imposes on the Bank directors a corresponding obligation to conduct them in conformity with the strictest rules of legitimate banking, the regularity with which the Government payments occur, and the certainty with which their amount may be foreseen, render an adherence to these rules in the conduct of the Government business peculiarly facile.

III. A very important part of the deposits of the Bank of England consists of the reserves of other banks. When the directors diminish their reserve to a dangerous extent, they endanger the reserves of other banks. The stoppage of the Bank of England would be tantamount to a general stoppage of the whole of the London banks and discount houses. This great establishment, from the vast amount of the capital at its disposal, from its being the depository of the public revenue, and of the banking reserves of the subordinate banking establishments of

the metropolis, wields a tremendous power, the mis-
direction of which might lead not only to its own
insolvency, but to a general insolvency of all subordinate concerns, and to national bankruptcy. Let us
proceed to inquire into the manner in which this
tremendous power was exercised from the time at
which the Act of 1844 came into operation to the
close of the year 1847.

In July 1846, the bullion in the issue department
was 15,320,000*l.*; while in the banking department
the additional capital, over and above the capital of
the proprietors, placed at the disposal of the directors
by the depositors, amounted to 22,196,000*l.*; the
portion of this additional capital advanced for the
accommodation of trade upon private securities was
18,145,000*l.*; the Bank rate of interest was 3½ per
cent.; and the reserve of coin and notes retained to
meet the liabilities, consisting of deposits and seven
days' bills, and amounting together to 23,083,000*l.*,
was 9,928,000*l.* This was a highly-satisfactory position. While intrusted with the disposal of so large
an amount of capital, and holding so ample a reserve,
the directors were justified, according to the strictest
principles of legitimate banking, in having advanced
to the public 18,145,000*l.* at 3½ per cent. But the
indications of a less prosperous state of things became
soon apparent. The diminution of capital from the
failure of the potato crop, our increased imports, and
our diminished exports, were premonitory symptoms
of impending danger; and although no drain of bullion
had as yet set in, and although the reserve of notes
and coin in the banking department was still as high
as 9,940,000*l.*, yet as the amount of banking capital

G

at the disposal of the directors, in so far as represented by deposits, had been reduced from 22,196,000*l.* to 16,917,000*l.*, their policy in reducing the rate of interest from 3½ to 3 per cent. on the 22nd of August, must be regarded as at least questionable. A decrease of 5,000,000*l.* in the deposits indicated the necessity of some reduction in the amount of the securities, while lowering the rate of interest could only tend to increase the advance on securities, at the very time at which the funds from which these advances were to be made, viz., the deposits, were diminishing.

In October 1846, the drain of bullion set in. In the first week of January 1847, the amount of coin and bullion in the issue department was reduced from 15,322,000*l.*, its amount in the first week of July, to 14,258,000*l.* ; while the banking capital, as represented by deposits, was reduced from 22,196,000*l.*, its amount in the first week of July, to 17,894,000*l.* in the corresponding week of January 1847 ; and while the reserve of coin and notes in the banking department had fallen from 9,927,000*l.* to 8,920,000*l.* Throughout the latter months of 1846, the condition of the Bank in both departments presented positive and unequivocal signs of a progressive decline in the national resources. The continuous drain of bullion showed that diminished production had caused the quantity of commodities to bear a less proportion to the quantity of money in this than in other countries ; the reduction in the private deposits to little more than half the amount at which they had stood during the first eight months of the year, indicated a serious diminution in the amount of floating capital ;

and the diminution of banking capital, as represented by these deposits, gave warning of an inevitable diminution in the means of commercial accommodation, which would remain at the disposal of the Bank of England. Under these circumstances, the conduct of the Bank, in continuing to discount at 3 per cent., cannot be defended. At length, on the 9th of January, they raised the rate of discount to 3½ per cent.; and on the 16th, when they had lost upwards of a million of treasure in the course of fourteen days, they raised the rate to 4 per cent. But they counteracted the effects of even these late precautions, by increasing, notwithstanding the diminished amount of the capital at their disposal, their advances upon commercial securities from 12,153,000*l.* and 13,880,000*l.*, their amounts in November and December, to 14,450,000*l.* and 15,819,000*l.*, their amounts in January and February. In March, the advances upon private or mercantile securities were increased to 17,650,000*l.*, and in April to 18,627,000*l.*, being an increase of 6,474,000*l.*, or more than 50 per cent. above their amount in November. During the whole of the period through which these extraordinary advances were being made, the reserve in the banking department was undergoing rapid diminution. Nothwithstanding that there had been no increase of its available capital by an increase of its deposits, and that a severe drain of bullion was in steady operation, the Bank increased its advances for the accommodation of trade between six and seven millions. These advances necessarily fell upon the banking reserve; and, consequently, on the 10th of April, the notes and coin in the Bank till were re-

G 2

duced to 3,464,000*l.* against liabilities, on account
of deposits and seven days' bills, of 17,229,000*l.*
The publication of this account created panic. A
further continuance of this system of constantly-in-
creasing accommodation by the Bank was considered
impossible, and stringent measures of contraction
were apprehended. Bankers, bill-brokers, merchants,
and traders, therefore, sought security by increasing
the amounts of their immediately available cash.
The Bank directors were compelled to a sudden
withholding of accommodation in order to protect
their establishment. The discount of commercial
bills of unquestionable credit was refused; and for
some days the monetary pressure was more severe
than any which had previously occurred since the
panic of 1825.

It is an extraordinary fact, and one which demands
the most serious consideration, that during the greatest
intensity of the monetary panic in April 1847, the
amount of the advances of the Bank in aid of commerce was very considerably greater than in 1845—
the year of the greatest commercial prosperity which
the country had ever seen. The highest and lowest
amounts of the private securities, representing the
extent of the accommodation afforded to commerce
were, in 1845, 16,329,000*l.* and 8,561,000*l.*; and
in April 1847, 18,627,000*l.* and 16,079,000*l.*: the
lowest amount of aid afforded to commerce during
the panic of April 1847, being equal, within 250,000*l.*,
to the highest amount afforded during the most prosperous year in the annals of British commerce. These
figures demonstrate, that the commercial pressure
and the monetary panic of April 1847, were not

caused by a diminution of the customary accommodation afforded by the Bank. The depression was the necessary sequence of a diminution of the national capital; and the panic was the natural result of the abortive efforts of the Bank to supply the loss of capital by a departure from the rules of legitimate banking. Those who contend that the commercial pressure of 1847 was caused by a contraction of the circulation and a diminution of banking accommodation, are not only oblivious of the fact that that pressure was accompanied by a larger circulation and by a more extended accommodation than had existed or had been granted in periods of prosperity, but maintain the absurdity that a nation may lose a part of its wealth without any portion of the loss falling on the individuals who compose the nation. Had the Bank directors possessed a mine of virgin gold beneath their vaults, from which they could have advanced the capital required to purchase foreign corn and pay up railway calls, they might have averted the commercial pressure. But as they could not create an article of export which would purchase in foreign markets the commodities required to balance our diminished production and increased consumption; as they had no power of creating additional capital; as their functions were strictly limited to loaning out that portion of the diminished capital of the country which was placed at their disposal—no effort of theirs could by possibility have prevented individual members of the community from participating in the loss of wealth which the community at large had suffered.

In a country in which trade is conducted upon an extensive system of credit, every temporary diminu-

tion of the national capital, whether arising from a
deficient harvest or other cause, must be followed by
a proportionate extent of insolvency amongst the
commercial community. Every observer of passing
events must have witnessed examples of the inevitable
process. A wholesale merchant in good credit, and
with a money capital of 10,000*l.*, may purchase goods
to the value of 100,000*l.*, making his payments in
bills of exchange, and may sell those goods at a profit
to retail dealers, receiving his payments in bills of
exchange. If the two sets of bills should have been
drawn so as to fall due about the same time they will
balance each other: the merchant, making the bills
he granted payable at his bankers, and endorsing to
his bankers the bills he received, might adjust the
whole of the transactions without finding it necessary
to draw a single cheque against his cash account.
The process may be repeated. While trade is prosperous and confidence unimpaired, a money balance
of 10,000*l.* may prove adequate to the conducting
of transactions to the extent of 200,000*l.* or 400,000*l.*
But a deficient harvest occurs; the increased price
of food diminishes the consumption and reduces the
value of the goods in which the merchant dealt; the
retail dealers delay to renew their purchases, and
some of them are unable to provide for the bills they
passed for purchases already made; the bills which
the merchant has endorsed to the bank no longer
balance those he has made payable there; the difference must be drawn from his cash balance; the
depression in trade increases; his transactions have
been so extensive that his outstanding bills amount
to 200,000*l.*, while, from the fall in prices and the
defalcation of the retail dealers, the good bills which

he holds on account of the resale of his goods amount
to no more than 180,000*l.* : the difference is twice
the amount of his money capital, and he becomes
insolvent.

It is evident that, in cases analogous to that above
described, no possible extent of credit or of banking
accommodation can avert insolvency. When the
amount of the wholesale merchant's acceptances exceeded that of the bills he had received on the resale
of his goods, he might have continued in business,
although in a state of insolvency, had he been able
to discount the latter before the former became due :
but such aid, instead of averting ultimate insolvency,
would have increased his losses by the amount of the
discount paid. Other means of continuing an illegiti-
mate trade, and postponing the ultimate result, might
be resorted to. Purchases might be increased, not
with the view of realizing profit, but for the purpose
of keeping up a cash balance by resales at short
credit and reduced prices; and this fraudulent, yet
losing process, might be prolonged through the aid of
incautious bankers, to the certain injury of themselves,
of the honest trader, and of the community at large.

When there is a diminution of floating wealth—of
the vendible commodities of the country—there must
be an inevitable loss somewhere; and that inevitable
loss necessarily falls in the first instance upon that
portion of the trading community whose credit transactions have been most extensive in relation to the
capital at their command. And when, from the fall
of prices, the loss of those whose purchases have been
made upon credit exceeds their reserve of capital,
advances from banks to be repaid with interest serve

but to increase the losses which must ultimately fall upon their creditors. Nor is this all. When the loanable capital placed at the disposal of bankers is advanced to insolvent traders, the accommodation to solvent houses, whose assets, though not immediately available, exceed their liabilities, is diminished; and such houses, for want of the aid thus mischievously misapplied, may be driven to an otherwise unnecessary sacrifice of property, or compelled to suspend payment. When the floating wealth—the vendible commodities—of a credit-dealing country suffer diminution, a commercial pressure, involving the less stable portion of the trading community in inextricable difficulties, is an inevitable evil, which cannot be mitigated, but, on the contrary, must be aggravated, by a departure from the rules of legitimate banking to save insolvents from insolvency.

It has been urged that during the commercial and monetary pressure of April 1847, the directors of the Bank of England were compelled to depart from the rules of legitimate banking, by the necessity under which they were placed of advancing the dividends upon the public debt then falling due. This is disproved by the 'Gazette' returns. On the 27th of March, the Government deposits were 6,616,000*l.*, the Government securities 11,990,000*l.*, and the private securities 17,824,000*l.* Now, the directors were fully aware that during the ensuing four weeks, the demands of Government, on account of the dividends and of the ordinary public expenditure, would considerably exceed the receipts on account of the revenue during those weeks, and that a heavy drain must consequently fall upon the Government deposits.

With perfect foreknowledge of the demands which must be made upon their coffers, it was the obvious duty of the directors to have so arranged their loans from the public money intrusted to them, that the securities upon which they were advanced should have fallen due as the dividends were drawn out. The directors adopted a directly opposite course. As the payment of the dividends approached, their advances upon securities were not diminished, but increased. From the 20th of February to the 10th of April, the public securities were increased from 11,990,000*l.*, to 13,574,000*l.*, and the private securities from 15,039,000*l.* to 18,136,000*l.* By this most improvident increase of securities, the reserve of coin and notes in the banking department was reduced from 6,732,000*l.*—its amount on the 20th of March—to 3,464,000*l.* on the 10th of April. It is palpable, on the face of the 'Gazette' returns, that this unsafe position was in no way caused by advances to Government on account of the dividends. The directors made no advances to Government. On the 3rd of April the public deposits held by the Bank amounted to 6,000,000*l.*; and on the 1st of May, after the dividends had been paid, their deposits still amounted to 2,299,000*l.* Thus the Bank did nothing more than return to the public 3,721,000*l.* out of the 6,000,000*l.* of the public money intrusted to its keeping; still holding a balance of 2,299,000*l.*—a balance which it might safely employ as loanable capital, from the certainty that so far from its being drawn out for Government purposes, it must, during the next ensuing three months, be steadily increased from the accumulating proceeds of the revenue.

When the directors of the Bank of England increased their securities in March, they knew the amount of the dividends to be paid in April; they knew the average amount of the ordinary public expenditure, and they also knew the average amount of the inflowing revenue; and knowing all these, they could not but know that in the first three weeks of April there must be a diminution in their Government deposits of nearly 4,000,000*l.* Under these circumstances, the rules of legitimate banking required that this demand upon their deposits should have been provided for by such a diminution of the securities as would have maintained their reserve at a safe proportion to their liabilities. Had they abstained from increasing these by about 3,000,000*l.* between the 6th of March and the 10th of April, or had they in the first week in April sold securities to that amount, they would have maintained their reserve at a safe proportion to their liabilities, and would have prevented the occurrence of an inevitable pressure from being accompanied by a gratuitously-inflicted panic.

It has been urged in defence of the Bank, that if it were, at a time of monetary pressure and under a heavy drain upon its deposits, to adhere to the rules of legitimate banking, and to recruit its reserve by a sale of securities, the pressing of securities upon a declining market would reduce their value to an extent most injurious to public confidence and to commercial credit. The answer to this defence is, that when the floating wealth—the vendible commodities of the country—have suffered a serious diminution, and when, as a necessary consequence, the deposits of the Bank are reduced under a drain of bullion, one of the most effectual means by which the national loss can be replaced, and public confidence restored, is· a fall in the value of securities. The relative value of the public securities of different countries is determined by the relative degrees of credit which different countries possess in the estimation of the capitalists of the world. When, from any temporary disaster, the value of the securities of any particular country fall below their relative value as thus determined, foreign capital flows in for profitable investment. This influx of capital is a restorative—a replenishing process; and any attempt to arrest it by withholding securities from the market, can have no other effect than that of prolonging the exhaustion of which it is an appropriate, and to whatever extent it may be carried, an effectual, remedy. Besides, when there is a diminution in the floating capital of the country, creating a demand upon deposits, the Bank has not the power to prevent the sale of a portion of its securities. All it can do is to suspend their sale in order to render it more sudden and extensive. This is most distinctly shown by the 'Gazette' returns. The securities which stood at 31,710,000*l.* on the 10th April, were reduced to 26,840,000*l.* on the 1st of May; being a reduction of nearly 5,000,000*l.* in twenty days. Had the directors not perilled their stability by failing to bring their securities *gradually* to market to replenish their reserve, this abrupt contraction of banking accommodation, and consequent paralysis of monetary transactions, could not have occurred.

That the aggravated commercial pressure, which

occurred in April 1847, was caused, not by any
contraction of the circulation,—not by any diminution
in the means of banking accommodation, beyond the
proportion in which the national wealth had declined,
—but solely and entirely by the capricious and fitful
manner in which the inevitably diminished amount
of loanable capital was unduly advanced and suddenly
withdrawn, is fully established by the fact, that
confidence recovered as rapidly as it had declined.
On the 1st of May, the deposits, representing the
amount of loanable capital over and above that of the
Bank proprietary, placed at the disposal of the
directors, had sunk to 11,611,000*l.* On the 5th of
June it reascended to 15,923,000*l.*, and on the 26th
of June to 17,717,000*l.*, the amount within less than
200,000*l.* at which it had stood on the 2nd of January.
The rapid increase in the private securities representing the amount of accommodation afforded to commerce, and in the reserve of coin and notes in
the banking department, representing the stability
of that branch of the establishment, was equally
remarkable.   On the 5th of June the private
securities had risen from 16,113,000*l.*, their amount
on the 1st of May, to 17,085,000*l.*, and on the 26th
of June to 18,315,000*l.*, while, within the same
period, the reserve of coin and notes had risen from
3,572,000*l.* to 5,891,000*l.*, and to 6,475,000*l.*

Here an important question demands consideration.
On the 26th of June, the amount of the circulation out
of the walls of the issue department exceeded its
amount on the 1st of May by no more than 1,170,000*l.*;
while in the banking department, the amount of the
deposits and of the reserve of notes on this same 26th

of June exceeded their amounts on the 1st of May by 6,106,000*l.* and 2,884,000*l.* The curious and important question which demands our consideration is, how did it come to pass that an increase of the circulation out of the walls of the issue department, to the amount of only 1,170,000*l.*, was accompanied by an increase of the deposits and reserve in the banking department to the amount of 8,990,000*l.* ? Now, the only answer which can be given to this question is, that the currency had ceased to circulate as confidence collapsed under the mismanagement of the Bank, and that its circulation was restored as confidence revived. When the Bank, after having, during the three previous months of the year, and while its bullion was steadily flowing out, continued to increase its securities and to reduce its reserve, was compelled, on the 17th of April, to publish an account which no private bank could have exhibited without inviting insolvency, merchants, bankers, discount houses—all, in fact, who had engagements to provide for—sought to strengthen their position by contracting their engagements and hoarding their cash. And when the consequent fall in the value of securities, and in the prices of commodities, caused an influx of foreign capital, and an increased demand for goods for exportation, the hoards were returned to the channels of circulation.

During the months of May and June the bullion in the issue department, and the deposits, the reserve, and the private securities in the banking department, continued to increase. In July, however, the process was reversed, and the signs of impending danger again became apparent. Between the 3rd of July

and the 7th of August, the bullion had fallen
from 9,562,000*l.* to 8,634,000*l.*, the deposits from
17,706,000*l.* to 13,456,000*l.*, and the reserve of notes
from 5,156,000*l.* to 3,946,000*l.* Under these circumstances, the Bank directors adopted the wise precaution of diminishing their private securities and raising
the rate of interest from 5 to 5½. The railways were
rapidly absorbing the circulating capital of the
country, and outbidding commerce in the discount
market. Bankers were deprived of the power of
affording the customary accommodation to trade, by
the withdrawal of deposits to pay up railway calls.
In Scotland, persons who had obtained cash credits
with the banks drew against their credits, in order
that they might reloan the borrowed capital on
railway securities, at a higher rate of interest than
that which they paid to the banks. The banks
checked the practice by contracting their cash credits,
and appropriating to themselves the higher rate of
interest obtainable upon railway securities.

While the customary accommodation was thus
withdrawn from trade, circumstances occurred which
rendered that withdrawal peculiarly embarrassing.
The rapid conversion of floating to fixed capital, the
destruction of a large proportion of the national
subsistence, the enormous outlay in the purchase of
foreign provisions, and the unprecedented extension
of credit transactions, had induced such a complica-
tion of industrial derangement, that the remedies
essential to permanent restoration could not be
brought into operation without exciting a temporary
paroxysm of intenser suffering. The blessing of an
abundant harvest brought down the price of corn

from 102*s*. to 48*s*. per quarter, and occasioned a most distressing amount of individual loss. Houses long established, and supposed to be possessed of the most ample resources, stopped payment. At first it was believed that the failures would be confined to the corn trade; but it was soon discovered that over-speculation and consequent insolvency had extended to other branches.   During the month of September, failures of houses engaged in various departments of commerce took place in rapid and melancholy suc-cession.*

These failures excited not merely surprise, but astonishment. A few weeks before, the merchants, bankers, and traders of London had presented a petition to Parliament, affirming that there was " no undue extension of the ordinary commerce of the country, or any spirit of speculation or overtrading afloat, so far as the trading interest was concerned." The failures of September and October disclosed the otherwise incredible fact, that this petition, averring that there was no spirit of speculation or overtrading afloat amongst the trading interest, bore the signature of parties who had been speculating and overtrading to an unexampled extent, who had been for years insolvent, and whose liabilities exceeded their assets in a proportion so enormous as to prove that their purchases upon credit must have been effected, not with any view of realizing a profit, but for the purpose of discounting bills to be obtained upon the resale of the merchandise thus surreptitiously acquired. The London petition, speedily followed as it was by the utter falsification of its statements, shook commercial

* Speech of the Chancellor of the Exchequer.

confidence to its centre. The questions current in
the City were, who can be safely trusted? and what
establishment will be the next to stop payment?
Bankers, who had been in the habit of placing their
balances in the hands of bill-brokers, locked up their
cash in their own drawers. The discount houses were
thus deprived of the means of affording the accustomed
accommodation to trade. Two bill-brokers stopped
payment; two others were nearly paralyzed; and
the remaining houses, for the purpose of securing their
own position, were obliged seriously to contract, if
not altogether to suspend, their usual advances; and
thus the whole business of the discount market was
thrown upon the Bank of England. The pressure
upon the Bank was so intense, that although the usual
demand for accommodation had not exceeded 20,000l.,
30,000l., or 70,000l. a-day, the call for loans on the
29th of September amounted to 149,000l., and on the
30th to 362,000l.*

Under these accumulating difficulties the Bank
directors redeemed, as far as in them lay, the error
into which they had fallen in the early months of the
year. Early in September they advanced to the
public the Government balances in their hands,
adopting the precaution of so limiting the period of
their loans as to make them repayable in sufficient
time to provide for the October dividends. This
salutary precaution, imperatively necessary as it was,
in order that faith might be kept with the public
creditor, was regarded by the unreflecting portion of
the mercantile community as a measure of injurious
and unjustifiable stringency. This condemnation was

* Speech of the Chancellor of the Exchequer.

inconsistent and irrational. In April the directors had been censured, and justly censured, for having reduced their reserve below the measure of security, and perilled public faith by not so limiting the period of their advances from the Government balances as to have them returned as the dividends fell due; and now that they had corrected their former mistake, conformed to the rules of legitimate banking, and secured the means of keeping faith with the public creditor, the former censure was most inappropriately revived. In October, as in April, there was panic. But the two panics originated in widely-different causes. That in April was produced by the publication of an account exhibiting a dangerous diminution of the Bank reserve; that in October was produced by the astounding disclosure that establishments of the highest standing had been long engaged in a system of ruinous overtrading, and that parties who had been looked up to as the merchant princes of the land, and against whom a breath of discredit was never cast, had not been solvent within the memory of a living partner. But at both periods there was monetary pressure; and the mercantile community were not in that calm and dispassionate mood which might have enabled them to trace the dissimilar causes of the similar effects. They had been falsely told by the concoctors of the London petition that there was " no undue speculation or overtrading afloat," and that " the Bank of England was restrained by legislative enactment from giving those facilities by which, when duly supported, commercial dealings rectify the derangement produced by temporarily disturbing causes." The whole of the daily

H

press of the metropolis,* with one glorious exception, echoed the cry that the commercial collapse was caused by the contraction of the currency and the limitation of banking accommodation which had been enforced by the Act of 1844. It was in vain that the 'Gazette' returns demonstrated from week to week that the amount of the circulation in the hands of the public, and the extent of accommodation afforded by the Bank, were greater than they had been during periods of the greatest prosperity; and it was all in vain that the most influential journal in the civilized world, in a series of articles of unrivalled power, reiterated the salutary though melancholy truth, that the commercial collapse had been caused, not by a deficiency of paper money, but by the destruction and absorption of commercial capital. The pearls were cast before swine. The cry was still, " The " commerce of the country cannot be carried on if the " continuance of the facility of discounting legitimate " commercial bills be practically withdrawn:" the existing law, " instead of sustaining public confidence " —the vital element of a commercial body—has " shaken it to its centre." As " the great commercial " revulsions of 1825 were traced to the Bill of 1819," and as every man who had chanced to impair his fortune by absurd and hazardous adventures found a salve for his self-reproaches in attributing to the Act the consequences of his own folly and improvidence, so, with a like disregard of the relation of cause and effect, the commercial revulsions of the present year

* Some admirable papers on the Currency, of which I have freely availed myself, appeared in the " Spectator." The principles of the Act were also ably defined by the " Examiner."

were attributed to the complementary Act of 1844.
And, again to borrow the appropriate language of Mr.
Fullarton—" There were no bounds to the vehemence
" with which those whose interests were touched em-
" braced and propagated opinions the most monstrous."

As prophecies have sometimes been the causes of
their own fulfilment—as fear creates the danger it
apprehends—so the popular delusion, that the circulation had been forcibly contracted, realized the ideal
mischief. The belief that money was scarce made it
scarce. The declaration of the merchants, bankers,
and traders of London, that commercial confidence
was shaken to its centre, shook it to its centre, and
made falsehood truth.

Thus was superinduced a panic scarcely less intense
than that of 1825. About the middle of October the
Royal Bank of Liverpool failed; and although that
failure was caused by the grossest mismanagement,
yet its occurrence aggravated the prevalent distrust,
and shook the credit of other establishments. Another
bank in Liverpool, and also the North and South
Wales Bank, stopped payment, and great, although
groundless, apprehensions were entertained regarding
the solvency of an eminent broker in that town. The
contagion spread. A bank in the West of England
failed; the Union Bank of Newcastle-upon-Tyne
stopped payment; and there was a severe run upon
the district bank of that town, an establishment of
the most undoubted solidity, but which could not
have made its resources immediately available so as
to have averted a suspension of payment, had it not
been sustained by advances of an almost unlimited
amount from the Bank of England.

H 2

The panic was fearfully aggravated by an application for assistance to the Bank of England from some banks in Scotland. It had always been supposed that the banks of Scotland rested on so secure a footing as to be able to take care of themselves, and that it would never be necessary for them to ask assistance from the Bank of England. But whether it was that their customers were drawing out their deposits, or that they themselves, under the temptation of the high rates of interest offered by railway speculators, had unduly diminished their reserves, they found it necessary to resort to the Bank of England for aid in rendering their securities immediately available.

Although a departure from the rules of legitimate banking may create a panic, yet an adherence to those rules cannot of itself arrest the progress of a panic after it has set in. Exceptional cases may arise, in which a temporary relaxation of ordinary rules, instead of aggravating distrust, may contribute to the restoration of confidence. Under no state of the law, and under no system of banking, can banks, whether of deposit or of issue, pay the whole of their liabilities on demand. All banks, including the Bank of England, must stop payment under a panic terror so extensive and intense as to cause a simultaneous drawing out of the whole, or a large proportion of their deposits. When, in periods of monetary panic, the withholding of extended accommodation would so aggravate the prevalent pressure and alarm as to increase the run upon deposits, the granting of such accommodation may become a measure of wise precaution, even although its immediate effect should be to diminish the reserve of the Bank below the safe proportion.   In such extreme and exceptional cases timely advances to any amount within the competence of the Bank might prevent the withdrawal of deposits to a still greater amount, and thus render the position of the Bank more stable than before.   Bankers must always expose themselves to more or less of danger by reducing their reserves below the proportion prescribed by the rules of legitimate banking; but in periods of panic they may expose themselves to still greater danger by attempting to maintain their reserves at the proportion so determined.   Upon the self-same principle upon which the rules of banking are founded, a departure from them in periods of extreme monetary pressure may become not only expedient but necessary.

On the grounds which have now been stated, it must be admitted that there is much to be said in defence of the course pursued at this period by the Bank, in making advances, otherwise of an exceptional character, for the special purpose of arresting panic by sustaining the credit of provincial banks, at the hazard of an undue diminution of their own reserve.   On the 30th of October their reserve was reduced below 2,000,000*l.*, against liabilities amounting to 14,200,000*l.*; and it was believed that, at a later period, the coin and notes in the till of the banking department fell short of 1,000,000*l.*   A further diminution of the reserve might have led to the stoppage of the banking department.   The directors intimated to the Government that they could not, without compromising the security of their own establishment, go on rendering assistance to the various parties, both banks and private concerns, in England and Scotland, from which the most pressing applications were made to them. Promptly and effectually the Government interfered. The First Lord of the Treasury and the Chancellor of the Exchequer recommended that the Bank should increase its issues upon securities beyond the amount of the 14,000,000*l.* prescribed by the Act, engaging, at the same time, to introduce a Bill of Indemnity in the event of a violation of the law. The effect was magical. The panic was at an end.

The inference to which the facts thus briefly recorded naturally lead are instructive and interesting.

It would seem to be a self-evident conclusion from these facts, that the commercial revulsion was not caused by a contraction of the circulation. On the 13th, 23rd, and 30th of October, during the greatest intensity of the monetary pressure, the circulation in the hands of the public was respectively 20,394,000*l.*, 19,359,000*l.*, and 20,309,000*l.*, being equal, to within about 200,000*l.*, of the actual circulation during the corresponding weeks of January before the commercial pressure had commenced; while the private securities which represented the extent of the advances of the Bank in support of commercial credit, and which had been only 12,700,000*l.* in the three last weeks of January, swelled to 19,900,000*l.*, 18,000,000*l.*, and 19,400,000*l.*, in the corresponding weeks of October.

It has been contended that, although the circulation in the hands of the public, and the aid afforded to commerce by the Bank, were greater during the intensity of the pressure than they had been in periods of high confidence, yet that that pressure was materially aggravated by the knowledge on the part of the public, that as the Bank could no longer meet the demands on its deposits by unlimited issues, it was deprived of the power of supporting commercial credit by indefinite advances. But it must be apparent, upon a dispassionate review of the facts, that the knowledge on the part of the public and of the Bank directors, that unlimited issues and indefinite advances were no longer practicable, so far from having increased the monetary pressure, saved the Bank of England from insolvency, and the country from the disgrace and the anarchy which that insolvency would have involved. Had the Bank retained the power of recruiting its reserve by increasing its issues upon securities, it could not, by any possible exercise of that power, have maintained the circulation at a higher amount than that determined by the monetary equilibrium of the commercial world. The sole result, as far as regards the amount of the circulation, would have been that the issues upon bullion would have decreased as the issues upon securities increased. Had the Bank persisted through the month of April in the course which it had steadily pursued from January to that time, the result here stated must have ensued. The bullion would have all disappeared, and suspension would have become inevitable. That the Bank did not so proceed, and that suspension did not occur at the end of April, or in the course of the following month, is solely attributable to the Act of 1844.

Persons ignorant of the necessary and natural law which governs the amount at which a convertible currency can be maintained, have occasionally con-

tended that, had it not been for the Act of 1844, the
Bank might have supported commercial credit by
increasing the circulation by the amount of the bullion
in the issue department; and that it was as absurd as
it was injurious to contract the currency while there
were eight or nine millions of treasure locked up in
the vaults of the Bank. Now, whatever the amount
of treasure in the vaults of the issue department, that
amount was, under the provisions of the Act, represented by an equal amount of bank-notes out of the
walls of the issue department. An increased issue,
equal to the whole amount of the bullion, could not
have added a single note to the maintainable amount
of the circulation. To whatever extent a further
amount of notes might have been issued, to the same
extent bullion would have been displaced and exported, until there remained no bullion, but securities
alone, to represent the whole amount of the notes
issued. This would have been a repetition of the
vicious process by which the bullion was reduced to
almost total exhaustion in 1825, and again in 1837
and 1839; and the necessity of obviating which
caused the discussions which terminated in the passing
of the Act of 1844.

It is sometimes affirmed that the Act of 1844 has
been a failure, because, on the first occurrence of one
of those monetary panics which it was its object to
avert, the Government was compelled to authorize its
suspension. The affirmation betrays an utter ignorance of the objects of the Act. These objects were
to secure the convertibility of the bank-note, and to
cause our mixed currency of coin and notes to vary
in amount and in value as a purely metallic currency

would have varied. These objects, as is shown in the preceding chapter, have been completely fulfilled. The following passage from a masterly tract by Lord Overstone, published in 1844, will establish the fact, that the prevention of panic was no object of the Act :—

" To guard against commercial convulsions is not " the direct or real purpose of the Bill. To subject " the paper issues to such regulation as shall secure " their conformity in amount and value with, and, " consequently, their immediate convertibility at all " times into, metallic money, is the purpose to which " the provisions of the measure are avowedly directed; " and if the Bill further exerts any indirect influence " in restraining the oscillations of commercial excite- " ment or the fluctuations of prices, it can only do " this to the extent to which mismanagement of the " circulation has hitherto, under the existing system, " been the means of originating or fomenting these " evils. It has, however, been urged, as an objection " to this measure, that it will not effectually prevent " the recurrence of commercial revulsions. The " answer to this cannot be so well given as in the " words of one of the ablest supporters of the measure, " to whose unwearied industry, singularly acute per- " ception, and sound philosophic views, as Chairman " of the Parliamentary Committee of Inquiry, the " public are mainly indebted for the successful con- " duct of that investigation, and for whatever public " benefit may result from it:—' I anticipate from the " adoption of this measure a less fluctuation in the " amount of the circulation—a less fluctuation in the " range of prices; but I am not so unreasonably

"'sanguine as to suppose that it will put an end' to
" all speculation and to all miscalculation in commer-
" cial matters. Prices will necessarily vary according
" to the relative supply and demand for commodities
" at various times. Speculators will make mistakes
" in their calculations as to the amount of the supply
" and the urgency of the demand. Prices may be
" unnaturally forced up, and individuals may be
" ruined in the collapse. All this cannot be put an
" end to, so long as competition exists in trade, and
" hope of gain influences human minds; but it is no
" reason why we should not remedy what is in our
" power because we cannot attain' everything.' We
" can prevent an additional stimulus being given to a
" rise of prices and 'undue speculations, by the influ-
" ence of an ill-regulated currency; and this it' is the
" duty of the Legislature to attempt.'"*

To the high authority of the present Chancellor 'of
the Exchequer, Lord Overstone adds that of Mr.
Huskisson:—

" The consequences of sudden alarm cannot be
" measured : they baffle all ordinary calculation.
" Cash is then withdrawn, not because the circula-
" tion is excessive, but by the country banks and the
" town bankers, for the purpose of meeting possible
" demands upon them ; and by the community at
" large, either directly from the Bank or indirectly
" through the former channels, for the purpose of
" hoarding, from the dread of some imaginary or con-
" tingent danger. In such a crisis every reduction in
" the amount of bank paper is so far from checking
" the drain that it aggravates the general distress;

* Thoughts on the Separation of Departments, pp. 4, 5.

" because the gold which is taken out of the Bank,
" instead of being substituted in circulation for the
" notes withdrawn from it; is for the most part locked.
" up: and thus, in proportion as the stagnant and
" straitened circulation wants life and aid, it be-
" comes every day more embarrassed, whilst each
" new calamity produced by such a state of things
" contributes to spread and increase the general ap-
" prehension. It is therefore manifest, that, by a
" possible combination of circumstances, the Bank
" might be driven to part with its last guinea, not
" only without having checked the drain, but with the
" certainty of increasing it in proportion as the
" amount of their notes was diminished. At such a
" moment, the preservation of the Bank from actual
" failure, though an important, is but a secondary
" consideration—that of the country is the first. The
" possible cases, however, which may call for such an
" intervention of power, are not capable of being
" foreseen or defined by law. The necessity may not
" occur again; if it should, the application of the
" remedy must be left to those who may then be at
" the head of affairs, subject to their own respon-
" sibility and to the judgment of Parliament."

Advocates and opponents of the Act of 1844 admit,
with one accord, that there had occurred in October
1847 a crisis, the remedy for which was to be sought,
not in the provisions of the existing law, but through
an interposition of power on the part of those who
were at the head of affairs, subject to their own
responsibility and the judgment of Parliament. That
the interposition of the executive authority had become necessary is not denied. Questions, neverthe-

less, continued to be raised regarding the time, the
manner, and the consequences of that interposition.
On these, some brief observations may be required :—

1st. It has been contended that Government ought
to have interposed at an earlier period of the year.
Now, the effects of an earlier relaxation of the provisions of the Act would have been, that insolvent
establishments would have been enabled to protract
their overtrading, to increase the already enormous
amount of their liabilities, and to involve a wider
circle of creditors in their ultimate and inevitable fall;
that there would have been a more rapid and extensive conversion of circulating into fixed capital, a
greater withdrawal of banking accommodation from
the support of trade, a less production of domestic with
a greater consumption of imported commodities, and a
more unfavourable balance of foreign payments; that
every additional note which might have been issued
by the Bank would have caused an abstraction of
bullion from its coffers to an equivalent amount; and
that Government would have been compelled to resort
to a second and more violent exercise of power, for
the purpose of averting national bankruptcy, by a
suspension of cash payments.

2nd. The origin of the crisis was traced to two
different sources: one party contending that the panic
was caused by a deficiency in the circulation, another
party maintaining that the deficiency in the circulation was caused by the panic. In this divided state
of public opinion, the measure adopted by Government
was the most judicious which could have been devised.
It was calculated not only to mitigate the monetary
pressure, but to decide, by actual results, the contro-

verted question regarding the cause in which that pressure had originated.

The contraction and pressure which actually occurred in the spring was only just sufficient to stop the drain of bullion, and keep the exchanges in equilibrium. The severer crisis of October was absolutely necessary for the effectual rectification of the exchanges; and it was only after that rectification had been effected that the Government interference could have been safely resorted to. Had it been resorted to earlier, it would have prevented the correctives which brought the exchanges into a safe state in October, and suspension would have been the consequence.

Whether the pressure had been caused by the restriction imposed by the Act on the issues of the Bank, or by a withdrawal of the circulation under the influence of alarm, the power of unlimited issue given to the Bank, under the recommendation and guarantee of Government, would have been equally effectual in removing it. Now, had the pressure originated in a deficiency in the bank-note circulation, it could not have been removed, unless that deficiency had been supplied by the actual exercise of the power of unrestricted issue conferred upon the Bank; but it was relieved without the exercise of the extra legal power intrusted to the Bank. The knowledge of the existence of an unlimited power to increase the circulation dissipated the alarm under which the circulation had been contracted. As soon as the Government measure was announced, " thousands and tens of " thousands were taken from the hoards; some from " boxes deposited with bankers, although the parties

" would not leave the notes in their bankers' hands;
" large parcels of notes were returned to the Bank of
" England, cut into halves, as they had been sent
" into the country; and so small was the real demand
" for additional notes, that the whole amount taken
" from the Bank, when the unlimited power of issue
" was given, was under 400,000*l.*" * By a masterly
and most successful stroke of financial policy the
monetary pressure was relieved, and the unsettled
question regarding its origin and its character practically solved.

3rd. The ultimate effect of the interposition of
Government upon our monetary system may not be
unimportant. The only objection worthy of serious
consideration urged against the Act of 1844 was that
contained in the memorial of some of the London
bankers, praying for the introduction of a special
clause to facilitate the suspension of the operation of
the Act in periods of peculiar pressure on the money
market. Lord Overstone, in the publication before
referred to, gave, in the words of Mr. Huskisson, a
sufficient—it may now be said, a prophetic—answer
to the objection : "*Should a crisis ever arise, baffling
" all ordinary calculation, and not amenable to ordinary
" principles, the remedy must be sought, not in the pre-
" vious provisions of the law, but in the discretion of those
" who may be then at the head of affairs, on their own
" responsibility, and subject to the judgment of Par-
" liament.*" That this was the true answer to the
memorial of the London bankers has been verified by
actual results. A crisis, baffling all ordinary calculations, had occurred—the contemplated interposition,

* Speech of the Chancellor of the Exchequer.

on the responsibility of ministers and subject to the judgment of Parliament, was effected ; and the panic was made to subside without its having been found necessary to resort to an actual violation of the provisions of the law.

The event has proved, that a provision investing the executive with the power to suspend the operations of the law would have been unnecessary ; but this is not all. Such a provision, as was distinctly shown by Lord Overstone, would have been not only unnecessary but mischievous. It is one thing for the ministers of the Crown to suspend the operation of a law in virtue of a special authority derived from Parliament ; and it is another, and quite a different thing, for a minister to violate the law upon his own responsibility, subject to the judgment of Parliament. The former course might be adopted in the absence of any very stringent necessity, under a moderate pressure from without ; the latter course could not be resorted to in a constitutional country, except in cases of real emergency, in which the public safety required a prompt interposition on the part of the executive authority. Unless we could be assured that the integrity of our monetary system will be ever defended against the assaults of popular delusion by Courage standing on the rock of Science, the engrafting of a suspensive provision on the Act of 1844 might lead to the most injurious tampering with the currency.

The demand for relaxation in April was such as no Government could have resisted, had it been invested with a legal power to relax. Yet it is perfectly clear, that relaxation at that time would have been not only highly injurious, but absolutely fatal. Suspension of cash payments would have been the certain result. All the pressure which actually occurred—that of October superinduced upon that of April 1847—was absolutely necessary for bringing the exchanges into that state into which it was necessary that they should be brought before the Government interference could be useful or even safe. But had there been a legal power of relaxation, the Government would have been inevitably compelled, by the ignorant impatience of public feeling, to resort to that power before the proper time, and when its exercise would have necessarily led to a suspension of cash payments.

CHAPTER III.

CRITICAL EXAMINATION OF MR. J. S. MILL'S CHAPTER ON
THE REGULATION OF A CONVERTIBLE PAPER CUR-
RENCY.

MR. MILL devotes this chapter to the theory and
practical operation of Sir Robert Peel's Act of 1844,
for the renewal of the charter of the Bank of England.
The chapter commences thus:—

" The frequent recurrence during the last half cen-
" tury of the painful series of · phenomena called a
" commercial crisis, has directed much of the atten-
" tion both of economists and of practical politicians
" to the contriving of expedients for averting, or at
" the least mitigating, its evils. And the habit which
" grew up during the era of the Bank restriction, of
" ascribing all alternations of high and low prices to
" the issues of banks, has caused inquirers in general
" to fix their hopes of success in moderating those
" vicissitudes, upon schemes for the regulation of
" bank-notes. A scheme of this nature, after having
" obtained the sanction of high authorities, so far
" established itself in the public mind, as to be, with
" general approbation, converted into a law, at the
" last renewal of the charter of the Bank of England;
" and the regulation is still in force, though with a

I

" great abatement of its popularity, and with its
" *prestige* impaired by a temporary suspension, on the
" responsibility of the executive, little more than
" three years after its enactment. It is proper that
" the merits of this plan for the regulation of a con-
" vertible bank-note currency should be here consi-
" dered."

This account of the origin and object of the Bank
Charter Act of 1844 is at once incomplete and erroneous. It is incomplete, inasmuch as the circumstances
which led to the enactment were not only the frequent
recurrence of commercial crises, but also and mainly
the frequent and imminent danger to which the convertibility of the bank-note circulation had been
exposed; and it is erroneous, inasmuch as the primary object of the Act was, not to mitigate commercial vicissitudes, but to provide effectual security
against a suspension of cash payments.

Mr. Mill proceeds: " It is proper that the merits
" of this plan for the regulation of convertible cur-
" rency should be here considered. But before touch-
" ing upon the practical provisions of Sir Robert
" Peel's Act of 1844, I shall briefly state the nature
" and examine the grounds of the theory on which the
" Act is founded."   He then enters at once upon his
self-imposed task, the preliminary and indispensable
labour of acquiring a competent knowledge of the
nature of the theory and of the grounds upon which it
is founded being conveniently evaded. A tissue of
misconception and error has been the natural result
of the inquiry thus entered upon. In order to avoid
the possibility of misinterpretation, suppression, or
exaggeration, I will present, in extenso, the whole of

Mr. Mill's facts and arguments in relation to the Act of 1844, and proceed toexamine them separately, paragraph by paragraph, commencing with what Mr. Mill terms a statement of the nature, and an examination of the grounds upon which the Act is founded.

" It is believed by many that banks of issue uni-
" versally, or the Bank of England in particular, have
" a power of throwing their notes into circulation,
" and thereby raising prices arbitrarily; that this
" power is only limited by the degree of moderation
" with which they think fit to exercise it; that when
" they increase their issues beyond the usual amount,
" the rise of prices thus produced generates a spirit of
" speculation in commodities, which carries prices
" still higher, and ultimately causes a reaction and
" recoil amounting in extreme cases to a commercial
" crisis; and that every such crisis which has oc-
" curred in this country within mercantile memory,
" has been either originally produced by this cause,
" or greatly aggravated by it."

Whether this passage can be regarded as a logical exposition of a theory of currency, it is unnecessary to inquire. It will be enough to show that it is not an exposition of the theory of metallic variation upon which the Act of 1844 is founded. According to that theory the value of the circulation and the scale of prices may be altered by two several causes, namely, by an alteration in the amount of the currency, while the quantity of commodities remains the same, or by an alteration in the quantity of commodities, while the amount of the currency remains the same. When the currency is increased, commodities remaining the same, prices rise, and the monetary equilibrium with

I 2

other countries is disturbed until restored by an exportation of specie.   And when the quantity of commodities is diminished, the amount of the currency
remaining the same, precisely analogous results are
produced upon prices, upon the circulation, upon the
exchanges, and upon the coffers of the banks.   Nevertheless, while these opposite effects are strictly analogous in kind, they are widely different in degree.
Alterations in the quantity of commodities are more
frequent and more considerable than alterations in the
amount of the currency; and as a necessary consequence, the most frequent and the most violent fluctuations in the money market are those which are
caused by variation in the supply of commodities.
Such, as propounded and recorded by its authors, is
the theory of metallic variation upon which the Act
of 1844 is founded.   It is thus expounded by Lord
Overstone :—

" Fluctuations in the amount of the currency are
" seldom, if ever, the original and exciting cause of
" fluctuations in prices, and in the state of trade.
" The buoyant and sanguine character of the human
" mind; miscalculations as to the relative extent of
" supply and demand; fluctuations of the seasons;
" changes of taste and fashion; legislative enact-
" ments and political events; excitement or depres-
" sion in the condition of other countries, connected
" with us by active trading intercourse; an endless
" variety of casualties acting upon those sympathies
" by which masses of men are often urged into a
" state of excitement or depression; these, all or
" some of them, are generally the original exciting
" causes of those variations in the state of trade; to

" which the report refers. The management of the
" currency is a subordinate agent; it seldom origi-
" nates, but it may, and often does, exert a consider-
" able influence in restraining or augmenting the
" violence of commercial oscillations."

It will be seen by the following extracts from
his evidence before the Bank Charter Committee in
1832, that Mr. Norman's views coincide with those of
Lord Overstone :—

" 2543. It appears there was at the period of 1825
" a great increase in the amount of paper circulating
" in the country, and there was, contemporaneously
" with that, a great rise in prices generally through-
" out the country. Do you attribute the rise of prices
" on that occasion solely to the increased issue of
" paper, or do you think that it was in proportion
" only to the increased issue of paper ?—I certainly
" should not either think that it was wholly owing to
" the increased issue of paper, nor do I conceive that
" it was in exact proportion to the increased issue of
" paper. I consider that in 1825, a sort of moral
" epidemic prevailed, and that you might have the
" same extent of currency, perhaps ten times over,
" without an equal degree of commercial excitement
" and subsequent distress. I do not consider that at
" all times even a similar amount of currency will
" perform exactly a similar amount of work, because
" there may be, in periods of great commercial ex-
" citement, a considerable increased velocity of circu-
" lation.

" 2544. Do you consider, then, that a spirit of specu-
" lation engendered by particular circumstances, at
" any particular time, may cause a great rise of prices

" entirely independent of any increase in the issues of
' paper-money ?—I think there might be a spirit of
" speculation abroad in the first instance, unconnected
" with an increased currency ; and when that specu-
" lation had raised prices, an increase in the circula-
" tion would probably follow ; but I do not think it
" should necessarily, though it does sometimes, pre-
" cede it.

" 2545. Therefore a spirit of speculation may be
" engendered, and there may be a rise of prices, and
" that rise of prices may be followed by an increase
" of issue as a necessary consequence ; but the ori-
" ginal rise of prices may happen entirely apart from
" any increase of the circulating medium, and owing
" solely to the speculation itself ?—Decidedly so, sup-
" pose the case of new markets opened.

" 2546. Are you at all acquainted with the state
" of things in 1720, at the time of the bubble ?—It is
" stated in Mr. M'Culloch's ' Dictionary of Commerce,'
" that the

Bank circulation in 1718 was about 1,829,000*l*.
,,   1721 ,, 2,054,000*l*.
,,   1730 ,, 4,224,000*l*.

The increase, then, from 1718 to 1721 was 225,000*l*., or about 75,000*l*. per
annum ; and from 1721 to 1730 it was 2,170,000*l*., or about 241,000*l*.

" Thus the bubble year, 1721, was preceded by a
" low, and succeeded by a high, rate of increase, the
" latter unattended by any commercial excitement ;
" there is, then, no necessary connection between a
" morbid spirit of speculation and a great augmenta-
" tion of bank issues. We might, perhaps, for all
" practical purposes, consider the circulation of the
" country in 1721 to have been metallic ; neverthe-

" less, at that time the excitement that prevailed
" seems to have much surpassed what we saw in
" 1825."

It is impossible that Mr. Mill should have been
guilty of wilful misinterpretation when he states that
the authors and supporters of the Act of 1844 held
the opinion that " an excessive issue of bank-notes is
" the primary cause of monetary crises ;" and " that
" every such crisis which has occurred in this country
" within mercantile memory, has been either origin-
" ally produced by this cause, or greatly aggravated
" by it." The gravest charge which can be brought
against him is, that of undertaking to state the nature
and examine the grounds of a theory respecting which
he had acquired no accurate conception.

" To this extreme length," continues Mr. Mill,
" the currency theory has not been carried by the
" eminent political economists who have given to a
" more moderate form of the same theory the sanction
" of their names.   But I have not overstated the
" extravagance of the popular version, which is a
" remarkable instance to what lengths a favourite
" theory will hurry, not the closet-students, whose
" competency in such questions is often treated with
" so much contempt, but men of the world and of
" business, who pique themselves on the practical
" knowledge which they have, at least, ample op-
" portunities of acquiring.   Not only has this fixed
" idea of the currency, as the prime agent in the
" fluctuations of price, made them shut their eyes
" to the multitude of circumstances which, by influ-
" encing the expectation of supply, are the true causes
" of almost all speculations, and of almost all fluctua-
" tions of price; but in order to bring about the

" chronological agreement required by their theory
" between the variations of bank issues and those of
" prices, they have played such fantastic tricks with
" facts and dates as would be thought incredible, if
" an eminent practical authority had not taken the
" trouble of meeting them, on the ground of mere
" history, with an elaborate exposure ; I refer, as all
" conversant with the subject must be aware, to
" Mr. Tooke's 'History of Prices.' The result of
" Mr. Tooke's investigations was thus stated by him-
" self in his examination before the Commons' Com-
" mittee on the Bank Charter question in 1832 ; and
" the evidences of it stand recorded in his book : ' In
" point of fact, and historically, as far as my re-
" searches have gone, in every signal instance of a
" rise or fall of prices, the rise or fall has preceded,
" and therefore could not be the effect of, an enlarge-
" ment or contraction of the Bank circulation.' "

The theory which regards the currency as the
prime agent in the fluctuation of prices may have had
its advocates. The late Mr. Hume may have maintained, " that the markets for commodities are
" directly influenced by every alteration in the
" quantity of money in the hands of, or issuing from,
" the Bank of England."* Mr. J. B. Smith may
have stated in the Report of the Manchester Chamber
of Commerce, " that alternations of excitement are to
" be attributed entirely to mismanagement of the
" circulation." Mr. Tooke himself may have been
an early propounder of the currency theory ; may
have denounced the " increased issue of the Bank of
" England, and of the country banks." " The great

* Speech in the House of Commons on the 8th July 1839, revised by
Mr. Hume.

"factitious increase of nominal monied capital
"coming into competition with the pre-existing real
"monied capital seeking investment." "The artificial
"incentive to speculation thus afforded, and the conse-
"quent very general extension of private paper and
"of transactions on credit, operating as cause and
"effect in a great rise of colonial produce, and of
"many other commodities."* And he may have even
gone so far as to express "great doubts whether a
"system of currency consisting of so large a portion
"of paper money is not of necessity liable to great
"and preponderating evils; evils quite sufficient to
"outweigh the consideration of the cheapness of such
"a medium of exchange."† But it is scarcely necessary to repeat that the currency theory thus advocated
by these authorities, is not the theory of metallic
variations upon which the Act of 1844 is founded.
And scarcely necessary is it to point out that Mr.
Tooke's "elaborate exposure of the fantastic tricks
"which have been played with facts and dates in
"order to bring about the chronological agreement
"required by the currency theory between the varia-
"tions of bank-notes and those of prices," however
forcibly it may apply to the currency theory propounded in his previous publications, does not apply
to the theory of metallic variation which regards
fluctuations in the supply of commodities as a primary,
and of variations in the amounts of bank-notes as a
minor and comparatively inefficient cause, of fluctuations in prices. The result of Mr. Tooke's investigations, that "in every signal instance of a rise or fall of
"prices, the rise or fall has preceded, and, therefore,

* Consideration on the State of the Currency, pp. 83, 84.
† Ibid., p. 87.

"could not be the effect of, an enlargement or con-
"traction of the Bank circulation;" while it amounts
to a complete refutation of the currency theory, of
which he had been a leading advocate, presents us
with a practical verification of the opposite theory of
metallic variation—a theory of which the leading
element is, that all the most signal fluctuations of
prices are caused, not by an expansion or a contraction of the bank-note circulation, but by a redundancy
or deficiency in the supply of commodities. It would
be amusing were it not melancholy to observe the
hallucination under which Mr. Tooke imagines that
he refutes the principles of the Act of 1844 by
parading, as the results of his historical researches,
that deficient harvests have raised, and that abundant
harvests have lowered, the prices of agricultural
produce.

"The extravagance of the currency theorists in
"attributing almost every rise or fall of prices to an
"enlargement or contraction of the issues of bank-
"notes, has raised up, by reaction, a theory the
"extreme opposite of the former, of which, in scien-
"tific discussion, the most prominent representatives
"are Mr. Tooke and Mr. Fullarton. This counter-
"theory denies to bank-notes, so long as their con-
"vertibility is maintained, any power whatever of
"raising prices, and to banks, any power of increasing
"their circulation, except as a consequence of, and in
"proportion to, an increase of the business to be
"done. This last statement is supported by the
"unanimous assurances of all the country bankers
"who have been examined before successive Parlia-
"mentary Committees on the subject. They all bear
"testimony that (in the words of Mr. Fullarton) 'the

"amount of their issues is exclusively regulated by
" the extent of local dealings and expenditure in their
" respective districts, fluctuating with the fluctuations
" of production and prices, and that they neither can
" increase their issues beyond the limits which the
" range of such dealings and expenditure prescribes,
" without the certainty of having their notes imme-
" diately returned to them, nor diminish them, but at
" an almost equal certainty of the vacancy being filled
" up from some other source.' From these premises
" it is argued by Mr. Tooke and Mr. Fullarton, that
" bank-issues, since they cannot be increased in
" amount unless there be an increased demand,
" cannot possibly raise prices; cannot encourage
" speculation, nor occasion a commercial crisis; and
" that the attempt to guard against that evil by an
" artificial management of the issue of notes, is of no
" effect for the intended purpose, and liable to pro-
" duce other consequences extremely calamitous.

" As much of this doctrine as rests upon testimony
" and not upon inference appears to me incontro-
" vertible. I give complete credence to the assertion
" of the country bankers, very clearly and correctly
" condensed into a small compass, in the sentence just
" quoted from Mr. Fullarton. I am convinced that
" they cannot possibly increase their issue of notes in
" any other circumstances than those which are there
" stated. I believe, also, that the theory, grounded
" by Mr. Fullarton upon this fact, contains a large
" portion of truth, and is far nearer to being the ex-
" pression of the whole truth than any form whatever
" of the currency theory."

Mr. Mill's strange misconception—he cannot be
suspected of wilful misrepresentation—in making the

advocates of the Act of 1844 participators in the currency theory, which attributes almost every rise or fall of prices to an enlargement or contraction of the issues of bank-notes—has already been disposed of. I proceed to examine the contrary theory which denies to convertible bank-notes any power whatever of raising prices, and to banks any power of increasing their circulation. Mr. Mill affirms that so much of this doctrine as rests upon testimony and not upon inference is incontrovertible. I affirm, and am prepared to prove, that it receives a complete refutation from the principles which Mr. Mill has himself propounded, and the facts which Mr. Tooke has himself recorded.

Mr. Mill has correctly stated that prices may be raised above their ordinary level either by an increase in the quantity of the currency or by a diminution in the quantity of commodities. In either of these cases the currency is rendered redundant in relation to foreign currencies, and a contraction of the circulation, through the action of the foreign exchanges, takes place, until prices are brought down to the ordinary level. Now, it is a necessary consequence of the principle correctly stated by Mr. Mill, that a rise of prices, when caused by a diminution in the quantity of commodities, must be followed by a contraction of the currency, unless the tendency to contraction should be counteracted by an increased issue of bank-notes. When Mr. Tooke tells us, that in every signal instance of a rise of prices, within mercantile memory, the rise has been followed by an enlargement of the Bank circulation, he tells us in effect that the Bank not only possesses, but has exercised, the power of unduly extending its issues.

For if, in all the signal instances in which a rise of prices has been caused by deficient supply of commodities, the Bank had not possessed and exercised the power of increased issue, the rise of prices would have been followed by a contraction of the Bank circulation.

But Mr. Tooke has shown by testimony more direct and positive, that the Bank possesses and exercises the power of increasing its issues. He tells us * that the harvest of 1838 was deficient by one-third; that the price of wheat, the average of which had been 68s. 2d. in July, advanced to 77s. in August, and to 81s. 6d. in January 1839. And he further informs us that, coincident with this great diminution in the supply and rise in the price of corn, there was a great deficiency in the supply and rise in the price of cotton, from the failure of the crops in the United States; and that the deficiency in the supply of food and of the material of our most important manufacture was attended by an adverse exchange and a decided efflux of bullion. Under the circumstances thus stated by Mr. Tooke, a contraction of the circulation would have been inevitable, had not the Bank possessed the power of increasing its issues upon securities as its deposits were drawn out in gold for exportation. But, as Mr. Tooke has shown, it did possess and did exercise the power of increased issue. It not only maintained undiminished issue in the face of an adverse exchange, but increased its issues from 17,000,000l., their average amount on the 9th of January, to 19,655,000l., their average amount on the 18th September.† When Mr. Tooke

---

* History of Prices, vol. iii. pages 12 and 13.

† Ibid., p. 78.

maintains that the Bank does not possess the power
of increasing its issue, he " plays such fantastic tricks
with dates and figures as would have been incredible
had he not himself taken the trouble of proving their
existence on the ground of mere history by an
elaborate exposure" of his own inconsistency.

Mr. Mill gives complete credence to the assertion
of the country bankers. He is convinced that they
cannot possibly increase the issues of their notes
in any other circumstances than those expressed by
Mr. Fullarton in the passage above quoted. Let
us analyse the statement of the country bankers,
as expressed by Mr. Fullarton, and endeavour to
ascertain whether it does not establish rather than
refute the doctrine that they do possess the power
of issuing their notes to excess. The testimony,
as condensed by Mr. Fullarton, is " that the amount
" of their issues is exclusively regulated by the
" extent of their local dealings' fluctuating with the
" fluctuations of produce and price." Here it is
expressly affirmed that the country banks have the
power of increasing their issues with every increase
in the amount of local dealings and expenditure ;
and the unavoidable inference is, that as often as the
local transactions are unduly increased, the corresponding increase in the issue of the banks is an
issue in excess. Mr. Mill must establish the fact
that local transactions and expenditure cannot be
unduly extended, before he can logically infer that
the country banks do not possess the power of unduly
extending the local circulation. But this fact he
cannot establish. Uniform experience shows us that
a deficient harvest increases transactions in the corn
trade ; that the rise of prices exceeds the proportion

in which the crops are deficient; that farmers demand increased advances in order to withhold their stock, and millers and dealers in order to replenish their stocks; and that the country bankers, acting upon their avowed principle of regulating their issues by the extent of local transactions and expenditure, cause a temporary extension of the circulation at the very time at which the diminution in the quantity of produce, and the consequent importation of corn and exportation of gold, require that the circulation should be contracted.

A further doctrine maintained by the country bankers, and indorsed by Mr. Fullarton and Mr. Mill, is, that they neither can increase their issues beyond the limits which the range of local dealings and expenditure prescribe, without the certainty of having their notes immediately returned to them, nor diminish them without an almost equal certainty of the vacancy being filled up from some other source. Regarding this doctrine, it is to be observed that, when the increased issues are paid back into the banks, they assume the character of additional deposits, which the depositors may draw out upon demand, and which consequently occasions as clear an addition to the paying power—the command of money-capital—as if the depositor had retained them in his private drawer. Thus it appears that when strictly analysed, the testimony of the country bankers, to which Mr. Mill gives perfect credence, establishes the fact that they possess the power of unduly increasing the local currencies, and of creating what Mr. Tooke not inappropriately denominates a " factitious increase of " nominal monied-capital coming into competition with

" the pre-existing real monied-capital seeking invest
" ment."*

Mr. Mill proceeds :—

" There are two states of the markets: one which
" may be termed the quiescent state, the other the
" expectant, or speculative state. The first is that
" in which there is nothing tending to engender in
" any considerable portion of the mercantile public a
" desire to extend their operations. The producers
" produce and the dealers purchase only their usual
" stocks, having no expectation of a more than
" usually rapid vent for them. Each person transacts
" his ordinary amount of business, and no more, or
" increases it only in correspondence with the increase
" of his capital or connections, or with the gradual
" growth of the demand for his commodity, occasioned
" by the public prosperity. Not meditating any
" unusual extension of their own operations, producers
" and dealers do not need more than the usual
" accommodation from bankers and other money-
" lenders; and as it is only by extending their loans
" that bankers increase their issues, none but a
" momentary augmentation of issues is in these
" circumstances possible. If at a certain time of the
" year a portion of the public have larger payments
" to make than at other times, or if an individual,
" under some peculiar exigency, requires an extra
" advance, they may apply for more bank-notes,
" and obtain them; but the notes will no more
" remain in circulation, than the extra quantity of
" Bank of England notes which are issued once in
" every three months in payment of the dividends.

* State of the Currency, 2nd edition, p. 83.

" The person to whom, after being borrowed, the
" notes are paid away, has no extra payments to
" make, and no peculiar exigency, and he keeps them
" by him unused, or sends them into deposit, or
" repays with them a previous advance made to him
" by some banker: in any case he does not buy·
" commodities with them, since by the supposition
" there is nothing to induce him to lay in a larger
" stock of commodities than before.　In this case,
" therefore, there can be no addition, at the discretion
" of bankers, to the general circulating medium : any
" increase of their issues either comes back to them,
" or remains idle in the hands of the public, and no
" rise takes place in prices."

In this passage, Mr. Mill limits to quiescent states
of the market the doctrine laid down by Mr. Tooke
and Mr. Fullarton, that " bank issues cannot be
" increased unless there be an increased demand;
" cannot possibly raise prices, cannot encourage
" speculation, nor occasion a commercial crisis; and
" that the attempt to guard against that evil by an
" artificial management of the issue of notes is of no
" effect for that purpose, and is liable to produce
" other consequences extremely calamitous."　But
Mr. Mill, in limiting the doctrine to states of the
market when there is no immediate demand for
increased advances from the banks, excludes from
his consideration the important fact, that banks
possess in themselves the power of increasing and
diminishing the demand for banking accommodation.
When they raise the rate of discount, the demand for
accommodation contracts, and when they lower the
rate it expands; and Mr. Mill expressly and truly

K

informs us " that it is by extending their loans that
" bankers increase their issue;" and unless he is
prepared to disprove the fact that banks can lower
the rate of discount, he cannot consistently maintain
that their power of increasing their issue is limited to
quiescent states of the market. Neither can he refer
to his " highest authority" for the purpose of dis-
proving that banks have the power of lowering the
rate of discount, because the gravest charge which
Mr. Tooke brings against the directors of the banks
is, that they are in the habit of lowering the rate of
discount when they ought to raise it. Neither can he
refer to his other great authority to disprove the fact,
that the increased application for banking accommodation, resulting from a reduction in the rate of
discount, causes an increased issue of bank-notes,
because he tells us that " it is justly remarked by
" Mr. Fullarton that if the Bank complies with such
" applications, it must comply with them by an issue
" of notes, for notes constitute the only instru-
" mentality through which the Bank is in the habit of
" lending its credit." Mr. Tooke possesses in perfection the faculty of self-refutation. While he
propounds the doctrine that the Bank has not the
power of increased issue, he establishes the fact that
it has the power of increased issue. No one has
affirmed more distinctly, no one has more fully
explained the power which the Bank possesses of
contracting and expanding its issues on securities by
raising and lowering its rate of discount. In his
review of the state of the circulation in 1838–1839,
he attributes the difficulties and the dangers of that
period to the mischievous conduct of the Bank

directors in not contracting the circulation by timely advances in the rate of discount. He sums up as follows:—

" As to the result of the impartial review in the " preceding pages of the management of the Bank, " in as far as a judgment can be formed of it from its " public measures, and from the monthly ' Gazette ' " returns of its liabilities and assets on the average " of the three months preceding, the following appear " to be the main points open to criticism :—

" 1. The impatience manifested at the commence-" ment of 1838 to reduce the stock of bullion.

" 2. The forcible operation of the Bank towards " the close of 1838, for the purpose of extending its " securities by increased facilities for loans, at a " time when the market rate of interest was rising " above the Bank rate, and when the proceedings " of the banks in America (particularly with re-" ference to the cotton trade), and the state of " commercial credit on the Continent, were calcu-" lated to suggest, as a measure of precaution on the " part of the Bank, rather to reduce than to extend " its securities.

" 3. The continuing, during nearly six months, " namely, till 16th May 1839, the same relatively " low rate of interest, and the extended facilities for " loans, notwithstanding the continued rise in the " market rate of interest, and notwithstanding the " notoriety of the large importations of American " securities then in progress, the negotiation of which " was of course greatly promoted by the compara-" tively low rate of interest and discount charged by " the Bank. The effect of this state of things being,

" that the Bank had, by the end of May, lost five
" millions of treasure, while its securities had increased
" three millions.

" 4. The inefficiency of the measures taken between
" May and July to stop the further progress of the drain.

" 5. The hesitation and inconsistency of the pro-
" ceedings of the Bank in respect of the dead weight.

" 6. The recourse to the bankers of Paris for
" assistance : a measure, the resort to which could
" not be justified on any ground but that of its being
" considered as the only remaining resource against a
" suspension of cash payments ; and doubtless, it was
" the lesser evil ; but so discreditable an expedient
" ought not to have been resorted to until the dead
" weight, or a considerable portion of it, had been
" converted, and such conversion found to be in-
" effectual.

" The general conclusion, with reference to the
" management of the Bank being, that while, *à priori*,
" the inference is irresistible, that there must be
" something essentially erroneous in the system or in
" the regulation by which, in a state of profound
" peace, and without any counteraction from the
" country banks, the Bank of England should have
" sustained so narrow an escape from suspension of
" cash payments ; so it appears, by a reference to
" particulars, that the measures of the Bank were
" characterised by anything but a due and vigilant
" regard for the interests of the public in the main-
" tenance of the convertibility of Bank paper, or for
" its own credit, which has been much impaired in
" public estimation, both at home and abroad, by its
" resort for aid to the bankers of Paris."

These facts are correctly stated; but how do they harmonise with the Tookean theory, that the Bank does not possess the power of enlarging the circulation? Do they not present a practical proof that the Bank does possess that power? Is not a " for-" cible operation for the purpose of increasing its " securities by increased facilities for loans " the same thing as a forced extension of the circulation? Does not a " relatively low rate of interest and extended " facilities for loans " increase the demand for loans? and does not the supplying of this increased demand by the Bank create an addition to the pre-existing " factitious monied-capital keeping the currency in " excess, in relation to foreign currencies? " Was not the driving out of 5,000,000*l.* the necessary effect of the excessive loaning out of factitious monied-capital? And could an increase of securities of 3,000,000*l.* have been effected in any other way than by advancing to the presenters of such securities additional issues of notes either *in esse* or *in posse* to the amount of 3,000,000*l.*?

The last of these questions Mr. Tooke has himself set finally at rest. He has demonstrated by facts and figures that banks of issue, through the rate of discount, possess to an indefinite extent the power of increasing the issue of their notes. He tells us that on the 6th of February 1838, the directors reduced the rate of discount from five to four per cent.; and he informs us that the consequence of this reduction was, that the circulation, which had stood at 17,900,000*l.*, rose to 18,600,000*l.*, and on the 3rd of April to 18,987,000*l.*, being in the two months an increased issue of upwards of 1,000,000*l.*; and on the 18th September to 19,665,000*l.*, being, as compared with the circulation in the previous January, of nearly 2,000,000l. And Mr. Tooke further informs us* that while the circulation was thus expanded under a reduction in the rate of discount, it was contracted under an increase in the rate of discount. He tells us that in May 1839 the directors, on the abstraction of 5,000,000l. of treasure from their coffers, raised the rate of discount from 3½ per cent., to which they had previously reduced it, to 5, and subsequently to 6 per cent.; and he shows, by reference to the ' Gazette' returns of the Bank of England, that this advance in the rate of discount was followed by a rapid contraction of the circulation, continued until January 1840, when it amounted to only 16,336,000l., showing a total contraction, within a period of sixteen months, of 3,329,000l. That the Tookean doctrine that banks of issue do not possess the power of increasing their issues—a doctrine the falsehood of which its author has thus demonstrated—should be advocated by Mr. J. S. Mill, is a psychological miracle, the existence of which could not have been credited, had it rested on any testimony other than his own.

In the following passage light appears to break through the Cimmerian darkness of those which preceded it:—

" But there is another state of the markets, strik-
" ingly contrasted with the preceding, and to this
" state it is not so obvious that the theory of Mr. Tooke
" and Mr. Fullarton is applicable; namely, when an
" impression prevails, whether well founded or ground-
" less, that the supply of one or more great articles of
" commerce is likely to fall short of the ordinary

* History of Prices, vol. iii. page 78.

" consumption.   In such circumstances all persons
" connected with those commodities desire to extend
" their operations.   The producers or importers desire
" to produce or import- a larger quantity, speculators
" desire to lay in a stock in order to profit by the
" expected rise of price, and holders of the commo-
" dity desire additional advances to enable them to
" continue holding.   All these classes are disposed to
" make a more than ordinary use of their credit, and
" to this desire it is not denied that bankers very
" often unduly administer.   Effects of the same kind
" may be produced by anything which, exciting more
" than usual hopes of profit, gives increased briskness
" to business; for example, a sudden foreign demand
" for commodities on a large scale, or the expectation
" of it; such as occurred on the opening of Spanish
" America to English trade, and has occurred on va-
" rious occasions in the trade with the United States.
" Such occurrences produce a tendency to a rise of
" price in exportable articles, and generate specula-
" tions, sometimes of a reasonable, and (as long as a
" large proportion of men in business prefer excite-
" ment to safety) frequently of an irrational or immo-
" derate character.   In such cases there is a desire in
" the mercantile classes, or in some portion of them,
" to employ their credit, in a more than usual degree,
" as a power of purchasing.   This is a state of busi-
" ness which, when pushed to an extreme length,
" brings on the revulsion called a commercial crisis;
" and it is a known fact, that such periods of specula-
" tion hardly ever pass off without having been
" attended, during some part of their progress, by a
" considerable increase of bank-notes."

The light was but a glimmer—the objects on which it flecked were not seen under their true proportions and relations—the blind guides were again blindly followed.

" To this, however, it is replied by Mr. Tooke and " Mr. Fullarton, that the increase of the circulation " always follows instead of preceding the rise of " prices, and is not its cause, but its effect. That, in " the first place, the speculative purchases by which " prices are raised, are not effected by bank-notes but " by cheques, or still more commonly, on a simple " book credit; and, secondly, even if they were made " with bank-notes, borrowed for that express purpose " from bankers, the notes, after being used for that " purpose, would, if not wanted for current transac- " tions, be returned into deposit by the persons receiv- " ing them. In this I fully concur, and I regard it as " proved, both scientifically and historically, that " during the ascending period of speculation, and so " long as it is confined to transactions between dealers, " the issues of bank-notes are seldom materially in- " creased, nor contribute anything to the speculative " rise of prices."

In examining this passage, the first thing to be no- ticed is, that the doctrine that " the increase of the " circulation always follows instead of preceding the " rise of prices," is utterly erroneous. It is equally opposed to theory and experience, to the law of me- tallic equilibrium, and to the daily-recurring pheno- mena of the money market. A rise of prices is caused either by an increase in the amount of the currency, or by a diminution in the quantity of commodities. It is obvious that when the rise is caused by an increase

in the amount of the currency, the cause must precede
and cannot follow the effect which it has produced.
And it will be equally obvious, upon a moment's consideration, that when a rise of prices is caused by a
diminution in the quantity of commodities, the rise
cannot be followed by an extension of the currency,
unless there should be a coincident and undue enlargement of the bank-note circulation. A rise of prices
caused by a diminution in the quantity of commodities, when not accompanied by an undue extension of
advances from the banks, is always followed by a contraction of the currency, for a diminution in the quantity of commodities renders the previous amount of
the currency redundant in relation to foreign currencies, and the necessary consequences of such redundancy are an exportation of bullion and á contraction
of the currency until it is restored to par with foreign
currencies. Thus it is strictly demonstrable, that
when a rise of price is caused by an extension of the
currency, the extension, instead of following, precedes
the rise; and that when the rise is caused by a diminution in the quantity of commodities, it is always
followed, not by an extension but by a contraction of
the currency, unless the contraction should be counteracted by a coincident increase of advances by the
banks.   When Mr. Tooke and Mr. Fullarton tell us
" that the increase of the circulation follows, instead
" of preceding the rise of prices," they tell us, in so
many words, that the note circulation has been issued
in excess.

Mr. Mill's inconsistency, in indorsing the doctrine
that an increase of the circulation follows a rise of
prices, is altogether unaccountable, inasmuch as he

had previously advocated the contrary doctrine, that a
rise of prices, when caused by an increase of the circulation, is preceded by that increase, and that when
caused by a diminution in the quantity of commodities, is followed not by an extension, but by a contraction of the circulation. He had previously affirmed
" that an increase in the quantity of money raises
" prices, and a diminution lowers them, is the most
" elementary proposition in the theory of currencies,
" and without it we should have no key to any of the
" others ;" and he had further stated, " that the very
" same effect would be produced on prices if we sup-
" pose the goods diminished instead of the money
" increased, and the contrary effects if the goods were
" increased or the money diminished." *   From the
proposition thus affirmed by Mr. Mill, the self-evident
inferences are, that a rise of prices, when caused by
an increase in the quantity of money, must be preceded by that increase ; and that when the rise of
prices is caused by a diminution in the quantity of
goods, it cannot be followed by an increase in the
amount of money, unless the action of the law of
equilibrium should be counteracted by an extension
of the bank-note circulation. I would venture to ask
Mr. Mill to reconcile the propositions just quoted with
his laudatory adoption of Mr. Tooke's celebrated
statement that, " in point of fact, and historically, as
" far as my researches have gone, in every signal in-
" stance of a rise or fall of prices, the rise or fall has
" been preceded by an enlargement or contraction
" of the Bank circulation."

So much for the doctrine that an extension of the

* Vol. ii. pages 16, 19.

currency is caused by a rise of prices. Let us proceed to the examination of the several other propositions which Mr. Mill affirms in the paragraph last
quoted. They are, that the speculative purchases by
which prices are raised are not effected by bank-notes,
but by cheques, or still more commonly, by a simple
book credit; that even if they were made by bank-
notes borrowed for that express purpose from bankers,
the notes, after being used for that purpose, would, if
not wanted for current transactions, be returned into
deposit by the person receiving them; and that, so
long as speculation is confined to transactions between
dealers, the issue of bank-notes is seldom materially
increased, nor contributes anything to the speculative
rise of prices.

These propositions are fundamentally erroneous.
Purchases and payments are never made by cheques.
Cheques are nothing more than orders for cash drawn
against deposits, and it is only by the transfer of the
deposits against which cheques are drawn that purchases and payments are effected. When notes are
returned to banks in deposit, the depositor continues
to possess, so long as the banks remain solvent,
the same amount of money-capital as he would have
possessed had he retained the notes in his private
desk; and the power of making purchases and payments, and of acting upon prices, is in either case
one and the same. Again, transactions between
dealers contribute most powerfully to a speculative
rise of prices. That they should so contribute is a
necessary consequence of the elementary principle of
currency which Mr. Mill has propounded. It is by
wholesale purchases between dealers that artificial deficiencies in the supply of goods are created; and on

Mr. Mill's own principle, a deficiency in the supply of goods has the same effect in raising prices as an increase in the amount of money. When he affirms that speculative purchases between dealers do not cause a rise of prices, and that deficiencies in the supply of goods do cause a rise of prices, does he not affirm in effect two contradictory propositions?

In the following passages, however, a step is taken in the right direction :—

" It seems to me, however, that this can no longer
" be affirmed when speculation has proceeded so far
" as to reach the producers. Speculative orders given
" by merchants to manufacturers induce them to ex-
" tend their operations, and to become applicants to
" bankers for increased advances, which, if made in
" notes, are not paid away to persons who return
" them into deposit, but are partially expended in
" paying wages, and pass into the various channels of
" retail trade, where they become directly effective in
" producing a further rise in prices. I cannot but
" think that this employment of bank-notes must have
" been powerfully operative on prices at the time
" when notes of one and two pounds value were per-
" mitted by law. Admitting, however, that the pro
" hibition of notes below five pounds has now rendered
" this part of their operation comparatively insig-
" nificant, by greatly limiting their applicability to
" the payment of wages, there is another form of their
" instrumentality which comes into play in the later
" stages of speculation, and which forms the principal
" argument of the more moderate supporters of the
" currency theory. Though advances by bankers are
" seldom demanded for the purpose of buying on spe-
" culation, they are largely demanded by unsuccessful

" speculators for the purpose of holding on; and the
" competition of these speculators for a share of the
" loanable capital, makes even those who have not
" speculated more dependent than before on bankers
" for the advances they require. Between the ascend-
" ing period of speculation and the revulsion, there is
" an interval, extending to weeks, and sometimes
" months, of struggling against a fall. The tide
" having shown signs of turning, the speculative
" holders are unwilling to sell in a falling market,
" and in the meantime they require funds to enable
" them to fulfil even their ordinary engagements. It
" is this stage that is ordinarily marked by a con-
" siderable increase in the amount of the bank-note
" circulation. That such an increase does usually
" take place, is denied by no one. And I think it
" must be admitted that this increase tends to prolong
" the duration of the speculations; that it enables the
" speculative prices to be kept up for some time after
" they would otherwise have collapsed; and therefore
" prolongs and increases the drain of the precious
" metals for exportation, which is a leading feature of
" this stage in the progress of a commercial crisis; the
" continuance of which drain at last endangering the
" power of the banks to fulfil their engagement of
" paying their notes on demand, they are compelled to
" contract their credit more suddenly and severely
" than would have been necessary if they had been
" prevented from propping up speculation by increased
" advances, after the time when the recoil had become
" inevitable."

The step in the right direction is not sustained.
The immediately succeeding paragraph evinces a com-

plete misconception of the objects and spirit of the Act
of 1844 :—

" To prevent this retardation of the recoil, and ulti-
" mate aggravation of its severity, is the object of the
" scheme for regulating the currency, of which Mr.
" Loyd, Mr. Norman, and Colonel Torrens, were the
" first promulgators, and which has, in a slightly-
" modified form, been enacted into law."

The objects of the Act of 1844 were, first and
mainly to secure at all times the perfect convertibility
of the bank-note circulation. Second, to maintain the
currency, in so far as respects its amount and its
value, in the same state in which it would exist under
a purely metallic circulation. Third, to prevent the recurrence of any alternations of speculative excitement
and depression other than those which would equally
occur were the whole of the bank-note circulation displaced by coin. It is obvious that the attainment of
the third and last of these objects must necessarily
result from the attainment of the second ; and it is not
only extraordinary, but altogether unaccountable, how
Mr. Mill should so far misconceive the purport and
intent of the Act as to represent its incidental operation in accelerating a recoil as its one and only object,
and to exclude from all consideration its primary
and most important object, that of securing the convertibility of the note circulation. Even Mr. Tooke
himself has not fallen into a misapprehension so entire.
He fully admits that in the regulation of the currency
the primary object should be to secure convertibility.
Writing in 1841, he says,*—" If greater security

---

* History of Prices, vol. iii. pages 173, 174.

" against the recurrence of the danger of suspension,
" which we have so narrowly escaped, cannot be pro-
" vided consistently with the maintenance of the
" existing establishment in all its main functions,
" there ought to be no hesitation in taking early mea-
" sures with the view to the substitution of some other
" system. Of any system so substituted, the primary
" object should be to afford the fullest security for the
" preservation, under any possible circumstances, of
" the present standard of value, or, in other words,
" of the constant and perfect convertibility of paper
" into gold, according to the present Mint regula-
" tions."

While Mr. Mill excludes from consideration this
primary and all-important object of the Act of 1844,
he presents us with a partial and imperfect view of the
provisions which it contains for the securing of that
object. He says—

" According to the scheme in its original purity,
" the issue of promissory notes for circulation was to
" be confined to one body. In the form adopted by
" Parliament, all existing issuers were permitted to
" retain this privilege, but none were to be thereafter
" admitted to it, even in the place of those who might
" discontinue their issues; and, for all except the
" Bank of England, a maximum of issues was pre-
" scribed on a scale intentionally low. To the Bank
" of England no maximum was fixed for the aggregate
" amount of its notes, but only for the portion issued
" on securities, or, in other words, on loan. These
" were never to exceed a certain limit, fixed for the
" present at fourteen millions. All issues beyond
" that amount must be in exchange for bullion; of

" which the Bank is bound to purchase, at a trifle
" below the Mint valuation, any quantity which is
" offered to it, giving its notes in exchange. In re-
" gard, therefore, to any issue of notes beyond the
" limit of fourteen millions, the Bank is purely passive,
" having no function but the compulsory one of giving
" its notes for gold at 3*l.* 17*s.* 9*d.*, and gold for its
" notes at 3*l.* 17*s.* 10½*d.*, whenever and by whomsoever
" it is called upon to do so."

Here a most important provision of the Act is
omitted, namely, that of dividing the business of the
Bank into two separate departments, totally distinct
from, and independent of each other, the functions of
one being strictly limited to issuing of notes in exchange for gold, and paying out gold in exchange for
notes, and the functions of the other being as strictly
assimilated to those of an ordinary bank of deposit
and discount. The practical effect of this separation
of functions is that there is no more connection
between the issue department and the banking department, than there is between the issue department
and any private or joint-stock bank within the limits
of the realm. Mr. Mill's failure to perceive the
existence of this complete separation of functions,
occasions ambiguity and vagueness in the language in
which his propositions are expressed, and, as we shall
hereafter see, renders it uncertain to which of the
departments, that of issue or that of banking, his
statements and inferences are intended to apply.

In the immediately-following paragraph, however,
the ambiguity is not apparent :—

" The object for which this mechanism is intended
" is, that the bank-note currency may vary in its

" amount at the exact times, and in the exact degree,
" in which a purely metallic currency would vary.
" The precious metals being the commodity that has
" hitherto approached nearest to that invariability in
" all the circumstances influencing value, which fits a
" commodity for being adopted as a medium of ex-
" change, it is an essential requisite of any substitute
" for those metals that it should conform exactly in its
" value to a metallic currency, and for that purpose it
" is very plausibly considered necessary that it should
" conform in its quantity likewise."

How far this purpose is really fulfilled by the
means adopted, we shall presently examine. First,
however, let us consider whether the measure effects
the practical object, chiefly relied on in its defence, by
the more sober of its advocates, that of arresting speculative extensions of credit at an earlier period with
a less drain of gold, and consequently by a milder and
more gradual process. I think it must be admitted
that to a certain degree it is successful in this object.

The only objection to the above passage is, that it
produces the misconception that the practical object
chiefly relied on by the supporters of the Act is, that
of correcting speculative extensions of credit at an
earlier period, and by a milder and more gradual
process. In the passage which immediately follows,
Mr. Mill relapses into graver errors.

" I am aware of what may be urged, and reason-
" ably urged, in opposition to this opinion. It may
" be said, that when the time arrives at which the
" banks are pressed for increased advances to enable
" speculators to fulfil their engagements, a limitation
" in the issue of notes will not prevent the banks, if

L

" otherwise willing, from making these advances ;
" that they have still their deposits as a source from
" which loans may be made beyond the point which
" is consistent with prudence as bankers; and that
" even if they refused to do so, the only effect would
" be, that the deposits themselves would be drawn
" out to supply the wants of the depositors, which
" would be just as much an addition to the bank-notes
" and coin in the hands of the public, as if the notes
" themselves were increased. .This is true, and is a
" sufficient answer to those who think that the ad-
" vances of banks to prop up failing speculators are
" objectionable, chiefly as an increase of the cur-
" rency."

The propositions here advanced are not true. They
are not only theoretically untrue, but are directly at
variance with fact and experience. Banks can make
advances to a far greater extent when they make them
with their own notes, than when they make them
from their deposits. When made by an increased
issue of notes, liabilities are increased; when made
from deposits, reserves are diminished. This is an
important difference as regards the proportion between
reserves and liabilities, inasmuch as that proportion is
more affected when advances diminish reserves, than
when they increase liabilities. This will be sufficiently obvious to those who are familiar with the
rules of practical banking; but as there is a numerous
class, including Mr. Tooke, Mr. Fullarton, Mr. Mill,
and their followers, who ignore these rules, some illustration of the fact that the effect upon the proportion
between reserves and liabilities is different in the
two cases, may be desirable.

Let us suppose that a banker's capital consists of deposits to the amount of two hundred thousand pounds; that he has advanced one hundred and fifty thousand pounds upon securities, and retained fifty thousand pounds as a reserve, and consequently that the proportion of his reserve to his liabilities is as one to four. It is evident, that should he now make to his customers an additional advance of fifty thousand pounds with his own notes, his liabilities would be increased from two hundred to two hundred and fifty thousand pounds; and that the proportion of his reserve to his liabilities would be diminished from one to four to one to five; while it is equally evident, that the banker could not make the additional advance of fifty thousand pounds from his reserve without the exhaustion of his coffers; and that were he to advance only two hundred and fifty thousand pounds from his reserve, the remaining reserve of twenty-five thousand pounds would bear to his liabilities of two hundred thousand, the proportion of one to eight. But had the banker made an additional advance of twenty-five thousand pounds in his own notes, his liabilities would be increased to two hundred and fifty thousand pounds, while his reserve would remain undiminished at fifty thousand pounds, so that the proportion of the latter to the former would be as one to four and a half.

2nd. The statement that were bankers to refuse to make advances from their deposits, " the only " effect would be, that the deposits themselves would " be drawn out to supply the wants of the depositors, " which would be just as much an addition to the " bank-notes and coin in the hands of the public, as if

" the notes themselves were increased," is so mani-
festly erroneous, that one marvels how it could possibly have been made.   When depositors draw out
that portion of the deposits which the bankers retain as
reserves, the bankers, in order to maintain a safe proportion between their reserves and liabilities, are compelled to contract the issue of their notes upon
securities.   Let the deposits be as before, 200,000*l.*;
of which 50,000*l.* are held as reserve, and 150,000*l.*
advanced to the public on securities, and let the depositors draw 250,000*l.* to supply their wants.   This
would reduce the proportion of the reserve to the
liabilities from one to four, to one to eight; and the
banker would be compelled, in self-defence, to restore
the safe proportion of one to four, by reducing his
advances to the public from 150,000*l.* to 75,000*l.*   It
is not too much to say, that no one acquainted either
with the theory of banking, or with the practical rules
under which the business of banking is conducted,
could have hazarded the proposition that increased
advances, when made from deposits, have the same
effect upon the circulation as when they are made by
additional issues of notes; and that the drawing out
of deposits to supply the wants of depositors would be
just as much an addition to the notes and coin in the
hands of the public, as if the notes themselves were
increased.

The following paragraph, although pervaded by
some of the misconceptions already pointed out, might
have been written by an advocate of the Act of 1844,
and an opponent of the currency theory, as originally
propounded by Mr. Tooke :—

" But the mode in which they are really objection-

" able is as an extension of credit. If, instead of
" lending their notes, the banks allow the demand of
" their customers for disposable capital to act on the
" deposits, there is the same increase of currency, for
" a short time at least, but there is not an increase of
" loans. The rate of interest, therefore, is not pre-
" vented from rising at the first moment when the
" difficulties consequent on excess of speculation begin
" to be felt. Speculative holders are obliged to sub-
" mit earlier to that loss by resale, which could not
" have been prevented from coming on them at last;
" the recoil of prices, and collapse of general credit,
" take place sooner.

" To appreciate the effect which this acceleration of
" the crisis has in mitigating its intensity, let us ad-
" vert more particularly to the nature and effects of
" that leading feature in the period just preceding the
" collapse, the drain of gold. A rise of prices pro-
" duced by a speculative extension of credit, even
" when bank-notes have not been the instrument, is
" not the less effectual (if it lasts long enough) in
" turning the exchanges; and when the exchanges
" have turned from this cause, they can only be
" turned back, and the drain of gold stopped, either
" by a fall of prices, or by a rise of the rate of interest.
" A fall of prices will stop it by removing the cause
" which produced it, and by rendering goods a more
" advantageous remittance than gold, even for paying
" debts already due. A rise of the rate of interest,
" and consequent fall of the prices of securities, will
" accomplish the purpose still more rapidly, by in-
" ducing foreigners, instead of taking away the gold
" which is due to them, to leave it for investment

" within the country, and even send gold into the
" country to take advantage of the increased rate of
" interest. Of this last mode of stopping a drain of
" gold, the year 1847 afforded signal examples. But,
" until one of these two things takes place—until
" either prices fall, or the rate of interest rises—
" nothing can possibly arrest, or even moderate, the
" efflux of gold. Now, neither will prices fall nor in-
" terest rise, so long as the unduly-expanded credit
" is upheld by the continued advances of bankers. It
" is well known that when a drain of gold has set in,
" even if bank-notes have not increased in quantity,
" it is upon them that the contraction first falls, the
" gold wanted for exportation being always obtained
" from the Bank of England in exchange for its notes.
" But under the system which preceded 1844, the
" Bank of England, being subjected, in common with
" other banks, to the importunities for fresh advances
" which are characteristic of such a time, could, and
" often did, immediately reissue the notes which had
" been returned to it in exchange for bullion. It is a
" great error, certainly, to suppose that the mischief
" of this reissue chiefly consisted in preventing a con-
" traction of the currency. It was, however, quite as
" mischievous as it has ever been supposed to be. As
" long as it lasted, the efflux of gold could not cease,
" since neither would prices fall nor interest rise
" while these advances continued. Prices having
" risen without any increase of bank-notes, could well
" have fallen without a diminution of them ; but
" having risen in consequence of an extension of
" credit, they could not fall without a contraction of
" it. As long, therefore, as the Bank of England

" and the other banks persevered in this course, so
" long gold continued to flow out; until so little was
" left, that the Bank of England, being in danger of
" suspension of payments, was compelled at last to
" contract its discounts so greatly and suddenly, as to
" produce a much more extreme variation in the rate
" of interest, inflict much greater loss and distress on
" individuals, and destroy a much greater amount of
" the ordinary credit of the country than any real
" necessity required.

   " I acknowledge (and the experience of 1847 has
" proved to those who overlooked it before) that the
" mischief now described may be wrought, and in
" large measure, by the Bank of England, through its
" deposits alone. It may continue, or even increase
" its discounts and advances, when it ought to con-
" tract them; with the ultimate effect of making the
" contraction much more severe and sudden than
" necessary. I cannot but think, however, that banks
" which commit this error with their deposits, would
" commit it still more, if they were at liberty to make
" increased loans with their issues as well as their
" deposits. I am compelled to think that the being
" restricted from increasing their issues, is a real
" impediment to their making those advances which
" arrest the tide at its turn, and make it rush like a
" torrent afterwards.   If the restrictions of the Act of
" 1844 were no obstacle to the advances of banks in
" the interval preceding the crisis, why were they
" found an insuperable obstacle during the crisis? an
" obstacle which nothing less would overcome than a
" suspension of the law, through the assumption by
" Government of a temporary dictatorship.   Evi-

" dently they are an obstacle ; and when the Act is
" blamed for interposing obstacles at a time when;
" not obstacles, but facilities are needed, it must, in
" justice, receive credit for interposing them when
" they are an acknowledged benefit. In this par-
" ticular, therefore, I think it cannot be denied that
" the new system is a real improvement upon the
" old."

So far so good. But Mr. Mill, " to one view con-
" stant never," forthwith deserts the principle he had
apparently espoused, and turns to re-embrace the
Tookean fallacies. He says—

" But although I am compelled to differ thus far
" from the opinion of Mr. Tooke and of Mr. Fullarton,
" I concur with them in thinking that these advan-
" tages, whatever value may be put on them, are
" purchased by still greater disadvantages.

" In the first place, a large extension of credit by
" bankers, though most hurtful when, credit being
" already in an inflated state, it can only serve to
" retard and aggravate the collapse, is most salutary
" when the collapse has come, and when credit, instead
" of being in excess, is in distressing deficiency, and
" increased advances by bankers, instead of being
" an addition to the ordinary amount of floating
" credit, serve to replace a mass of other credit which
" has been suddenly destroyed. Antecedently to 1844,
" if the Bank of England occasionally aggravated the
" severity of a commercial revulsion by rendering
" the collapse of credit more tardy, and thence more
" violent than necessary, it, in return, rendered in-
" valuable services during the revulsion itself, by
" coming forward with advances to support solvent

" firms, at a time when all other paper and almost all
" mercantile credit had become comparatively value-
" less. This service was eminently conspicuous in
" the crisis of 1825–6, the severest probably ever
" experienced; during which the Bank increased
" what is called its circulation by many millions,
" in advances to those mercantile firms of whose ulti-
" mate solvency it felt no doubt; advances which,
" if it had been obliged to withhold, the severity of
" the crisis would have been even greater than it
" was. If the Bank, it is justly remarked by Mr.
" Fullarton, complies with such applications, ' it
" must comply with them by an issue of notes, for
" notes constitute the only instrumentality through
" which the Bank is in the practice of lending its
" credit. But those notes are not intended to circu-
" late, nor do they circulate. There is no more
" demand for circulation than there was before. On
" the contrary, the rapid decline of prices which the
" case in supposition presumes, would necessarily
" contract the demand for circulation. The notes
" would either be returned to the Bank of England,
" as fast as they were issued, in the shape of deposits,
" or would be locked up in the drawers of the private
" London bankers, or distributed by them to their
" correspondents in the country, or intercepted by
" other capitalists, who, during the fervour of the
" previous excitement, had contracted liabilities which
" they might be imperfectly prepared on the sudden
" to encounter. In such emergencies, every man
" connected with business, who has been trading on
" other means than his own, is placed on the defen-
" sive, and his whole object is to make himself as

" strong as possible, an object which cannot be more
" effectually answered than by keeping by him as
" large a reserve as possible, in paper, which the
" law has made a legal tender. The notes themselves
" never find their way into the produce markets ; and
" if they at all contribute to retard ' (or, as I should
" rather say, to moderate) ' the fall of prices, it is
" not by promoting in the slightest degree the effective
" demand for commodities, not by enabling consumers
" to buy more largely for consumption, and so giving
" briskness to commerce, but by a process precisely
" the reverse, by enabling the holders of commodities
" to hold on, by obstructing traffic and repressing
" consumption.' "

Here Mr. Mill present us with a striking example
of the " fantastic tricks which may be played with
" facts and figures." He suppresses the fact that
while the Act of 1844 confers the important advantage of arresting speculative excitement and mitigating the severity of the consequent collapse, it at the
same time confers the still more important advantage
of securing the convertibility of the circulation, and
he also suppresses the fact that, previous to the Act
of 1844, the Bank, while prolonging the periods of
speculative excitement, and intensifying the severity
of subsequent recoil, endangered the convertibility
of the note circulation, and that so far from having
been able " to render invaluable service during a
" revulsion, by coming forward with advances to
" support solvent firms, when all other paper and
" almost all mercantile credit had become compara-
" tively valueless," the Bank itself became included
in the list of firms verging on insolvency. These

facts were strictly exemplified during the commercial crisis of 1839–40.

Mr. Mill offers no proofs of his assertions that the disadvantages of the restriction on the Bank circulation, under the Act of 1844, exceed the advantages, and that the advantages of unrestricted issues exceed the disadvantages. The best and shortest way of testing their correctness will, probably, be to contrast the results of unrestricted issues during the commercial crisis of 1839–40 with the results which would have been produced, had the provisions of the Act of 1844 been then in force.

A drain of gold commenced on the 3rd of April 1838, when the securities were 18,947,000*l.*, and the bullion 10,125,000*l.* ; and on the 26th of June, the bullion had declined to 9,722,000*l.*, being a diminution of 403,000*l.* Now, had the principle of metallic variation been in force, this diminution of the bullion would have been accompanied by a corresponding diminution of the circulation, which would, consequently, have fallen on the 26th of June from 18,987,000*l.*, its amount on the 3rd of April, to 18,544,000*l.* But on the 26th, the circulation, instead of being reduced to 18,544,000*l.*, was increased to 19,047,000*l.* Consequently the actual amount of the circulation on the 26th of June, exceeded by 463,000*l.* the amount at which it would have stood under metallic variation.

On the 3rd of April 1836, the bullion had declined from 10,125,000*l.*, its amount on the 2nd of April, 1839, to 7,073,000*l.*, being a diminution of 3,052,000*l.* Had the principle of metallic variation been in force, the diminution of the bullion would have been accom-

panied by a corresponding diminution in the securities
from 18,987,000*l*., the amount at which they stood in
the previous April, when the bullion was 10,125,000*l*.
to 15,935,000*l*.   Now a contraction of the circulation
to 16,732,000*l*. on the 12th of December, arrested the
drain, and the bullion, which on that day had fallen
to 2,887,000*l*., rose on the 7th of January 1840, to
3,454,000*l*.   Now it is evident that, as a contraction
to 16,732,000*l*. was sufficient in December to turn the
exchanges in our favour, and terminate the monetary
crisis, a contraction in April to 15,935,000*l*. would
have been equally efficacious, at least in turning the
exchanges and terminating the crisis.   But while in
these two cases the crisis would have been equally terminated, the statics of the Bank, and its power to restore commercial confidence, would have been widely
different.   In the actual case of unrestricted issue, the
Bank, paralysed by the fear of endangering the convertibility of its notes, and flying to foreign aid to avert
its own insolvency, was not in the condition to run to
the rescue of inferior firms.   In the assumed case of
issues restricted within the limit of metallic variation,
the Bank, holding, as it did on the 2nd of April,
1839, when the drain would have been stopped, a
reserve of 7,000,000*l*. of bullion, and thus freed from
all anxiety on account of the convertibility of the
note circulation, would have been in a condition to
afford invaluable aid in relieving the collapse of
commercial confidence.   Besides, the collapse would
have been far less severe in the assumed than it was
in the actual case.   Under the principle of metallic
variation, the drain of bullion and the contraction of
the circulation would have ceased in April 1839 ;

under the principle of unrestricted issues, they proceeded with increased intensity to December.

The *modus operandi* by which, under the case above
assumed, the Bank would have sustained solvent
houses, and hastened the restoration of commercial
credit, may be easily explained.   As soon as the cessation of the drain ceased to require a further contraction of the circulation, the banking department, secured
against a further diminution of its reserve, might
have safely given from its deposits increased advances
to firms, of whose ultimate solvency it was assured.
This increase of money capital could not, so long as
the exchanges were favourable, have the effect of
rendering the currency excessive in relation to foreign
currencies, because the exchange could not be favourable, unless the currency were deficient in relation to
foreign currencies.   It thus appears evident, that
when the currency is regulated on the principle of
metallic variation, the Bank, relieved from the necessity of protecting its own coffers, acquires the
power of mitigating the commercial revulsion consequent upon undue speculation.   But it possessed,
as we have seen, no such salutary power during the
commercial revulsion of 1838-39, when, acting on the
principle of unrestricted issue, it had endangered its
coffers by not contracting its advances as its gold
flowed out, and when any forcible increase of the
circulation might have protracted the drain and suspended cash payments.

In the concluding sentences of the paragraph on
which we have been animadverting, Mr. Mill's logic
is in fault.   Forgetful of the rules of deductive
reasoning which he has elsewhere laid down, he

falls into the fallacy of drawing similar conclusions
from dissimilar premises.   There is no analogy, there
is a positive contrariety, between the causes of the
monetary crisis of 1825 and the causes of the crises
which have subsequently occurred.   In the crisis of
1825 there was a sudden diminution in the amount
of the currencies—in that of 1839 in the quantity of
commodities.   In 1825 the stoppage of provincial
banks annihilated the greater part of the provincial
circulation, at that time consisting, almost exclusively, of one-pound notes, and caused a heavy domestic drain upon the Bank for sovereigns to supply
the void.   In 1839, a deficient harvest, and a diminished supply of cotton, rendered the proportion of
currency to commodities greater in this than in foreign
countries, and caused a heavy drain of gold for exportation.   These opposite states required opposite
treatment.   A further contraction of the circulation
by the Bank of England in 1825 would have increased
the domestic drain and intensified the panic of that
disastrous period—a further extension of the Bank
circulation in 1839 would have increased the foreign
drain, and issued in a suspension of cash payments.
When Mr. Mill contends, that because an unrestricted
issue of bank-notes was efficacious in mitigating a
monetary crisis, originating in a deficiency of currency, it would be equally efficacious in rectifying a
derangement originating in a relatively redundant
currency, he shows us how wide is the difference
between teaching logic as a science and practising it
as an art.

   " The opportune relief thus afforded to credit,
" during the excessive contraction which succeeds to

" an undue expansion, is consistent with the principle
" of the new system ; for an extraordinary contraction
" of credit, and fall of prices, inevitably draw gold
" into the country, and the principle of the system is
" that the bank-note currency shall be permitted, and
" even compelled, to enlarge itself, in all cases in
" which a metallic currency would do the same.   But
" what the principle of the law would encourage, its
" provisions in this instance preclude, by not suffer-
" ing the increased issues to take place, until the
" gold has actually arrived; which is never until the
" worst part of the crisis is past, and almost all the
" losses and failures attendant on it are consummated.
" The machinery of the system withholds, until for
" many purposes it comes too late, the very medicine
" which the theory of the system prescribes as the
" appropriate remedy."

The argument urged in the above passage has been
already answered.   It has been already shown, that
limiting the issue of banks on the principle of metallic
variation would not, even were there no separation of
departments, preclude the Bank, when the exchanges
have become favourable, from affording opportune
relief to credit during the excessive contraction which
succeeds undue expansion.   It remains to be shown,
that under the separation of functions, the power of
granting such relief is very considerably increased.
Under the provisions of the Act, the banking department is, like all other banks of deposit and discount,
placed under the necessity of maintaining a reserve of
notes to meet the demands of its depositors.   Now,
this banking reserve may bear a varying proportion
to the deposits, the payment of which it is held to

secure. When an adverse exchange causes a withdrawal of deposits to be exchanged for gold, the Bank
is obliged to replenish its reserve by a contraction of
its securities; and on the other hand, when gold has
ceased to flow out and begins to flow in, and when
the deposits, instead of diminishing, show a tendency
to increase, the banking department may, without
endangering its position, diminish its reserve and
increase its securities. Thus we see that when excessive contraction succeeds to undue expansion; when
a rapid fall of prices, with a consequent increase of
exports and a diminution of imports, indicate a speedy
rectification of the exchanges, the banking department,
should it have maintained an adequate reserve during
the pressure, will be in a position to anticipate the
influx of gold, and to make advances to solvent firms
from its now superabundant reserve. Mr. Mill's statements become true when reversed. The opportune
relief which the principle of the law would encourage,
its provisions *secure*, by *allowing* increased advances to
be made *before* the gold has actually arrived. The
machinery of the system *provides*, *before* it is too late,
the very medicine which the theory of the system
prescribes as the appropriate remedy.

" This function of banks in filling up the gap made
" in mercantile credit by the consequences of undue
" speculation and its revulsion, is so entirely indis-
" pensable, that if the Act of 1844 continues un-
" repealed, there can be no difficulty in foreseeing
" that its provisions must be suspended, as they were
" in 1847, in every period of great commercial diffi-
" culty, as soon as the crisis has really and com-
" pletely set in. Were this all, there would be no

" absolute inconsistency in maintaining the restriction
" as a means of preventing a crisis, and relaxing it
" for the purpose of relieving one."

The indispensable function of filling up the gap
made in commercial credit by undue speculation,
and its revulsion, is, as already shown, far more
effectually secured under the provisions of the Act
of 1844 than it was or could have been under the
previous system of unrestricted issue.   Mr. Mill
falls into a complete misconception of the actual
facts of the case, when he implies that it was the
restrictions imposed on the issue department, which
disabled the banking department from coming in aid
of commercial credit when the crisis of 1847 had set
in.   The banking department had postponed, and
thereby intensified, the collapse by a premature increase of their securities and reduction of their reserve ; and the consequence was, that when the aggravated collapse occurred and the exchanges turned,
the banking department, instead of having a disposable reserve to advance in aid of commercial
credit, was itself in danger of suspending payment.
Had the banking department been conducted in accordance with the ordinary rules of legitimate banking,
the commercial embarrassments of 1847, instead of
being prolonged and intensified into panic, would
have been early palliated and early relieved.

" But there is another objection, of a still more
" radical and comprehensive character, to the new
" system. Professing, in theory, to require that a
" paper currency shall vary in its amount, in exact
" conformity to the variations of a metallic currency,
" it provides, in fact, that in every case of an efflux

M

" of gold, a corresponding diminution shall take place
" in the quantity of bank-notes; in other words, that
" every exportation of the precious metals shall be
" virtually drawn from the circulation; it being
" assumed that this would be the case if the currency
" were wholly metallic. This theory, and these prac-
" tical arrangements, are adapted to the case in which
" the drain of gold originates in a rise of prices pro-
" duced by an undue expansion of currency or credit;
" but they are adapted to no case beside."

When Mr. Mill penned this passage, it must not
only have escaped his recollection that he had previously indorsed Adam Smith's doctrine that the
value of money is determined by its proportion to
commodities, but that he had himself affirmed the
proposition that a diminution in the quantity of commodities has the same effect upon the value of prices
as an increase in the quantity of money. He cannot,
without self-contradiction, deny the truth of the doctrine, that a diminution in the quantity of commodities
has the same effect upon prices as an increase in the
quantity of money; and he therefore cannot, upon
reflection, continue to maintain that the theory and
practical arrangements of the Act of 1844 are applicable to no case except that in which a drain of gold
originates in a rise of prices produced by an undue
expansion of currency or credit.

" When the efflux of gold is the last stage of a
" series of effects arising from an increase of the cur-
" rency, or from an expansion of credit tantamount in
" its effect on prices to an increase of currency, it is
" in that case a fair assumption that in a purely
" metallic system, the gold exported would be drawn

" from the currency itself; because such a drain,
" being in its nature unlimited, will necessarily con-
" tinue as long as currency and credit are undi-
" minished.   But an exportation of the precious
" metals often arises from no causes affecting cur-
" rency or credit, but simply from an unusual exten-
" sion of foreign payments, arising either from the
" state of the markets for commodities, or from some
" circumstance not commercial.   In this class of
" causes, four, of powerful operation, are included, of
" each of which the last fifty years of English history
" afford repeated instances.   The first is that of an
" extraordinary foreign expenditure by Government,
" either political or military, as in the last war, and
" particularly in the latter years of it.   The second is
" the case of a large exportation of capital for foreign
" investment, such as the loans and mining operations
" which partly contributed to the crisis of 1825, and
" the American speculations which were the principal
" cause of the crisis of 1839.   The third is a failure of
" crops in the countries which supply the raw material
" of important manufactures, such as the cotton fail-
" ure in America, which compelled England, in 1847,
" to incur unusual liabilities for the purchase of that
" commodity at an advanced price.   The fourth is a
" bad harvest, and a great consequent importation of
" food, of which the years 1846 and 1847 present
" an example surpassing all antecedent experi
" ence."

Here the glaring inconsistency of the preceding
passage reappears.   As Mr. Mill admits that the
value of money is increased by a diminution of its
quantity, he cannot consistently maintain that dimi-

nution in the quantity of money originating in an
extraordinary foreign expenditure by Government,
by a large exportation of capital for foreign investment, and by a failure of the crops of the countries
which supply the raw materials, "arise from no causes
"affecting currency or credit." Neither can he,
without the most glaring inconsistency, maintain that
a bad harvest and a great importation of food have no
effect upon currency or credit; because he has not
only admitted, but expressly affirmed, that a diminution in the quantity of commodities, of which deficient
harvest is the most frequent and the most powerful
temporary cause, has the same effect in lowering the
value of money and raising prices as an increase in the
quantity of money. Mr. Mill proceeds :—

"In none of these cases, if the currency were
"metallic, would the gold or silver exported for the
"purposes in question, be necessarily or even pro-
"bably drawn from the circulation. It would be
"drawn from the hoards which, under a metallic
"currency, always exist to a very large amount; in
"uncivilised countries, in the hands of all who can
"afford it; in civilised countries, chiefly in the form
"of bankers' reserves. Mr. Tooke, in his 'Inquiry
"into the Currency Principle,' bears testimony to
"this fact; but it is to Mr. Fullarton that the public
"are indebted for the clearest and most satisfactory
"elucidation of it. As I am not aware that this part
"of the theory of currency has been set forth by any
"other writer, or with anything like the same degree
"of completeness, I shall quote somewhat largely
"from this able production."

Mr. Mill's statement that in none of the cases enumerated, if the currency were metallic, would the gold and silver exported for the purposes in question, be necessarily or even probably drawn from the circulation, is directly opposed to fact. In all these cases, if the currency were metallic, the specie exported would be withdrawn from the Bank of England, diminishing at one and the same time the amount of its loanable capital and the amount of its reserve of bullion. As these were diminished, the advances of the Bank would also be diminished, and as these were diminished the currency of the metropolis would be reduced below its due proportion to that of the pro vinces, and coin would flow in from the provinces until the equilibrium should be restored.

The theory of the Act of 1844 requires that under our system of banking, our mixed circulation of coin and notes should vary in amount and in value as it would vary were it wholly metallic. But the theory of the Act does not require that the circulation should vary in accordance with the variations to which a purely metallic circulation may be liable in those countries in which banks of deposit and discount are either not established at all, or established to a very limited extent. Mr. Fullarton's doctrine of hoards, derived from the customs of some barbarous countries, however true it may be in relation to states of society in which the practice of keeping all spare cash with bankers does not extensively prevail, has no bearing whatever, either upon the theory or upon the practical operation of the Act of 1844; nevertheless, as this doctrine of hoards has been adopted with such high approval by Mr. Mill, we shall give it, as he has done, in the words of Mr. Fullarton :—

" No person who has ever resided in an Asiatic
" country, where hoarding is carried on to a far larger
" extent in proportion to the existing stock of wealth,
" and where the practice has become much more
" deeply engrafted in the habits of the people, by
" traditionary apprehensions of insecurity, and the
" difficulty of finding safe and remunerative invest-
" ments, than in any European community ; no person
" who has had personal experience of this state of
" society, can be at a loss to recollect innumerable
" instances of large metallic treasures extracted in
" times of pecuniary difficulty from the coffers of
" individuals by the temptation of a high rate of
" interest, and brought in aid of the public neces-
" sities ; nor, on the other hand, of the facility with
" which those treasures have been absorbed again,
" when the inducements which had drawn them into
" light were no longer in operation. In countries
" more advanced in civilisation and wealth than the
" Asiatic principalities, and where no man is in fear
" of attracting the cupidity of power by an external
" display of riches, but where the interchange of com-
" modities is still almost universally conducted through
" the medium of a metallic circulation—as is the case
" with most of the commercial countries on the conti-
" nent of Europe—the motives for amassing the pre-
" cious metals may be less powerful than in the
" majority of Asiatic principalities ; but the ability
" to accumulate being more widely extended, the
" absolute quantity amassed will be found probably
" to bear a considerably larger proportion to the
" population. In those states which lie exposed to
" hostile invasion, or whose social condition is un-

" settled and menacing, the motive indeed must still
" be very strong; and in a nation carrying on an
" extensive commerce, both foreign and internal,
" without any considerable aid from any of the bank-
" ing substitutes for money, the reserves of gold and
" silver indispensably required to secure the regu-
" larity of payments, must of themselves engross a
" share of the circulating coin which it would not be
" easy to estimate.

" In this country, where the banking system has
" been carried to an extent and perfection unknown
" in any other part of Europe, and may be said to
" have entirely superseded the use of coin, except for
" retail dealings and the purposes of foreign com-
" merce, the incentives to private hoarding exist no
" longer, and the hoards have all been transferred to
" the banks, or rather, I should say, to the Bank
" of England. But in France, where the bank-note
" circulation is still comparatively limited, the quan-
" tity of gold and silver coin in existence, I find
" now currently estimated, on what are described
" as the latest authorities, at the enormous sum of
" 120,000,000$l.$ sterling; nor is the estimate at all at
" variance with the reasonable probabilities of the
" case. Of this vast treasure there is every reason to
" presume that a very large proportion, probably by
" much the greater part, is absorbed in the hoards.
" If you present for payment a bill for a thousand
" francs to a French banker, he brings you the silver
" in a sealed bag from his strong room. And not the
" bankers only, but every merchant and trader, ac-
" cording to his means, is under the necessity of
" keeping by him a stock of cash sufficient not only

" for his ordinary disbursements, but to meet any
" unexpected demands. That the quantity of specie
" accumulated in these innumerable depôts, not in
" France only, but all over the Continent, where bank-
" ing institutions are still either entirely wanting, or
" very imperfectly organised, is not merely immense
" in itself, but admits of being largely drawn upon
" and transferred even in vast masses from one country
" to another, with very little, if any, effect on prices,
" or other material derangements, we have had some
" remarkable proofs :" among others, " the signal suc-
" cess which attended the simultaneous efforts of some
" of the principal European powers (Russia, Austria,
" Prussia, Sweden, and Denmark) to replenish their
" treasuries and to replace with coin a considerable
" portion of the depreciated paper which the neces-
" sities of the war had forced upon them, and this at
" the very time when the available stock of the pre-
" cious metals over the world had been reduced by
" the exertions of England to recover her metallic
" currency. . .   There can be no doubt that these
" combined operations were on a scale of very extra-
" ordinary magnitude, that they were accomplished
" without any sensible injury to commerce or public
" prosperity, or any other effect than some temporary
" derangement of the exchanges, and that the private
" hoards of treasure accumulated throughout Europe
" during the war, must have been the principal source
" from which all this gold and silver was collected.
" And no person, I think, can fairly contemplate the
" vast superflux of metallic wealth thus proved to be
" at all times in existence, and, though in a dormant
" and inert state, always ready to spring into activity

" on the first indication of a sufficiently intense de-
" mand, without feeling themselves compelled to
" admit the possibility of the mines being even shut
" up for years together, and the production of the
" metals altogether suspended, while there might be
" scarcely a perceptible alteration in the exchangeable
" value of the metal."*

Applying this to the currency doctrine and its
advocates, "one might imagine," says Mr. Fullarton,†
" that they supposed the gold which is drained off for
" exportation from a country using a currency exclu-
" sively metallic, to be collected by driblets at the
" fairs and markets, or from the tills of the grocers
" and mercers. They never even allude to the exist-
" ence of such a thing as a great hoard of the metals,
" though upon the action of the hoards depends the
" whole economy of international payments between
" specie-circulating communities, while any operation
" of the money collected in hoards upon prices must
" ever, according to the currency hypothesis, be wholly
" impossible. We know from experience, what enor-
" mous payments in gold and silver specie-circulating
" countries are capable, at times, of making, without
" the least disturbance of their internal prosperity ;
" and whence it is supposed that these payments come,
" but from their hoards? Let us think how the
" money market of a country transacting all its ex-
" changes through the medium of the precious metals
" only, would be likely to be affected by the necessity
" of making a foreign payment of several millions. Of
" course the necessity could only be satisfied by a

* Fullarton on the Regulation of Currencies, pp. 71-74.
† Ibid., pp. 139-142.

" transmission of capital ; and would not the compe-
" tition for the possession of capital for transmission
" which the occasion would call forth, necessarily raise
'' the market rate of interest ?   If the payment was to
" be made by the Government, would not the Govern-
" ment, in all probability, have to open a new loan on
'' terms more than usually favourable to the lender ?
'' If made by merchants, would it not be drawn either
'' from the deposits in banks, or from the reserves which
" merchants keep by them in default of banks, or would
" it not oblige them to obtain the necessary amount of
'' specie by going into the money market as borrowers ?
" And would not all this inevitably act upon the hoards,
'' and draw forth into activity a portion of the gold and
" silver which the money-dealers had been accumu-
'' lating, and some of them with the express view of
" watching such opportunities for turning their trea-
" sures to advantage ?

  '' I would desire, indeed, no more convincing evi-
" dence of the competency of the machinery of the
" hoards in specie-paying countries to perform every
" necessary office of international adjustment, without
'' any sensible aid from the general circulation, than
" tho facility with which France, when but just re-
" covering from the shock of a destructive foreign
" invasion, completed within the space of twenty-seven
" months, the payment of her forced contribution of
" nearly twenty millions to the allied powers, and a
'' considerable proportion of that sum in specie, with-
" out any perceptible contraction or derangement of
" her domestic currency, or even any alarming fluc-
" tuation of her exchanges.

  " Or to come to the present time [1844], the balance

" of payments with nearly all Europe has for about
" four years past been in favour of this country, and
" gold has been pouring in, till the influx amounts to the
" unheard-of sum of about fourteen millions sterling.
" Yet, in all this time, has any one heard a complaint
" of any serious suffering inflicted on the people of
" the Continent? Have prices there been greatly
" depressed beyond their range in this country?
" Have wages fallen, or have merchants been exten-
" sively ruined by the universal depreciation of their
" stock? There has occurred nothing of the kind.
" The tenor of commercial and monetary affairs has
" been everywhere even and tranquil; and in France,
" more particularly, an improving revenue and ex-
" tended commerce bear testimony to the continued
" progress of internal prosperity. It may be doubted,
" indeed, if this great efflux of gold has withdrawn
" from that portion of the metallic wealth of the
" nation which really circulates a single Napoleon.
" And it has been equally obvious, from the undis-
" turbed state of credit, that not only has the supply
" of specie indispensable for the conduct of business
" in the retail market been all the while uninterrupted,
" but that the hoards have continued to furnish every
" facility requisite for the regularity of mercantile
" payments. It is of the very essence of the metallic
" system, that the hoards, in all cases of probable
" occurrence, should be equal to both objects; that
" they should, in the first place, supply the bullion
" demanded for exportation, and in the next place
" should keep up the home circulation to its legiti-
" mate complement. Every man trading under that
" system, who, in the course of his business, may have

" frequent occasion to remit large sums in respect to
" foreign countries, must either keep by him a suffi-
" cient treasure of his own, or must have the means
" of borrowing enough from his neighbours, not only
" to make up when wanted the amount of his remit-
" tances, but to enable him, moreover, to carry on
" his ordinary transactions at home without inter-
" ruption."

The only thing in this passage worthy of special
remark is Mr. Fullarton's extraordinary disregard of
the facts, in stating that the forced contribution of
nearly twenty millions, which France paid to the
allied powers, was derived from private hoards of
treasure. It was derived from a loan contracted for
by an eminent London firm, and subscribed by leading capitalists in this as well as in other countries.
France paid and pays the interest of the loan, but
the raising of the loan had not and could not have had
any greater effect, probably not even so great an
effect upon the circulation of France as on the circulation of England. The loan was derived, not from
the hoards of France, but from the money-capital of
the world. The misconceptions of Mr. Fullarton and
Mr. Mill have been triumphantly disposed of by Mr.
Arbuthnot, in his recent publication, entitled, " Sir
Robert Peel's Act of 1844 vindicated."

Mr. Mill goes on :—

" In a country in which credit is carried to so great
" an extent as in England, one great reserve, in a
" single establishment, the Bank of England, supplies
" the place, as far as the precious metals are con
" cerned, of the multitudinous reserves of other
" countries. The theoretical principle, therefore, of

" the currency doctrine would require that all those
" drains of the metal, which, if the currency were
" purely metallic, would be taken from the hoards,
" should be allowed to operate freely upon the reserve
" in the coffers of the Bank of England, without any
" attempt to stop it, either by a diminution of the cur-
" rency or by a contraction of credit. Nor to this
" would there be any well-grounded objection, unless
" the drain were so great as to threaten the exhaus-
" tion of the reserve, and a consequent stoppage of
" payments; a danger against which it is easy to take
" adequate precautions, because in the cases which
" we are considering the drain is for foreign payments
" of definite amount, and stops of itself as soon as
" these are effected. And in all systems it is ad-
" mitted, that the habitual reserve of the Bank should
" exceed the utmost amount to which experience war-
" rants the belief that such a drain may extend;
" which extreme limit Mr. Fullarton affirms to be
" seven millions, but Mr. Tooke recommends an ave-
" rage reserve of ten."

This passage is false in its facts and illogical in its
conclusions. In the first place it is false, in point of
fact, that the theoretical principle of the Act of 1844
requires that all the drains of the metal which, if the
currency were purely metallic, would be taken from
the hoards, should be allowed to operate freely upon
the reserve in the coffers of the Bank of England,
without any attempt to stop it either by a diminution
or by a contraction of credit. The theory of the
Act requires the direct contrary. It expressly and
absolutely requires that for every hundred pounds
in gold withdrawn from the coffers of the Bank, the

currency shall be contracted by the withdrawal of a hundred pounds from the note circulation; and it further requires, as a necessary effect of a contraction of the note circulation, that there shall be a corresponding contraction of credit. Again, it is contrary to fact to affirm, that there would be no well-grounded objection to allow a drain to act freely upon reserve in the coffers of the Bank, " because when the drain " is for foreign payments of a definite amount, it is " easy to take adequate precautions against the danger " of the exhaustion of the reserve, and a consequent " stoppage of payment, by the adoption of Mr. Tooke's " regulations for maintaining a reserve at the average " amount of ten millions." In order to effect this object, Mr. Tooke proposes that the Bank rate of discount shall be kept above the market rate during a favourable exchange, so as to keep up the influx of bullion until the reserve shall be raised from the average amount of ten to fifteen millions; and that on the occurrence of an unfavourable exchange the Bank rate shall be kept below the market rate, so as to allow the drain upon the coffers of the Bank to proceed, until the reserve shall be reduced from the average amount of ten to five millions. Now this boasted arrangement, which Mr. Mill regards as an adequate precaution against the danger of an exhaustion of the reserve, and a consequent suspension of cash payments, has been tried and has been found wanting. The bullion in the Bank of England during the months of March, April, and May, 1838, exceeded by a slight fraction the average amount of ten millions. In May, however, the exchanges became adverse, and a drain of gold set in. The Bank directors adopting, as it were by anticipation, Mr. Tooke's me- thod of liquidating foreign debt, kept their rate of discount below the market rate, until the reserve was reduced from the average amount of ten to five millions. What was the practical result of this adoption of the Mill-Tookean theory? The foreign debt had been increased by deficient harvests at home and deficient crops of raw material in America. Was the debt thus increased liquidated as, according to the doctrine laid down by Mr. Mill, it should have been, either wholly or in part, by the unrestricted exportation of five millions of gold? It was not liquidated either wholly or in part. New debt was incurred as fast as the old was discharged. Circulation and securities were increased rather than diminished as the gold flowed out. There was no rise in the rate of discount, no fall in the prices of commodities or of securities. Speculation continued to be excited. The excess of imports over exports continued to be maintained. In June 1839, when upwards of five millions had been withdrawn from the reserve of the Bank to provide for foreign payments, foreign debts continued to accumulate, and before the drain could be arrested the Bank of England was reduced to the necessity of averting a suspension of cash payments, by accepting a loan of two millions of treasure from the Bank of France.

Such were the practical results of the adoption, in 1839, of Mr. Tooke's arrangements for securing the convertibility of the note circulation. The conduct of the Bank directors in venturing to adopt it drew down upon their unhappy heads the following unmitigated denunciation from Mr. Tooke himself. The denuncia-

tion is contained in the self-same volume in which Mr.
Tooke reiterates the unfailing efficacy of his proposed
arrangement.   This juxtaposition of denunciation and
recommendation must be regarded as the climax—the
culmination of Mr. Tooke's inconsistency.   We give
Mr. Tooke's denunciation of his own doctrine in his
own words :—

- " As the result of the impartial review in the pre-
" ceding pages of the management of the Bank, in as
" far as a judgment can be formed of it from its public
" measures, and from the monthly ' Gazette ' returns
" of its liabilities and assets on the average of the three
" months preceding, the following appear to be the
" main points open to criticism.

  " 1. The impatience manifested at the commence-
" ment of 1838 to reduce the stock of bullion.

  " 2. The forcible operation of the Bank towards the
" close of 1838, for the purpose of extending its securi-
" ties by increased facilities for·loans, at a time when
" the market rate of interest was rising above the
" Bank rate, and when the proceedings of the Banks
" in America (particularly with reference to the cotton
" trade), and the state of commercial credit on the
" Continent, were calculated to suggest, as a measure
" of precaution on the part of the Bank, rather to re-
" duce than to extend its securities.

  "3. The continuing during nearly six months, namely,
" till 16th May 1839, the same relatively low rate of
" interest, and the extended facilities for loans, not-
" withstanding the continued rise in the market rate
" of interest, and notwithstanding the notoriety of the
" large importations of American securities then in
" progress, the negotiation of which was of course

" greatly promoted by the comparatively low rate of
" interest and discount charged by the Bank. The
" effect of this state of things being, that the Bank
" had by the end of May lost five millions of treasure,
" while its securities had increased by upwards of
" three millions.

" 4. The inefficiency of the measures taken between
" May and July to stop the further progress of the drain.

" 5. The hesitation and inconsistency of the pro-
" ceedings of the Bank, in respect of the dead
" weight.

" 6. The recourse to the bankers of Paris for assist-
" ance: a measure the resort to which could not be
" justified on any ground but that of its being consi-
" dered as the only remaining resource against a
" suspension of cash payments; and doubtless it
" was the lesser evil, but so discreditable an expe-
" dient ought not to have been resorted to until the
" dead weight, or a considerable portion of it, had
" been converted, and such conversion found to be
" ineffectual.

" The general conclusion, with reference to the ma-
" nagement of the Bank, being, that while, _à priori_,
" the inference is irresistible, that there must be some-
" thing essentially erroneous in the system, or in the
" regulation by which, in a state of profound peace,
" and without any counteraction from the country
" banks, the Bank of England should have sustained
" so narrow an escape from suspension of cash pay-
" ments; so it appears, by a reference to particulars,
" that the measures of the Bank were characterised
" by anything but a due and vigilant regard for the
" interests of the public in the maintenance of the

N

" convertibility of bank paper, or for its own credit,
" which has been much impaired in public estimation
" both at home and abroad, by its resort for aid to the
" bankers of Paris."

Let us return to Mr. Tooke's co-labourer in the field
of currency reform. Having affirmed that the theoretical principle of the Act of 1844 requires that all
drains of the precious metals, which, under a purely
metallic currency, would be drawn from the hoards,
should be allowed to operate without check upon the
coffers of the Bank of England, Mr. Mill proceeds to
say—

"The machinery, however, of the new system in-
" sists upon bringing about by force, what its prin-
" ciple not only does not require, but positively
" condemns. Every drain for exportation, whatever
" may be its cause, and whether under a metallic
" currency it would affect the circulation or not, is
" now compulsorily drawn from that source alone.
" The bank-note circulation, and the discounts or
" other advances of the Bank, must be diminished to
" an amount equal to that of the metal exported,
" though it be to the full extent of seven or ten mil-
" lions. And this, be it remembered, when there has
" been no speculative rise of prices which it is indis-
" pensable to correct, no unusual extension of credit
" requiring contraction, but the demand for gold is
" solely occasioned by foreign payments on account of
" Government, or large corn importations consequent
" on a bad harvest. 'There is, at least, one object,
" therefore,' says Mr. Fullarton,* ' which would be
" effectually accomplished by acting on this system.

* P. 137.

" It would be perfectly calculated, I think, to insure
" that no derangement of the exchange, or none, at
" least, subsisting in coincidence with anything like
" pressure on the money market, should ever be per-
" mitted to pass off, without one of those crises,
" hitherto fortunately of rare occurrence, but of
" which the results, when they have occurred, have
" been so extensive and deplorable.'"

In the above passage, Mr. Mill's misconceptions
regarding the practical working of the Act of 1844
are as total as were his previous misconceptions regarding its theoretical principle. The machinery of
the Act does not insist upon bringing about by force
what its principle condemns. It does not require that
every drain for exportation, whatever may be its
cause, and whether under a purely metallic currency
it would affect the currency or not, must be compulsorily drawn from that source alone. The department
of issue exerts neither force nor compulsion; it is
purely passive. To adopt an Irish phraseology, it
does its work by doing nothing. Its essential function
is that of abstaining from every kind and species of
interference with the proportions, as determined by
the law of metallic equilibrium, between the amount
of money and the quantity of commodities. It is
absolutely precluded from the exercise of any active
function; it is acted upon by the exchanges, but it
cannot act upon them. When the public demand gold
in exchange for notes, it gives out gold in exchange
for notes; and when they demand notes in exchange
for gold, it gives notes in exchange for gold. In the
former case the circulation contracts, and in the latter
it expands; but it is self-evident that in either case the

effect would not be produced by a forced and compulsory action on the part of the Bank, but by the law of monetary equilibrium, and the action of the foreign exchanges. A reference to the phenomena of the money market during the crisis of 1847, will show that the Act of 1844, instead of exercising a forced and compulsory action on the circulation, as Mr. Mill supposes, deprived the Bank of the compulsory action on the circulation which it had previously possessed. After the passing of the Act, the amount of the circulation out of the walls of the issue department, increased or diminished in exact accordance with the increase or diminution of the bullion; while previous to its passing, the circulation, instead of constantly conforming to the increase or diminution of the bullion, sometimes increased as the bullion diminished, and diminished as it increased. Let us refer to dates and figures. On the 4th April 1846, under the operation of the Act, the bullion in the issue department stood at 13,182,000*l.*, the circulation out of its walls at 27,183,000*l.*; and on the 19th September the bullion stood at 15,758,000*l.*, and the circulation at 29,758,000*l.*, the increase of each being 2,576,000*l.* In 1838, under the old system, the bullion on the 3rd April stood at 10,126,000*l.*, the circulation at 18,987,000*l.*; and on the 14th September the bullion had fallen to 9,615,000*l.*, while the circulation had increased to 19,665,000*l.*, being a decrease of bullion by 511,000*l.*, accompanied by an increase of circulation by 678,000*l.* Again, on the 30th October 1847, when the depression of that period had reached its lowest point, the bullion in the issue department stood at 8,009,490*l.*, and the circulation out of its walls at

22,000,000*l.*, and on the 25th December the bullion rose
to 11,609,075*l.*, and the circulation to 25,609,075*l.*;
while on the 12th December 1839, the lowest point
of depression during the crisis of that period, the
bullion stood at 2,887,000*l.*, and the circulation at
16,732,000*l.*, and on the 7th January the bullion rose to
3,454,000*l.*, while the circulation sank to 3,454,000*l.*

Thus is it historically proved that under the Act of
1844 the circulation uniformly expanded as the bullion
in the issue department increased, and contracted as
the bullion diminished; and that, under the old system,
the circulation occasionally increased as the bullion
diminished, and diminished as the bullion increased.
What was the cause of this remarkable difference
between the practical operation of the two systems?
In 1847, as in 1839, there was a sudden diminution in
the ordinary proportion of commodities and currency,
and it became necessary, in order to restore that proportion, that there should be an exportation of gold
and a contraction of the circulation. Why did the
contraction of the circulation exactly correspond with
the diminution of the bullion in one case, and not
in the other? For no other reason, save that in the
one case the Bank directors were precluded from all
compulsory action on the amount of the circulation,
and that in the other they possessed and exercised the
power of compulsory action. Under the Act of 1844
the issue department is a simple reservoir through
which the gold and paper currents, freed from all
exterior pressure, ebb and flow in equal volumes and
in the same direction. Under the former system, the
Bank, exercising its double function of issue and discount, was a reservoir with a forcing pump attached,

by which these currents were driven in unequal volumes in contrary directions, and occasionally to the
exclusion of the metallic stream.   Mr. Mill, whose
mental vision is somewhat obscure when directed to
realities, is unable to perceive to which of these reser-
voirs the forcing pump was attached ; and, consistent
when in error, he joins with Mr. Fullarton in predict-
ing, that on every occurrence of an adverse exchange
and monetary pressure, the aggravated crisis caused
by the former forcing system would be infallibly re-
produced under the passive operation of the Act of
1844.   He goes on to ask,

   "Are not the events of 1847 a fulfilment of this
" prediction?   The crisis of that year was preceded
" by no inflation of credit, no speculative rise of
" prices.   The only speculations (the corn-market ex-
" cepted) were those in railway shares, which had no
" tendency to derange the imports and exports of
" commodities, or to send any gold out of the coun-
" try, except the small amounts paid in instalments
" by shareholders in this country to foreign railways.
" The drain of gold, great as it was, originated solely
" in the bad harvest of 1846 and the potato failure of
" that and the following year, and in the increased
" price of raw cotton in America.   There was nothing
" in these circumstances which could require either a
" fall of general prices or a contraction of credit.   An
" unusual demand for credit existed at the time, in
" consequence of the pressure of railway calls, and
" this necessitated a rise of the rate of interest.   If
" the bullion in the Bank of England was sufficient
" to bear the drain without exhaustion, where was the
" necessity for adding to the distress and difficulty of

" the time, by requiring all who wanted gold for
" exportation, either to draw it from the deposits,
" that is, to subtract it from the already insufficient
" loanable capital of the country, or to become them-
" selves competitors for a portion of that inadequate
" fund, thus still further raising the rate of interest?
" The only necessity was created by the Act of
" 1844, which would not suffer the Bank to meet
" this extra demand of credit by lending its notes,
" not even the notes returned to it in exchange for
" gold."

Mr. Mill is an inaccurate observer. He lacks the
faculty of seeing things as they are. He seems as
regardless of realities as if he denied, with Bishop
Berkeley, the existence of an external world.

In the passage just quoted the facts are so dis-
torted, so changed in their dimensions, bearings, and
aspect—so completely metamorphosed—that we fail to
recognise them as the antecedents and consequents of
the crisis of 1847. The whole passage does not contain a statement which is not either partially, or entirely incorrect, nor a conclusion which is not drawn
from premises contrary to facts. It is a perversion
of fact to say that " the crisis of that year was pre-
" ceded by no inflation of credit, no speculative rise
" of prices;" the actual fact being that between March
and September 1845, joint-stock speculations, for the
immediate investment of capital, were entered upon to
an extent involving a larger amount of capital than
had ever before been invested in this country.

It is a perversion of the fact to say that " the
" speculation in railway shares had no tendency to
" derange the export and import of commodities, or

" to send gold out of the country." The abstraction
of capital, to the amount of one million a week, from
the production of commodities to the construction of
railroads, was one of the principal causes which contributed to diminish the ordinary proportion of commodities to money, and consequently to increase the
exportation of the gold thus rendered relatively redundant, and the importation of the commodities thus
rendered relatively deficient. It was directly contrary
to fact to affirm that there was nothing in the bad
harvest, the potato failure, and the increased price of
raw cotton in America, which could require either a
fall of general prices or a contraction of credit. The
enormous rise in the price of corn, which was at one
time 114s. per quarter* in Mark Lane, diminished the
consumption, and reduced the prices of all the leading
articles other than food, while an extraordinary expenditure for foreign corn, to the amount of twenty
millions in 1847, diminished loanable capital at the
command of the Bank and other discount houses, and
consequently contracted credit to such an extent, that
the acceptances of some of the first merchants of
London were charged with a rate of interest, which,
combined with commission, raised the deduction for
discount to the rate of 10, 12, and even 15 per cent.
per annum.†

Misconceptions of the most extraordinary character
are involved in the question, " If the bullion in the
" Bank of England was sufficient to bear the drain
" without exhaustion, where was the necessity for
" adding to the distress and difficulty of the times by ·

* Hibbert, p. 16.
† Letter to the Chancellor of the Exchequer by Hubbard.

" requiring all who wanted gold for exportation, either
" to draw it from the deposits, that is, to subtract it
" from the already insufficient loanable capital of the
" country, or to become competitors for a portion of
" that inadequate fund, thus still further raising the
" rate of interest?"   The implied assumption that the
bullion in the Bank was sufficient to bear the drain
without exhaustion is utterly erroneous.   In the first
place the highest amount of the bullion in the issue
department, in 1847, was 14,258,000l. on the 2nd
January, while the extraordinary foreign payments on .
account of corn alone amounted to 20,000,000l.   In
the second place, against every hundred pounds in
gold deposited in the issue department, a hundred
pounds in bank-notes were issued to the public, so that
the effect upon the amount of the circulation was
exactly the same as if the gold itself had circulated
instead of the notes.   In the third place, had the gold
been issued to the public in addition to the notes
which represented it, the law of equilibrium would
have driven the gold out of the country as fast as it
passed out of the walls of the Bank, and a suspension
of cash payments would have ensued.

But the import of Mr. Mill's question is rather obscure.   It would be difficult to believe that it was his
intention to assume as a fact that the bullion in the
Bank of England was sufficient to bear the drain without exhaustion, seeing that its highest amount in
January 1847, was only 14,258,000l., while the foreign
balance to be paid amounted to 20,000,000l., and that
total exhaustion must have been the inevitable result
of allowing this balance to be drawn from the reserve
of treasure in the Bank.   And it seems all but incre-

dible that Mr. Mill should have intentionally inferred
that the drawing out of gold from the Bank for exportation, and the competition of the exporters for a share
of the diminished amount of loanable capital, were
caused by the Act of 1844, inasmuch as they were the
necessary effects of natural causes over which no conceivable regulation of the currency could by possibility
have exercised control—effects which could not have
been averted unless the directors of the Bank had,
through some superhuman agency, assumed with the
philosopher in 'Rasselas,' the regulation of the seasons,
or been endowed with the purse of Fortunatus, or
invested with power " to pluck bright *metal* from the
" pale-faced moon."

Mr. Mill, however, has relieved us from all uncer-
tainty regarding the import of his question.   He tells
us in so many words that the only necessity for drawing out the gold, and subtracting it from the loanable
capital of the country, was created by the Act of 1844,
which would not suffer the Bank to meet the extra
demand for credit by lending out its notes, or even
the notes returned to it in exchange for gold.   The
failure of the potato crop, the deficiencies in the crops
of corn and of cotton, and the consequent drain of
bullion, the diminution of loanable capital, the advance
in the rate of interest, and the aggravated difficulty of
the time, would all have been averted, had the Bank
of England possessed, in 1847, that power of unlimited
issue, the exercise of which, in 1839, landed it on the
very brink of insolvency !

" The crisis of 1847 was of that sort which the
" provisions of the Act had not the smallest ten-
" dency to avert; and when the crisis came, the

" mercantile difficulties were probably doubled by its
" existence."

These are propositions, the contraries of which are
true. The crisis of 1847 was of that sort which the
provisions of the Act had a peculiar and a special
tendency to avert; and when the crisis came, the mercantile difficulties were mitigated by its existence,
while a second suspension of metallic payments was
averted. In 1846-7, the diversion of one million a
week from the production of commodities to the construction of railways, a deficiency in the supply of the
cotton crop in America, and of the corn crops at home,
with the almost total destruction of the staple food of
one-third of the population, occasioned the greatest and
the most sudden diminution in the quantity of commodities which has been experienced in modern times.
The balance due to foreign countries on account of the
importation of food exceeded by many millions the
amount of treasure in the Bank. Nothing could have
enabled us to liquidate the adverse foreign balance,
save a fall in the prices of commodities and of securities, so decided as to invite foreign capitalists to
become the purchasers of both. Had the Bank, as in
1839, reissued the notes returned to it in exchange
for bullion for exportation, a contraction of the circulation, a rise in the rate of interest, and a fall in the
prices of commodities and of securities, would have
been postponed until the total exhaustion of the reserve of gold, and the stoppage of the Bank, induced a
universal collapse of credit. Fortunately this intensi-
fication of the crisis was averted by the Act of 1844.
The circulation out of the issue department was gradually contracted as the gold was withdrawn; and

notwithstanding the error of the Bank directors in unduly diminishing the amount of the reserve in the banking department, the rise in the rate of interest, and the fall in the prices of commodities and securities, enabled us to effect sales of both to an extent sufficient to liquidate the enormous foreign balance without jeopardizing the convertibility of the currency.* The Act of 1844 is especially calculated to provide against such a crisis as that of 1847. On the 7th of August, when that crisis was at its height, the amount of bullion in the Issue Department of the Bank never fell below 8,634,000*l.*

The Act of 1844 has triumphantly succeeded in accomplishing the primary object it was intended to secure—that of placing the convertibility of the bank-note beyond the reach of suspicion.

Mr. Mill meets these recorded facts by conjectures and assumptions regarding processes which might by possibility have occurred. He says—

" I am aware it will be said, that by allowing " drains of this character to operate freely upon the " Bank reserve, until they cease of themselves, a con- " traction of the currency and of credit would not be " prevented, but only postponed ; since, if a limitation " of issues were not resorted to for the purpose of " checking the drain in its commencement, the same, " or a still greater limitation, must take place after- " wards, in order, by acting on prices, to bring back " this large quantity of gold, for the indispensable " purpose of replenishing the Bank reserve. But in

---

* The way in which the foreign debt of 1847 was liquidated is fully explained by Mr. Hubbard in his letter to Sir Charles Wood, on the " Monetary Pressure of 1847."

" this argument several things are overlooked. In the
" first place, the gold might be brought back, not by
" a fall of prices, but by the much more rapid and
" convenient medium of a rise of the rate of interest,
" involving no fall of any prices except the prices of
" securities. Either English securities would be
" bought on account of foreigners, or foreign secu-
" rities held in England would be sent abroad for
" sale, both which operations took place largely
" during the mercantile difficulties in 1847, and not
" only checked the efflux of gold, but turned the tide
" and brought the metal back. It was not, therefore,
" brought back by a contraction of the currency,
" though in this case it certainly was so by a contrac-
" tion of loans. But even this is not always indis-
" pensable. For in the second place, it is not necessary
" that the gold should return with the same sudden-
" ness with which it went out. A great portion would
" probably return in the ordinary way of commerce,
" in payment for exported commodities. The extra
" gains made by dealers and producers in foreign
" countries, through the extra payments they receive
" from this country, are very likely to be partly ex-
" pended in increased purchases of English commo-
" dities, either for consumption or on speculation,
" though the effect may not manifest itself with suffi-
" cient rapidity to enable the transmission of gold to
" be dispensed with in the first instance. These extra
" purchases would turn the balance of payments in
" favour of the country, and gradually restore a por-
" tion of the exported gold ; and the remainder would
" probably be brought back, not by a rise of the rate
" of interest in England, but by the fall of it in foreign

" countries, occasioned by the addition of some mil-
" lions of gold to the loanable capital of those coun-
" tries. If it were necessary to accelerate the process
" by an artificial action on the rate of interest in Eng-
" land, a very moderate rise would be sufficient,
" instead of the very great one which is the conse-
" quence of allowing the whole demand for gold for
" exportation to act suddenly and at once on the
" existing resources of the loan market."

These conjectures and speculations as to the manner
by which a suspension of cash payments might by
possibility have been averted, require no answer
beyond that which may be supplied by a simple reference to the manner in which, under the greatest temporary and most sudden destruction of commodity-
wealth recorded in modern times, a suspension of cash
payments was actually averted.

Mr. Mill concludes his review of the theory and
practical working of the Act of 1844, with the following remark :—

" Thus stand, according to the best judgment I am
" able to form, the advantages and disadvantages of
" the currency system established by the Act of 1844,
" of which, as it seems to me, the disadvantages
" greatly preponderate. I am, however, far from
" thinking that on a subject at once so intricate and
" so new, a subject which has only begun to be under-
" stood through the controversies of the last few years,
" experience and discussion have nothing further to
" disclose. I give the foregoing opinions as the results
" to which I have been guided by the lights that have
" hitherto fallen on the subject ; conscious that addi-
" tional lights are almost sure to be struck out when

" the knowledge of principles and of facts necessary
" for the elucidation of the question becomes united in
" a greater number of individuals."

It is satisfactory to learn from this concluding passage, that Mr. Mill does not belong to the category designated by Mr. Fullarton as " the deaf fanatics " whom the voice of truth and reason cannot reach." As his mind is still open to the reception of additional evidence, let us hope that on further inquiry, he will endeavour to re-establish, what no hand other than his own could have impaired—the reputation, as an advanced and original thinker, which had been justly awarded to the author of ' Unsettled Questions in Political Economy.'

CHAPTER IV.

ON THE EFFECT OF THE NEW SUPPLIES OF GOLD UPON
THE CURRENCY OF THE AUSTRALIAN COLONIES.

THE anomalous state of the Australian money market, subsequent to the discovery of the gold-fields, presents a striking illustration of the limitations to which, in their practical applications, theoretical principles are liable. No induction within the compass of commercial science rests on a wider basis of fact and experience, than the principle, that variations in the value of raw materials extend to finished goods. It would sound like an absurdity, almost like a contradiction in terms, to affirm that a deficiency in the supply, and a rise in the price of bread, had been caused by an excess in the supply, and a fall in the price of corn. Previous to the discovery of the Australian gold-fields, no one acquainted, whether practically or theoretically, with commercial and exchange transactions, would have ventured to maintain that the value of a manufactured article could be raised by a fall in the value of the material of which it is composed. But political economy has no universal truths. Its abstract principles are practically

correct, in those cases only in which the circumstances
to which they are applied coincide with those from
which they are deduced.   When this coincidence
does not exist, scientific conclusions are contrary to
facts.   An economist who should have adopted, as a
universal truth, the theoretical principle, that variations in the value of raw materials extend to finished
goods, would have confidently predicted that the great
increase in the supply and fall in the value of gold in
Victoria and New South Wales, would have lowered
the value of money throughout the Australian markets.
That a rise in the value of currencies consisting of gold
coin, and of bank-notes convertible into it, should
have been caused by an increase in the supply, and a
fall in the value of gold, would have appeared to such
a theorist as incredible as the existence of a miracle
appeared to David Hume.   Nevertheless the most
implicit follower of Hume must admit that the commercial miracle—the rise in value of money from a
fall in the value of gold—is established by testimony
which it is impossible to resist.

    The peculiar circumstances which reversed, in Aus-
tralia, the general law, that the value of money con-
forms to that of the material of which it is composed,
admits of an obvious explanation.   In England,
where the Mint is open, and where no seignorage
is charged, gold in the form of coin is of the same
value as gold in the form of bullion, because either
can be converted into the other without loss.   The
slightest fall in the market price of bullion sends gold
to the Mint, while the slightest rise in the market
price of bullion sends coin to the melting-pot.   Hence

o

an ounce of gold, as bullion, and an ounce of gold, as coin, are always maintained at the same value in relation to each other; and as by the regulation of the Mint, an ounce of gold is coined into $3l.\ 17s.\ 10\frac{1}{2}d.$, the price of an ounce of gold in the market, as at the Mint, must always be, with scarcely any variation, $3l.\ 17s.\ 10\frac{1}{2}d.$

The case has been altogether different in Australia. There was no Mint there. While the increased supplies of gold thrown upon the market for sale increased the demand for coin, an increased supply of coin could not be produced. While the value of gold, in bullion, fell from increased supply, the value of gold, in coin, rose from increased demand. The rise in the value of money, and the fall in the value of the material of money, proceeded to such an extent, that while the price of gold in the British markets continued at $77s.\ 10\frac{1}{2}d.$ per ounce, the price in the Australian markets sank to $60s.$, $50s.$, and even $40s.$ per ounce.

This anomalous difference between the value of money and of gold produced some novel results, which it may be expedient to state and to explain.

The difference between the value of coined and uncoined gold occasioned the establishment of a cross, or counter trade in gold, between England and the Australian colonies. Gold, as merchandise, was less valuable in Sydney and Melbourne than in London, while gold, as money, was more valuable in Sydney and Melbourne than in London. Hence, while nuggets and dust were exported from the colonies to England, sovereigns were exported from England to

Australia. Mr. Bell, the experienced and able managing director of the London Chartered Bank of Australia, has stated in his instructive publication, ' The Philosophy of Joint-Stock Banking,' that the loss to the colonies, including risk, expense, and delay of remitting gold to England, to be returned in coin, was estimated at not less than 20 per cent.*

The exportation of gold, and the importation of coin, had an important effect upon the course of exchange between England and Australia. Previous to the gold discoveries, and while gold was an imported commodity in both countries, the exchanges between London and Melbourne or Sydney were determined on ordinary commercial principles, and their alternate deviations from par, whether adverse or favourable, were limited to the cost of transmitting specie. As often as the amount of wool, tallow, and copper, exported to England was equal to the amount of British goods imported in return, the amount of the bills which the importing merchant had to pay in England equalled the amount of those which the exporting merchant had to receive in England; debts were balanced by credits, and no remittances in specie were effected. The exporting merchants sold, while the importing merchants purchased, bills payable in England; the bankers and brokers through whom the transactions were conducted, charging upon each a slight per centage. Subject to this per centage the currencies of the colonies were of the same value as the currency of England, a given sum

---

* Philosophy of Joint-Stock Banking, p. 101.

in colonial currency purchasing a bill upon London for a similar sum in British currency.

This monetary equilibrium between Australia and England was of course disturbed as often as the colonial exports exceeded or fell short of the imports. When the exports were in excess, bills upon England fell to a discount, because the amount of those which exporters offered for sale exceeded that of those which importers wished to purchase ; and when imports were in excess, bills upon England rose to a premium, because the amount of those which importers desired to purchase exceeded that of those which importers offered for sale. In the former case sovereigns were imported, in the latter they were exported; the cost of their transmission constituting the limit beyond which the price of bills could not for any permanency either fall below or rise above par. The cost of transmitting sovereigns also constituted the limit beyond which the value of the currencies of the colonies could not, for any permanency, either rise above or fall below the value of the currency of England. When exports exceeded imports, the price in the colonial currency of a bill upon England for any given sum could not permanently fall short of that sum by more than the cost of importing its amount in sovereigns ; and when imports were in excess of exports, the price of a bill upon England for any given sum could not permanently exceed that sum by more than the cost of providing for it by the transmission of its amount in sovereigns.

This brief exposition of the ordinary exchange transactions between England and Australia while gold was an imported article in both, will aid us in acquiring a distinct conception of the alterations which these transactions underwent, on gold becoming a permanent staple in the Australian exports.

When Australia became an exporter instead of an importer of gold, the value of gold became less valuable, by the cost of transmission, in Sydney and in Melbourne than in London ; and had a branch of the Royal Mint been established in Australia, and had the colonial coinage, equally with the British coinage, been exempt from seignorage, then, the currencies of the colonies would also have been of less value, by the cost of transmitting gold, than the currency of England; for in this case the value of gold in Australia, when invested with the character of money, would have been identical with the value of gold while retaining the character of merchandise. Standard coin and standard bullion would have been equally eligible as articles of export, and it is self-evident that standard coin could not have been exported from Australia to England unless the convertible currencies of Australia should have been of less value, by the cost of the exportation, than the currency of England; or, to express the same thing in other words, unless the price in Australian currency of a bill for 100*l.*, payable in London, should have exceeded 100*l.* by the cost of transmitting a hundred sovereigns.

It is abundantly evident that had there been a free mint in Australia, as in England, the only permanent effect which the new supplies of gold could have produced upon the exchange transactions between the colonies and England, would have been that of keeping colonial bills drawn upon England at a premium equivalent to the cost, including bankers' commission, of transmitting specie.

When two countries, having commercial transactions with each other, are both importers of gold, the course of exchange may be in favour of either, and the balance of payments will alternate between them; but when commercial transactions take place between two countries, one of which is an importer, and the other an exporter of gold, the course of exchange must always be against the exporting and in favour of the importing country. Obvious as the truth of this position may appear, it has been occasionally controverted. It has been contended that the same law which governs the rate of exchange between two countries, both importers of gold, also governs it between two countries, one an importer and the other an exporter of gold; and that in a gold-exporting, no less than in a gold-importing country, an excess in the amount of exports over imports may so increase the supply of bills payable in the foreign market, as to reduce them from a premium to a discount: or, in other words, to raise the value of the currency of the gold-exporting in relation to the currency of the gold-importing country.

The answer to this objection is, that when in a gold-producing country having a free Mint, an excess of exports over imports—whether that excess consists of the precious metals or of other commodities—so increases the supply of foreign bills as to cause the premium upon them to be less than the cost of transmitting gold, the gold-producing must cease to be a gold-exporting country. No one would transmit specie to a foreign market should the premium of a bill drawn against it be less than the cost of the transmission. No one would send a hundred sovereigns from Australia to England at a cost, say of 3*l.*, were the price in the Australian market of a bill upon England for 100*l.* below 103*l.* It is quite possible that there might arise in the British markets such an increase in the demand for tallow, wool, and copper, as would cause the amount of the exports from Australia to exceed the amount of British goods imported ; but it is quite impossible that, in this state of the market, gold should, under a free colonial mint, form an item in the exports of Australia to England, because, in this state of the markets, a bill upon England for 100*l.* could be purchased in Australia for less than 100*l.*, and it would be the interest of all parties in Australia having payments to effect in England, to effect them by purchasing bills, instead of by remitting cash. But, while it may be possible that such states of the money markets should occur, it is quite impossible, so long as Australia continues to be a largely gold-producing country, that they should be permanent. The discount upon bills upon England would operate as a bounty on imports and as a tax upon exports, while, still assuming the existence of a free local mint, the accumulation of treasure from the diggings would lower the value of the currency, raise prices, and still further invite imports and arrest exports, until the exchanges should be restored to that permanent level at which bills upon England could be purchased in Australia at a discount equivalent to the cost of transmitting gold.

Having thus seen that, had there been in Australia as in England a free Mint and a costless coinage, the effect of the gold discoveries would have been to

keep the currencies of Australia at a permanently
lower value than British currency, by the cost of
transmitting gold from Australia to England,—let
us now proceed to consider the manner in which the
withholding from the colonies the liberty of coinage
reversed this natural result, and rendered the Australian currencies more valuable than the currency
of England, by the double cost of exporting nuggets
and importing sovereigns.

The currencies of the Australian colonies consist
of the standard coins of the British Mint, and of bank-
notes convertible into such coin upon demand ; and
the colonial banks are under the necessity of maintaining in their coffers an amount of coin sufficient
to secure the convertibility of their notes.   On the
discovery of the gold-fields, the sudden and vast
increase of mineral wealth caused a corresponding
increase in the demand for currency—in other words,
for notes and coin.   But the banks could not, with
safety to their coffers, supply the additional demand
for notes until they could themselves obtain an
additional supply of coin; and this could only be
obtained by the tedious process of exporting bullion
and importing sovereigns.   Thus, while the value of
bullion declined from increased supply, the value of
coin and of convertible notes advanced from deficient
supply.   The market price of gold, which, had there
been a free colonial coinage, could not have deviated
from the Mint price of 3l. 17s. 10½d., sank to 3l., to
2l. 10s., and, in some instances, to a still lower price ;
while the price of bills upon England which, with free
coinage, would have borne a premium equivalent to
the cost of transmitting bullion, fell to a discount

equivalent to the double cost of transmitting bullion and importing coin. This cost, as we have seen, was estimated by Mr. Bell, the manager of the London Chartered Bank of Australia, at 20 per cent.

The double cost incurred by the exportation of bullion and the importation of coin, formed but a small part of the injury resulting from the want of a colonial mint. The new gold was divested of the character of money. It was neither a measure of value, nor a medium of exchange, nor a legal tender. It could make no purchase, except in the way of barter. It could satisfy no legal demand, and it could close no pecuniary transactions. Instead of supplying the increased demand for currency, it was itself the cause of that increased demand. The circulation was rendered deficient in relative amount, and was increased in value, as the universal money of the world was increased in quantity and reduced in value.

The difference between the value of bullion and of coin was the measure of the immediate loss inflicted on the diggers. But the injury was not confined to them: it extended to all. The labouring population abandoned their accustomed occupations, and rushed to the gold-fields. The flocks were neglected, the fields were untilled, and all the branches of colonial industry, save that of gold-digging, appeared to be sinking into a state of suspended vitality.

Foreign transactions were scarcely less paralyzed than home production. As the expense and delay attending the importation of coin enhanced the value of the currency, bills drawn against exports fell to a heavy discount; and while this rise in the value of currency reduced the prices of wool and tallow and copper to their producers, the fall in the price of bills upon England was a deduction from the profits of exporters. Nor was the loss which the state of the exchanges inflicted upon the exporter balanced by a corresponding advantage conferred on the importer. The latter did not gain all that the former lost. For while the state of the exchanges held out a bounty upon the importation of foreign goods, the loss suffered by the producers of the new gold in exchanging it for coin, diminished their power of consumption, and rendered the demand for foreign goods less than it would otherwise have been.

Again, the rise in the value of the currency had a seriously injurious effect upon commercial credit. Existing contracts were deranged. Those who had entered into pecuniary engagements previous to the sudden and anomalous enhancement of the circulation, were involved in unexpected and inevitable difficulties. Debtors, dealers upon long credit, and producers were impoverished; creditors, moneyed capitalists, and the recipients of fixed incomes, were enriched, while fortunate adventurers bounded into unlooked-for opulence.

The profits of the bankers became enormous. The absence of a colonial Mint conferred on these establishments a species of monopoly in the gold discoveries. They purchased gold in the form of dust or nuggets at 60s. per ounce, sold it in England at 77s. 9d. per ounce, and reimported it in the form of sovereigns, to be readvanced in the purchase of uncoined gold at 60s. per ounce. But the extraordinary rate. of profit thus derived from the exportation of bullion and importation of coin, formed the smallest portion of the advantage accruing to the banks. The absence of a mint gave a scarcity-value to the imported coins, and this scarcity-value was not confined to that portion of the currency which consisted of the imported coin, but was communicated to the whole of the bank-note circulation convertible into it. Hence, as the rapid increase of population and of mineral wealth caused a corresponding increase in the demand for currency, the bank that imported one hundred sovereigns, and added them to its cash reserve, might, without departing from the received principles of legitimate banking, issue, upon interest-bearing securities, additional notes to the amount of three or four hundred pounds. Had the new surplus of gold been convertible into money by a free colonial Mint, the banks could not have absorbed so vast a proportion of the mineral wealth of the colonies at the expense of the diggers and of the community at large: the whole of the exported treasure would have been paid for, not in sovereigns, but in commodities; and all the evils consequent upon a sudden increase in the value of the currency would have been averted. These evils, as before stated, fell with most severity on the debtor classes, upon mortgagees, dealers upon credit, and all persons having fixed engagements to discharge. Those only who are aware of the extent to which the system of credit and deferred payments has prevailed in Australia, can form an adequate conception of the embarrassment and pecuniary derangement which, coincidently with the vast increase of mineral wealth, resulted from the increased value.

of the currency, as indicated by a fall in the price
of bills upon England, from the ordinary par to a
discount of 10 per cent.

The fall in the price of bills upon England is thus
explained by Mr. Bell :—" The principal exports
" from Australia to Europe, like those from many
" other parts of the world, are not spread equally
" over the whole year, but press more heavily at par-
" ticular seasons. Thus the influx of wool, from
" November to February, occasions a demand for
" money against that produce ; numerous bills are
" drawn against the anticipated proceeds in Europe,
" and offered to the banks and private parties for
" discount, to an extent which often occasions a con-
" siderable depression in their value. The introduc-
" tion of a new article of export in the shape of gold
" has, of course, added to the difficulties attending the
" operations of exchange. The value of gold exported
" in two months only, namely, in December and
" January 1851–2, was nearly as great as that of the
" whole annual export of the general produce of the
" colony previously. The enlarged application to the
" banks produced the usual effects in all such cases.
" The exchange on London increased to 10 per cent.
" upon drafts at thirty days' sight, and the rate of
" advance upon gold fell from 55s. and 50s. per
" ounce to 40s. Much of the pressure was with-
" drawn upon this change, and parties preferred to
" await returns from London for the gold consigned
" there, to accepting advances of money under such
" disadvantages, or to the forcing of sales at prices
" which this rate of exchange had so greatly reduced.
" On the first discovery of the gold-fields the ex-

" portation of gold was conducted ·in the following
" manner: it was remitted from the colonies to Eng-
" land, to bé returned back chiefly in the form of
" coin.   The risks, expenses, and delay of these re-
" mittances were lost to the colonies, and this opera-
" tion, with all its attendant agencies, was estimated
" to occasion an average loss of not less than 20 per
" cent.   This average loss of 20 per cent. in sending
" gold to London, in dust, nuggets, and bars, and re-
" ceiving it back in coin, partly suggested the idea of
" a colonial Mint; but with an assay-office properly
" constituted, and banks privileged to issue notes upon
" the deposit of bullion, this heavy loss upon the re-
" mittance of gold to London might be entirely avoided.

" The banks of Australia issue notes of various de-
" nominations, from 1$l.$ upwards ; the use of gold,
" therefore, as a currency, must necessarily be limited ;
" yet a great deal has been written on the advan-
" tages of a colonial Mint for coinage of gold into
" sovereigns.   In a colony enjoying the privilege of
" issuing paper money, the advantage of a Mint ap-
" pears very doubtful.   Gold, so abundantly obtained
" in Australia, is not required for circulation, it is
" simply an article of merchandise.   It is bought by
" the local banks, they issue their own notes or bills
" on London in payment; if by the gold brokers, it
" is paid for in bank-notes.   All that is wanted is a
" Government office of assay, to certify the quantity
" and quality of gold in bars or ingots.'   This is done
" at present chiefly by private individuals.   Now, it
" is well known that these private assays have, in
" innumerable instances, proved very different from
" the assays at the Bank of England ; the assays of

" some gold in the colonies and in London have ex-
" hibited a most unaccountable disparity.   The ne-
" cessity of a Government assay is above all question,
" but the utility of a branch of the Royal Mint is, as
" already remarked, very questionable.   The legisla-
" ture of Sydney recently advanced a large sum of
" money towards the establishment of a branch of the
" Royal Mint, which they at length succeeded in ob-
" taining; but it is believed that the expense of its
" maintenance, and the little coinage required in that
" colony, are gradually awakening them to the fact
" that it is an institution with which they may safely
" dispense." *

After much pressure and deliberation, and after
having actually received remittances for the requisite
machinery, the Home Government gave a reluctant
sanction to the establishment of colonial Mints.   The
Treasury issued a very elaborate minute upon the subject, and in a despatch addressed to the Governor-
General of Australia, and dated 20th February 1852,
Earl Grey, then Colonial Secretary, stated in the following passage his reasons for regarding the measure
as one of very doubtful expediency :—

" In considering the question whether it is desirable
" to establish a colonial Mint, you will bear in mind
" that it would be unsafe to infer from the apparent
" want of a ready mode of converting gold into coin,
" which was experienced during the first few months
" after the discovery of gold in the colony, that the
" same want would continue.   The value of gold

* A local Mint could not be safely dispensed with, unless notes issued
against standard bullion were made a legal tender. This is implied in
Mr. Bell's statement.

" thrown upon the market in a short time, when this
" unexpected discovery took place, was so large in
" proportion to the capital available for its purchase,
" and to the amount of coin then in the colony, that a
" great fall in the price of gold-dust and of uncoined
" gold generally was to be expected in the first in-
" stance.   Accordingly it appears that gold has been
" sold in the colony at 60s. an ounce, and even, I be-
" lieve, in some cases at a lower price, although its
" intrinsic value is known to be 77s. 10½d.; but the
" profit derived from the purchase of gold at so low a
" rate cannot fail to attract capital from other quar-
" ters, and especially from this country, into the
" business, and the deficiency of coin to carry on the
" increased transactions arising from the discovery of
" gold, is certain to be in like manner supplied by
" those who will find it advantageous to make remit-
" tances in this form; accordingly I am informed
" that a large amount of capital, and considerable re-
" mittances of specie, have already been sent to the
" colony, and this process will certainly continue so
" long as high profits can be made by it, and it is
" thus shown to be required.   But I entertain no
" doubt that in a very short time the price of uncoined
" gold will rise, and will approach so near the value
" the metal would bear when coined, as merely to
" leave the usual rate of mercantile profit on the trans-
" mission of gold to this country to be converted into
" coin; but whether gold is remitted to this country
" for the purpose of being coined, or is coined on the
" spot, the expense will directly or indirectly fall
" upon the colony, and more particularly on those by
" whom the gold is found."

In the above passage Earl Grey took a narrow, and, therefore, an erroneous view of the question at issue. While he saw with sufficient distinctness that the difference between the price of coined and uncoined gold must cause a large importation of coin, and that the effect of the increasing supplies of sovereigns must be to diminish the difference between the value of coin and bullion, his vision did not expand from these immediate results to the remote effects upon the exchanges, and through the exchanges on all the branches of home production and external trade, which could not fail to result from the process of sending gold from Australia to England, in order to be passed through the British Mint, and returned back to the colonies in the form of coin. Upon his Lordship's own showing, the effect of this process must be to make coin more valuable than bullion by the cost, including the ordinary rate of mercantile profit, of exporting the one and importing the other; but, with a free colonial Mint, coin and bullion would be of the same value. It follows, as a necessary consequence, that colonial currency, consisting of British coin and notes convertible into it, must be more valuable, by the cost of a double transit, than colonial currencies, consisting of colonial coin and of notes convertible into colonial coin.

Gold, as we have already seen, must be less valuable in Australia than in England by the cost of transit, and therefore a currency convertible into standard bullion in Australia must also be less valuable, by that cost, than a currency convertible into standard bullion in England. But this is not all; the currency of Australia was convertible, not into native bullion, but into British coin, and British coin was more valuable in Australia than in England by the cost of transit. The two following conclusions are, therefore, strictly demonstrable: 1st. That so long as Australia continues to be a gold-exporting country, a colonial currency, if based upon a colonial coinage, must be less valuable than British currency, by the cost of transmitting gold from Australia to England. 2nd. That the Australian currencies, while based upon a British coinage, must be more valuable than British currency, by the cost of transmitting sovereigns from England to Australia.

Lord Grey's assumption that when bullion is exported to be reimported as coin, the permanent difference between their values cannot be more than sufficient to yield the ordinary mercantile profit upon the capital employed in the transaction, would not, even were it in accordance with fact, be a valid objection to the establishment of a colonial Mint. Why should any portion of the capital of the colonies be employed in a transaction so useless and so wasteful? The arguments in favour of a colonial Mint were, that it would extinguish the difference between the value of coined and uncoined gold; disengage for productive occupation a considerable portion of capital then wholly unproductive; and prevent a large and fruitless expenditure on account of freight, insurance, and risk. Lord Grey replied to these arguments, not by showing that a colonial Mint could not remedy the existing evils, but by affirming the fact, that, in the absence of a Mint, they must continue to exist. He admitted that there would be a permanent difference between the value of bullion and of coin, measured by the cost of the double

P

transmission, and that a portion of the colonial capital would be expended in the unproductive business of effecting it.

But Lord Grey's assumption that the price of uncoined gold will rise and approximate so near the value the metal would bear when coined, as merely to leave the usual rate of mercantile profit on the transmission of gold to this country to be converted into coin, must be received with considerable limitations. It is true that in the absence of a colonial Mint the price of uncoined gold would have a tendency to approximate to, and to settle at, the level at which the profit upon the importation of coin would not exceed the ordinary mercantile rate. But then it is also true, that, under the frequently-recurring fluctuations of trade, this tendency would be counteracted, and that the price of uncoined gold would at one time rise so high as to leave no profit at all upon the importation of coined gold, and at another time would fall so low as to yield upon the importation of coin a profit considerably above the ordinary rate.

In the ordinary states of trade, and when nothing occurred to cause either an increase or a diminution in the demand for the colonial currencies, the value of imported coin and of uncoined gold would be so nearly equal as to reduce the profit on the importation of coin to the ordinary mercantile level. But let the supply of the colonial currencies become, from any cause, either excessive or deficient, in relation to the supply of commodities, and then, in either case, an immediate change would take place in the relative value of coined and uncoined gold. Should the existing amount of currency become excessive in relation to commodities, from a diminution of home production, or of foreign importation, then coin would become an article, not of importation but of exportation, in common with bullion. But, as an article of export, the value of coin can be neither greater nor less than that of bullion. In the case under consideration the difference between the value of coined and uncoined gold would disappear. Both would be exported, and the value of both would be less in the colonies than in the countries to which they were exported, by the cost of transmission. Hence the value of the colonial currency would be lower than that of British currency, by the same cost. The exportation of coin would diminish the cash reserves of the banks; and the banks would protect their coffers by a corresponding contraction of their issues, until the ordinary proportion between the amount of the circulation and the quantity of commodities should be restored.

On the other hand, as often as an increase of home production or of foreign trade should cause the amount of the circulation to bear a less than ordinary proportion to the quantity of commodities, results directly the reverse of those above described, would be produced. In this case the relative deficiency of the circulation would create a demand for such an increased amount of coin as might enable the banks, without danger to their coffers, to make good that deficiency by increased issues. But in the absence of a colonial Mint, the demand for an additional amount of coin could only be supplied by importations of sovereigns from England. Many months must elapse before these could arrive; and, during the long period

of unsatisfied demand, the value of coin would exceed
the value of bullion by an amount considerably exceeding the cost of sending bullion to be converted
into coin, and returned as such to the colonies. In
all cases in which increased production or extended
trade creates a demand for additional circulation, the
assumption upon which the argument of Earl Grey
proceeds would be contrary to facts. Had a local
Mint been denied to Australia, every diminution in
the demand for circulation, whether arising from
diminished home production or diminished trade,
would have reduced the value of coin, in relation
both to uncoined gold and to commodities, below the
level at which sovereigns could be profitably imported; while every increase in the demand for
circulation, whether arising from an increase in home
production or foreign trade, would have raised the
value of coin, in relation both to uncoined gold and to
other commodities, above the level at which the importation of sovereigns yields ordinary mercantile profits.

These fluctuations in the value of coin, or, in other
words, in the price of uncoined gold, would be accompanied by corresponding changes in the value of the
local currencies, and in the rates of the foreign exchanges; and while the colonial currencies consisted
of British coin and of bank-notes convertible into it,
every diminution in the demand for circulation,
which so reduced the value of coin as to render it,
in common with uncoined gold, an article of export,
would have rendered the colonial currency less
valuable than British currencies, by the cost of
transmitting sovereigns to England; while, on the
other hand, every increase in the demand for cir-

culation, which caused an importation of coin, would, during the period that preceded the actual arrival of the importation, have rendered the colonial currencies more valuable than British currency, not only by the cost, including the usual rate of profit of importing sovereigns, when at their ordinary value, but by that cost including the extra rate of profits yielded by importing them when at a scarcity-value.

Had a colonial Mint been withheld, these fluctuations in the value of the colonial currencies would have been accompanied by corresponding variations in the rate of the foreign exchanges. As the value of currency declined, bills upon England would have borne a premium equivalent to the cost of exporting sovereigns; and as the value of the colonial currencies rose, bills upon London would have been at a discount equivalent to the cost of importing sovereigns.

It has been already shown that these deep fluctuations in exchange transactions could not occur under the establishment of a colonial Mint. Make the new supplies of gold immediately convertible into coin, and the value of coin and of bullion will be identical. The price of gold will never fall below the Mint price of 3l. 17s. 10½d. As the production of additional quantities of gold creates a demand for additional circulation, that demand will be instantaneously supplied. So long as Australia continues to be a gold-producing and gold-exporting country, so long will the value of the colonial currency be less than that of British currency, and bills upon England be at a premium equivalent to the cost of exporting gold to England.

In England, as in Australia, the vicissitudes of trade occasion alternate expansions and contractions of the circulation. An abundant harvest, or an increase of exports, causes an influx of gold, and the currency expands ; a deficient harvest, or a diminution of exports, causes an efflux of treasure, and the currency contracts. In the former case, money becomes abundant, commercial confidence becomes high, and trade becomes flourishing; in the latter, monetary pressure is induced, confidence declines, trade is paralyzed, and prices continue to fall, until increased exports and diminished imports turn the exchange in our favour, and replenish the exhausted coffers of the banks. Now, if we can realize to ourself the effect which would be produced upon the money market in this country should the Government, under these latter circumstances, shut the Mint for a period of six months, and at the same time prohibit the banks from issuing notes against the uncoined gold flowing into their coffers—if we can picture forth the industrial devastation which would have aggravated the commercial crisis of 1836, 39, and 47, had the relief afforded in these years, as the exchange turned in our favour, been withheld by a legislative enactment suspending the coinage of gold, and interdicting the issue of notes against the uncoined metal—if we can succeed in doing this, then shall we be enabled to acquire some distinct perception of the manner in which the absence of a Mint, and the impossibility of monetising the new supplies of gold, contributed to prolong, and to aggravate, the severe commercial crisis through which the Australian colonies have so recently passed, and from which they are now slowly recovering. In this case, theory and experience coincide. The theory explains the phenomena of the market, and the phenomena of the market verify the theory. To recapitulate :—the absence of a Mint rendered the currency of Australia more valuable than the currency of England, by the double cost of exporting bullion and importing coin. The increase in the value of the colonial currencies caused bills upon England to fall to the extraordinary discount of ten per cent. The state of the exchange led to the realization of extraordinary profits upon importation, excited overtrading, and the glutting of the colonial markets with British goods. Prices fell, importation was arrested, and exportation encouraged. A proportion of the British imports had consisted of sovereigns ; and as sovereigns had been articles of import while bearing a scarcity-value, they became articles of export when their value declined from excessive supply and diminished demand. The dust, and the nuggets, and the bars, which had been sent to England as merchandize, and reimported in the form of money, were, while still retaining the form of money, again exported as merchandize, in common with the uncoined gold from the diggings— thus completing a treble voyage. The Australian currencies, which had been more valuable than British currency, by a double cost of transit, when sovereigns were imported, became less valuable than British currency, by a single cost of transit, as sovereigns were exported. Bills upon England, which had fallen to a discount of ten per cent. in the former case, rose to a premium of three or four per cent. in the latter case. On the 23rd of June, the

state of the money market at Sydney was as
follows:—

" There was a further improvement in almost every
" description of imports. Confidence seemed to be
" gradually returning. Bills upon England were
" quoted at thirty days' sight. Bank buying rate
" one to two premium, selling rate three to four
" premium. The discount of bills under three months
" six per cent. per annum ; ditto four months, seven
" per cent. Little or no change had occurred in the
" gold market from the 1st of January to the 1st of
" June; at the Mint the progress of coinage was
" going on rapidly ; and Australian sovereigns would
" shortly be in circulation."—*Times*, August 27,
1855.

The Australian Mint has been established under
the following conditions, namely :—that the coins
shall be of the same denomination, weight, and
fineness as those of the Royal Mint: that there shall
exist such supervision and control as may be requisite
to secure accuracy in the operations to be performed ;
and that the coins shall bear a distinguishing mark,
so as to exclude them from circulation in all parts
of the empire, except the colony in which they are
issued.

A brief recapitulation of the consequences which
may be expected to result from the establishment of
the Australian Mint will not be inexpedient.

1st. The issue of a colonial coinage, identical—as
regards denomination, weight, and fineness—with
British coinage, will prevent a recurrence of that
anomalous state of the money market under which the
value of money increased, as the value of the metal

composing it declined. The market price of gold, should no seignorage be charged, will be maintained with scarcely-perceptible variations at the Mint price of 3*l*. 17*s*. 10½*d*. per ounce.

2nd. The colonial currency, so long as Australia may continue to be a gold-producing and gold-exporting country, instead of being more valuable than British currency, by the cost of importing coin, will be less valuable than British currency, by the cost of exporting gold.

3rd. Extraordinary and anomalous fluctuations in the exchanges will be prevented; the price of colonial bills drawn upon England, instead of falling at one time to a discount equal to the cost of importing British coin, and rising at another time to a premium equal to the cost of exporting gold, will now be maintained, with only slight and occasional deviations, at a premium regulated by the cost of transmitting to England, whether in the form of bullion or of colonial coin, the produce of the gold-fields.

4th. The comparative steadiness in the exchanges will give more security and stability to commercial transactions; importers and exporters will be less exposed to risks resulting from variations in the prices of foreign bills; and, as the returns upon commercial operations are thus rendered more susceptible of accurate calculation, hazardous adventures will be avoided, and overtrading, and its consequent collapses, will become less frequent than they hitherto have been in the markets of Australia.

Against the advantages of a colonial Mint must be placed the cost of maintaining it. The opinion of Earl Grey is that the cost will be so considerable

as to render the experiment one of doubtful expediency.   But the question is not, as his lordship seems
to suppose, whether the cost of the Mint will be greater
or less than the cost of exporting gold to be coined in
England and reimported, but whether the cost of the
colonial Mint will outweigh the manifold advantages
of maintaining the currency of Australia at its intrinsic or bullion value.

This, the real question at issue, must be decided in the negative.   When we take a comprehensive view of the evils inflicted by a fluctuating,
and of the benefits secured by a uniform currency,
it becomes a matter of no inconsiderable surprise
that the home Government should have so long
withheld its sanction to the establishment of a
colonial Mint ; and that the legislators of New South
Wales and Victoria should not have anticipated the
tardy decision of the colonial secretary by the
adoption of some prompt and efficacious regulation
for monetising the new supplies of gold.   This
desirable object might have been effectually secured,
either by establishing, in conjunction with a Government assay office, a bank of deposit, analogous to the
famous bank of Hamburgh ; or, by applying (also
in conjunction with an authoritative assay) to the
existing colonial banks the principle embodied in
Sir Robert Peel's Act of 1844, for the regulation
of banks of issue in the United Kingdom.   Under
the last-mentioned arrangement the colonial banks
might have been authorized to issue, upon interest-
bearing securities, the same amount of notes for one
pound and upwards, which they had respectively
issued previous to the gold discoveries, while, at the

same time, required to make all their further issues against standard gold, actually held in their coffers; to purchase all such gold as might be offered to them at 3*l*. 17*s*. 9*d*., and to sell it to the holders of their notes at 3*l*. 17*s*. 10½*d*.

The immediate effects of this arrangement would have been, to diminish the demand for imperial coin, until it fell from its scarcity to its bullion value; to raise the market price of uncoined gold to the Mint price of 3*l*. 17*s*. 10½*d*.; to prevent the value of Australian currency from rising above the level of British currency by the cost of importing sovereigns; to retain it below that level by the cost of exporting gold; and, at the same time, to raise the price of Australian bills drawn upon England from a discount, regulated by the cost of importing coin, to a premium regulated by the cost of exporting bullion.

While New South Wales and Victoria were engaged in extorting from the home Government a reluctant sanction for the establishment of a colonial Mint, the adoption of measures for the monetisation of the new supplies of gold devolved on South Australia. While the sudden rise in the value of the standard coin obstructed, to some considerable extent, the rapid advance of the adjoining colonies, in which the gold had been discovered, it threatened to extinguish altogether the prosperity of South Australia. While the migration of the labouring population to the gold-field suspended production, the drain upon the banks, to supply the sudden and intense demand for sovereigns in Sydney and Victoria, deprived the trading classes of a circulating medium.

The intelligent author of ' South Australia and the Gold Discoveries,' thus describes the crisis :—

" It was in the autumn of 1851 that the colony
" began to be disturbed by the gold discoveries in
" Port Phillip.   The hardships and difficulties that
" many had endured at the New South Wales diggings
" somewhat checked the first impressions received;
" but when the reports arrived of the great wealth
" of Mount Alexander, the ardour and excitement for
" this alluring scene of labour became uncontrollable,
" and that portion of the population which could
" migrate began to make the necessary preparations
" for their departure.   Every vessel that proceeded
" to Melbourne was loaded with passengers; many
" people started with slender means, both for ordinary
" comfort and to meét the privations and hardships
" that were inevitable.   Nothing daunted, however,
" those who had a rage for the diggings knew no
" obstacles; and to so great a height did the excite-
" ment reach, that in many cases vessels having an
" insufficiency of accommodation, could only give
" bare standing room for the crowds who took posses-
" sion of the decks.   This was only one part of the
" stream, for many hundreds went overland through
" a tract of country which, though certain to lead to
" their destination, the great majority knew nothing
" whatever about.   The sufferings to many by this
" route were, in the first instance, very great.   With-
" out shelter, proper means of transport, or provisions
" necessary for the enterprise, they wandered over an
" extent of country five hundred miles in length, in a
" condition anything but enviable, and such as only
" the most tempting inducements could have stimulated

them to persevere in. It will of course be apparent
from the routes adopted, that no very accurate
account could be kept of the numbers who left the
province: but the Governor, in a despatch to the
Colonial Office, dated May 7th, 1852, states that
'the migrations to the gold-fields, chiefly of our adult
male population, still continue, and exceed 16,000.'
If, to the close of 1852, we reckon that 20,000 had
left the colony for Port Phillip, we shall doubtless
be within the truth; but what does such a number
represent? Recollecting the aggregate population,
it must represent all the available labour of the
colony, the source from which its vitality proceeded,
the very means by which the fabric of society was
cemented. A writer on the spot, alluding to the
effects of this withdrawal of labour, says, 'it was
with difficulty the harvest was got in. Mining and
other productive operations requiring numerous
hands were suspended. Property of every description was suddenly depreciated, but especially fixed
property. Houses, now tenantless, and fields, for
the cultivation of which farm labourers could no
longer be procured, were offered for sums equivalent
to no more than two or three years' rental.'

" Such a change from prosperity to what appeared
almost like annihilation, produced effects greater
than had been witnessed in any previous crisis.
The shares of the Burra Burra mine, which are to
South Australia what the 3 per cent. Consols are to
England, declined in a few weeks from 175*l.* to 75*l.*
each. All property that had to be sold suffered in
a similar manner; and the consequence was, that
traders and shopkeepers imagined for a time that

" nothing but insolvency awaited them; in fact, that
" every prospect of recovery from their perilous posi-
" tion was beyond hope. An authority as to the
" prevailing feeling reports that ' the condition of the
" colony was likened to a man in the vigour of
" youthful strength struck with sudden paralysis;'
" and there was no exaggeration in the simile. ' The
" deserted streets, the anxious and desponding coun-
" tenances of the few passers-by, recalled to memory
" scenes witnessed on the first visitation of the cholera
" in Great Britain. The loss of capital invested in
" productive pursuits, and the grievous deterioration
" of property consequent on the withdrawal of labour,
" were not alone sufficient to produce these effects
" upon a community eminent for resolute perseverance
" and indomitable energy, displayed under former
" disasters. To those losses was superadded a frightful
" monetary crisis, to withstand or evade which means
" did not for some time appear.' " *

The conduct of the local government in averting
a crisis which threatened to discolonize the province
is above praise. An Act (No. 1, 1852) to provide
for the assaying of the uncoined gold, and to make
bank-notes issued against ingots of standard purity
a legal tender, was promptly introduced, was passed
through the Legislative Council without a dissent-
ing voice, and received, on the 28th of January,
1852, the sanction of the Governor.

This Act provided that a Government assayer
should receive, melt, assay, and cast into one or more
ingots of convenient size, all such gold bullion or

---

* South Australia and the Gold Discoveries, p. 8.

dust, not less than twenty ounces, which might be
brought to him for that purpose; that these ingots
should bear a stamp specifying the quantity of
standard gold which they respectively contained;
that all persons should be entitled to demand from
any one of the banks of the province, the notes of
such banks in exchange for ingots at the rate of
3*l.* 11*s.* per ounce of standard gold; that the banks,
in addition to their issues at the time of the passing
of the Act, should be authorized to issue notes in
exchange for, or to the amount of, any gold bullion
purchased or required by them; that such additional
issues should be made at the same rate of 3*l.* 11*s.*
per ounce of standard gold; that the banks should
retain in their coffers, gold or silver coin to an
amount equivalent to one-third of that portion of
their circulation which consisted of notes over and
above those issued against bullion; that the banks
should not sell, export, or otherwise dispose of the
bullion against which their notes should be issued,
unless in exchange for other notes returned into
their coffers; that the notes so returned should
not be reissued, except in exchange for other
bullion, or unless the banks reissuing them should
possess coin of the realm equal in value, at the rate
of 3*l.* 11*s.*, to the gold bullion exported, or otherwise disposed of; that the banks should furnish
weekly returns, setting forth the average amount of
the notes respectively issued and kept in circulation
by them during the preceding week, the amount of
such notes issued against bullion, the amount of the
gold and silver or copper coin held by them respectively, and also the amount of the coin and bullion

paid, exported, or disposed of, during each week, by
each bank respectively; that such weekly returns
should be published by the Colonial Treasurer in
the ‘South Australian Government Gazette,’ at the
expiration of every two calendar months; and
that the notes issued by any of the banks of the
province should be a legal tender, so long as the
issuing bank should continue to pay its notes upon
demand in the legal coin of the realm, or in bullion
as before provided; provided always that no notes
issued by the banks should be a legal tender of payment by any of the banks; that the banks should
be authorized to pay all cheques drawn upon, and
all bills accepted by them, and to satisfy all pecuniary claims upon them by delivering to the persons
tendering such notes, cheques, or bill, or making such
pecuniary demand, such quantity of gold stamped
by the Government assayer, as should, at the rate
of $3l.$ $11s.$, be equal to the amount of the notes,
cheques, bills, or demands presented for payment;
and that the Act should cease and determine at the
expiration of twelve calendar months from the date
of its passing.

Such were the leading provisions of the South
Australian Bullion Act. Its first effect was to give
a premium on the importation of gold. The price of
gold at Melbourne was under $3l.$ per ounce. The
premium upon importing it, and converting it into
currency at the rate of $3l.$ $11s.$ per ounce, was consequently over 20 per cent. The amount imported
was immense. The restoration of prosperity resulting from this great and sudden increase of capital
is described in the following eloquent passage from

the Report of the Chairman of the Adelaide Chamber of Commerce :—

" The effect of this measure was little short of miraculous. Credit and confidence were almost instantaneously restored; the extreme tightness of the money market was relieved; our traders were enabled to meet their engagements; and the public mind was at once raised from a state of paralyzing despondency to one of hopefulness and vigour.   In its more permanent results the measure has greatly exceeded the expectations which were formed of it.   The most sanguine could only have calculated that it would break our fall—that it would save the colony from general bankruptcy.   No one could have foreseen that in less than six months, we would not only be rescued from impending ruin, but that our condition would be infinitely more sound, and healthful, and prosperous, than ever it had been before; and yet such is indisputably the case.   The enormous stock of goods, which formerly lay like an incubus on the market, has, by exports to Melbourne, where, generally speaking, they realized *saving* prices, been reduced to a manageable compass.   In point of fact, the demand now in many cases anticipates the supply.   The amount of paper under discount at the banks, which formerly was excessive in so small a trading community, has dwindled into, comparatively, an insignificant sum.   Cash payments in the transaction of business, which were wont to be the exception, are now becoming the rule.   Discounting on 'Change at extravagant rates of interest, which formerly was of the nature of a trade, has altogether ceased.   There is no longer any borrowing on mortgage.   Old arrears are being rapidly paid off.   A large amount of petty debts in the books of our traders, which were looked upon as incurably bad, are daily being liquidated. Added to all this, there is in the province, and at the diggings (where deposit receipts have already been signed by our Resident Commissioner for about 250,000*l.* worth), gold to the value of one million sterling, the property of our colonists, which will shortly be seeking investment in the purchase of land, and in other branches of our colonial industry."

It will be seen that the principles upon which the Bullion Act was founded are analogous to those embodied in Sir Robert Peel's Acts of 1844, for the regulation of banks of issue in the United Kingdom. The colonial, like the Imperial Act, limited the issues of the banks upon securities, while it left unlimited their issues against bullion, and thus provided that the currency should expand or contract as the incidents of production and trade caused gold to flow into or out of their coffers. In other particulars, however, the operation of the colonial was different from that of the Imperial Act. The value of the note circulation of the United Kingdom cannot permanently deviate from that of the coin which it represents. But under the Bullion Act, the value of the note circulation of South Australia was permanently higher than that of the ingots which it represented. The cause of this difference in the working of the two Acts is obvious. The ingots were not available as a legal tender, and consequently those who had a purchase or a payment to effect, were obliged to go through the preliminary process of exchanging their ingots for notes. Hence the value of notes exceeded that of ingots to an extent equivalent to the delay and trouble of selling the ingots in the open market, or of returning them upon the banks; and, to a like extent, the market price of gold ingots was kept below the Mint, or rather the assay price of 3l. 11s. This depression in the market price of ingots was increased by a defective provision in the Bullion Act. While it required the banks to pay their notes in ingots, it gave them the option of paying cheques drawn against deposits, and bills accepted by

them, or made payable at their firms, either in notes
or in ingots; and of this option they occasionally
availed themselves.   The parties receiving ingots in
payment for cheques and bills, could not go into the
market as purchasers, until they had previously sold
their ingots for notes, or exchanged them for notes
with one or other of the banks.   Additional difficulty
and delay was thus created in converting ingots into
currency, and consequently an additional depression
in their market price, below their assay price of
3*l.* 11*s.*   This depression proceeded so far, that the
average price of ingots in the market fell to 3*l.* 8*s.* 6*d.*
This gave a great and undue advantage to the banks,
which were enabled, while paying out ingots at the
assay price of 3*l.* 11*s.*, to buy them at the market
price of 3*l.* 8*s.* 6*d.*

The value of the currency, while raised in relation
to the bullion into which it was convertible, was
lowered in relation to coin; while the price of ingots
fell from their assay value of 3*l.* 11*s.* to 3*l.* 8*s.* 6*d.*,
the price of sovereigns rose from their Mint price of
1*l.* to 1*l.* 3*s.* 6*d.* and even 1*l.* 5*s.*

Previous to the passing of the Bullion Act, the
bank-note circulation was convertible into, and therefore equivalent to, sovereigns.   Consequently the
excess in the price of sovereigns above 1*l.* measured
the degree in which the value of the circulation was
reduced under the operation of the Act.

Again, the value of the currency of New South
Wales and Victoria was maintained at par with the
standard coin of the realm; and, consequently, the
rise in the price of sovereigns in the currency of South
Australia, measured the fall in the value of the

currency of this colony, in relation to the currencies of the adjoining colonies.

Once more, while the currency of the United Kingdom was equivalent to standard gold, at the rate of 3*l.* 17*s.* 10½*d.*, that of South Australia, under the operation of the Bullion Act, was equivalent to standard gold at the rate of 3*l.* 8*s.* 6*d.*; consequently the intrinsic value of the currency of South Australia, or, in other words, its value in relation to standard bullion, was higher than the intrinsic or bullion value of British currency by the difference between 3*l.* 17*s.* 10½*d.* and 3*l.* 8*s.* 6*d.*

The Bullion Act produced corresponding changes in the previously existing rates of exchange. So long as the currency of South Australia, in common with the currencies of the adjoining colonies, conformed to the high scarcity-value which had been conferred on the imperial coin, the exchange between South Australia and the adjoining colonies remained nearly at par; while the exchange between the whole of the Australian colonies and England was in favour of Australia by the cost of importing sovereigns. Before the passing the Bullion Act, bills upon London, whether drawn in Adelaide, Melbourne, or Sydney, were, in round numbers, at a discount of about 10 per cent. But after the passing of that Act, bills upon London, when drawn in Adelaide, were, in round numbers, at a discount of about 5 per cent.; or, in other words, a bill for 100*l.*, payable in London, was worth about 90*l.* in the currency of Melbourne or Sydney, and about 95*l.* in the currency of Adelaide.

It has been already remarked that while the

currencies of New South Wales and Victoria conformed to that of the standard coin, the value
of the currency of South Australia was depressed
below that of the standard coin, to such an extent
that the market price of sovereigns in Adelaide rose
to from 23s. to 25s. This difference between the
value of the bank-note circulation and that of the
standard coin, occasioned, amongst the economists of
Australia, a controversy regarding the question of
depreciation, somewhat analogous to that which had
occurred in this country forty years before, when the
restriction upon cash payments disturbed the equality
between bank notes and coin. The question of
depreciation, however, was neither so simple nor so
easy of solution in Australia as it had been in
England. Some of the leading facts on which it
turned were different in the two cases. In England,
under the restriction Act, a foreign demand for gold
gave bullion, which could be sworn off for exportation,
a higher value than coin, the exportation of which was
at that time prohibited. In Australia, a domestic
demand for sovereigns gave coin a higher value than
bullion which could not be there converted into coin.
In England, under the restriction Act, the value of
the bank-note was less than the value of the quantity
of gold which it is supposed to represent, whether
that quantity appeared in the form of bullion or in
the form of coin. In South Australia, under the Bullion Act, the bank-note circulation was of less value
than the standard coin; but of greater value than
the quantity of gold contained in the standard coin.
Under these circumstances, so different from those
which had existed in England during the suspension

of cash payments, was the bank-note circulation of
South Australia depreciated or not ?   On this question
the Australian authorities came to opposite conclusions: the Chairman of the Melbourne Chamber of
Commerce, the Manager of the Bank of Australia, and
the Colonial Treasurer of South Australia, contending
that the currency was depreciated; while the Chairman of the Adelaide Chamber of Commerce, the
Manager of the South Australian Bank, and the
Government Assayer, maintained that it was not
depreciated.

Before we can arrive at a correct decision upon the
question at issue between these opposite authorities,
it is necessary that we should have a distinct perception of what it is in which depreciation consists.   Depreciation is, reduction of price; reduction of price is,
reduction of value in relation to that which law or
custom has established as the standard measure of
value; and hence the term depreciation, when applied
to currency, means a reduction of its price or value in
relation to the established standard of value.   With
respect to metallic money, it is depreciated as often as
its value from adulteration, clipping, or other cause,
becomes less than that of the quantity of standard
metal, which, by the regulations of the Mint, it ought
to contain; and with respect to a paper currency, it
is depreciated as often as its value from any cause
becomes less than that of the standard coin which it
purports to represent.   A sovereign is depreciated
when its value is less than that of the quantity of
standard gold, which by the regulations of the Mint
it ought to contain, and a five-pound bank-note is
depreciated when its value is less than that of five

sovereigns. Now the imperial coin was the standard
of the Australian currency. Previous to the passing
of the Bullion Act, the value of the bank-note circulation of the whole of the colonies was equal to that
of the imperial coin into which it was convertible on
demand; or, to express the same thing in other
words, was not depreciated. After the passing of
the Bullion Act, the value of the bank-note circulation of South Australia was depressed below that
of the imperial coin, or, in other words, was depreciated. In the language of economical science, the
terms " depreciation of currency" are employed to
express depression of value in relation to a given
standard. When coin is the legalized standard of
value, it is a manifest contradiction of terms to say
that a currency is not depreciated when it ceases to be
equivalent to standard coin.

Let us now examine the arguments advanced by the
advocates of non-depreciation. The Chairman of the
Adelaide Chamber of Commerce contended that the
currency was not depreciated, because " bank bills
" could be purchased on London at 5 per cent. dis-
" count." This was a practical proof that the value
of the currency of South Australia was higher than
that of England; but it did not disprove the con-
temporaneous fact, that the currency was less valuable
than its standard. A rise or a fall in the price of
bills drawn upon a foreign country proves a fall or a
rise in the value of domestic currency in relation to
the currency of that foreign country; but does not
and cannot show any fall or rise in the value of domestic currency in relation to the standard. The
state of the foreign exchanges, to which the Chairman

of the Adelaide Chamber of Commerce triumphantly
referred, had no relation whatever to the question at
issue.

The Government assayer, another strenuous cham-
pion of non-depreciation, thought to establish his
position by a reference to the statistics of prices.
He compared the prices current of the several Australian colonies, and drew the conclusion that, as
prices were not higher in Adelaide than in Melbourne
and Sydney, the bank-note circulation of Adelaide
could not be depreciated. The conclusion was erroneous. It was disproved by Mr. Babbage's own
statistics. His facts, taken in conjunction with the
coexisting fact that South Australia was then not
only exporting agricultural produce, but re-exporting
British goods to Melbourne, present a practical demonstration that the currency of South Australia was
depreciated; for if the prices of agricultural produce
and foreign goods were the same in Adelaide as in
Melbourne, their exportation from the former to the
latter would have been attended by positive loss,
unless the currency in which prices were estimated in
Adelaide had been of less value than the currency in
which prices were estimated in Melbourne. But the
currency of Melbourne was at par with standard coin ;
and as the currency of Adelaide was of less value than
that of Melbourne, it was also of less value than the
standard coin, or, in other words, was depreciated.
Had the fact that sovereigns were at a premium in
Adelaide been practically unknown, its existence,
with its necessary consequence, depreciation of the
currency, might have been scientifically deduced from
Mr. Babbage's statistics.

Unable to controvert the fact that the Bullion Act had depreciated the currency in relation to the standard coin with which it had previously been at par, Mr. Babbage discards the coin of the realm as the standard of colonial currency, and substitutes in its stead, "a real value available in England." He says, " that sovereigns should be at a premium in a distant " colony results from the state of things. The ex- " pense of transmission on sovereigns to this country " (South Australia) is about 2½ per cent.; they " ought, therefore, if the note circulation here were " based on real value available in England (as it is " in fact under the Bullion Act), to bear a premium " to that amount, which corresponds very nearly to " the present state of things."

To give practical effect to this very novel and some-what startling doctrine, it would be necessary that the exchanges between the colonies and England should be constantly maintained at par; for if bills drawn upon England fell to a discount, or rose to a premium, 100*l.* in colonial currency would purchase a real value available in England for more than 100*l.* in the former case, and for less than 100*l.* in the latter: and in neither case would the colonial currency conform to the novel standard adopted by Mr. Babbage. And how would he propose to maintain the exchanges in that invariable state of equilibrium, without which the colonial currencies could not conform to his standard of real value available in England? Would he, when an excess of exports created a corresponding excess of bills drawn upon England, create a proportionate in-crease in the demand for them by an expansion of the circulation? or, on the other hand, when an excess of

R

imports rendered the supply of bills upon England
short of the demand for them, would he prevent their
rising to a premium, by contracting the circulation,
until its value rose in the same ratio with that of
bills? The high ability, theoretical and practical,
possessed by the late Government assayer, renders it
impossible to doubt that he will, upon reconsideration,
rectify opinions which seem to have been overhastily
advanced upon the question of depreciation.

The question whether the Bullion Act depreciated
the local currency, involved the further question
whether it violated existing contracts. On this further question opposite opinions were maintained, the
Chairman of the Melbourne Chamber of Commerce
and the Colonial Treasurer of South Australia contending that contracts were violated; the Chairman of the
Adelaide Chamber of Commerce and the Government
assayer that they remained undisturbed. This controversy was less complicated than the former. The
question regarding depreciation turned, to some extent, upon abstract principles and scientific classification; that regarding the violation of contracts turned
entirely upon admitted fact and law. It was an admitted fact, that previous to the passing of the Bullion
Act, the bank-note circulation was at par with the
standard coin; it was an admitted fact, that before
the Act came into operation, all creditors were legally
entitled to receive the amount of their demands
in a currency equivalent to standard coin; and it
was a palpable and unquestionable fact that, under
the provisions of the Act, creditors were compelled to
accept payment in a currency of less value than the
standard coin. It is difficult—it is impossible to

understand upon what logical grounds it could have been maintained, in the face of these admitted facts, that contracts were not violated. All the existing contracts which had been entered into previous to the passing of the Bullion Act were legal engagements to pay in sterling coin, or in bank-notes convertible into sterling coin. The Act relieving debtors from the fulfilment of their legal engagements, and compelling creditors to receive payment in bank-notes of less value than sterling coin, could not be otherwise designated than as an Act authorising the violation of contracts. And here another important question occurs. If it must be admitted that the Bullion Act depreciated the local currency and violated all existing contracts, on what conceivable grounds could it have been justifiable? The answer is, on the very conceivable and very obvious grounds of imperative necessity. The colony was being deprived of a circulating medium; and the only alternative was, should it have a note circulation five per cent. below the legal standard, or no circulation at all. The debtor classes were verging on insolvency; the creditor classes, unable to enforce payment of their legal demands, were, no less than the debtor classes, sinking into poverty. The question was, should universal bankruptcy be averted by a legislative compromise? To deny that the Bullion Act depreciated the local currency, and set aside legal contracts, is to deny that it did that which it was intended to do. Had it not reduced the value of the note circulation below that of the standard coin, and authorised an universal composition between debtors and creditors, it would have been an utterly nugatory instead of an

eminently successful measure. Those were not the
most judicious advocates of the Bullion Act who
sought to defend it by a denial of the fact that it was
a departure from the general principles, according to
which, under ordinary circumstances, currencies are
regulated and contracts enforced. Its adoption was a
palpable departure from general principles; and the
sagacity and practical wisdom of the local government were strikingly exemplified in discerning that
the condition of the colony presented one of those
anomalous and exceptional cases in which general
principles cannot be with safety applied. The highest
praise which can be bestowed upon the economist or
statesman is, that, not the slave, but the master of
scientific deductions, he can correct and adapt them
to the unforeseen emergencies into which disturbing
elements have entered, and for which the file affords
no precedent. This highest praise the future his-
torian of South Australia will not hesitate to award
to the Governor and Council by whom the Bullion
Act was passed. Nor will such praise be withheld
from the Principal Secretary of State for the Colonies,
under whose advice the Act of the Colonial Legislature
received the sanction of the Crown.

THE

ECONOMISTS REFUTED;

OR,

AN INQUIRY

INTO THE

NATURE AND EXTENT OF THE ADVANTAGES

DERIVED FROM

TRADE.

By R. TORRENS, Esq.

LONDON: PUBLISHED BY S. A. ODDY,
AND C. LA GRANGE, DUBLIN.
1808.

ECONOMISTS REFUTED.

CHAPTER I.

POLITICAL Economy, a branch of knowledge at all times highly important, derives a peculiar interest from the present circumstances of this country and of Europe. The ruler of France, adopting a new mode of warfare, has closed the ports of the European continent against British commerce, and it becomes extremely desirable that the people should be able to ascertain, with some exactness, the extent of the injury which their enemy may have power to inflict. The courage which arises from an ignorance of our danger may fail us in the day of trial; true magnanimity will contemplate the coming storm, and, with unswerving resolution, prepare to brave its fury. At the present awful crisis, when "England expects that " every man will do his duty," I know not that my time can be more beneficially employed than in an endeavour to diffuse among my countrymen just ideas

of the sources of wealth, and of the nature and extent of the benefits conferred by foreign trade.   In
the present chapter I intend to inquire into the sources
of wealth, and to urge some arguments, which, in my
opinion, are calculated to overthrow, completely, the
positions advanced by the economists.

The articles which supply our wants and gratify
our desires constitute what is called wealth.   The
primary sources of wealth are, the land and the waters.
The Designer of the Universe hath ordained, that the
earth shall supply, spontaneously, things adapted to
supply the wants, and to gratify the desires, of the
sensitive beings that dwell upon her surface.   Our
planet traverses in the path prescribed, the seasons
succeed each other in their order, and, by an agency
which we cannot comprehend, we are furnished with
whatever is necessary to preserve existence; but the
proposition which asserts that every article of wealth,
everything which supplies our wants or gratifies our
desires, must be derived, originally, either from the
land or from the water, is so obvious, that it requires
neither proofs nor illustrations.   We may proceed to
examine another source of wealth, namely, labour.

Labour creates wealth in three ways: by appropriating; by preparing; and by augmenting the productions of the land and water.

First, labour creates wealth by appropriating the
productions of the land and water.   The earth which
we inhabit does, indeed, abound with articles adapted
to our use; but before these articles can constitute
wealth, before they can supply any want or gratify
any desire, they must be appropriated by labour.
The rude savage, who plucks the fruit of the forest,

or turns up the ground in quest of roots, works before
he eats. Nature will part with none of her productions until we have paid her the stipulated price, and
this stipulated price is toil.

Secondly, labour brings wealth into existence, by
preparing the productions of the land and water.
Some of the productions of the earth, such as fruits,
may be consumed the instant they are appropriated.
Other productions of the earth, such as flax and iron,
require considerable preparation before they can
supply our wants or gratify our desires. Now, the
labour that renders this class of productions fit for
consumption is a source of wealth. From materials
which, without its intervention, would have possessed
no value, it creates articles useful and desirable to
man. But every article that is useful or desirable to
man comes under the denomination of wealth; and
everything that brings such article into existence
must be a source of wealth. In the rudest stages of
society we discover labour producing wealth, by preparing the productions of the earth for use. The
wretched inhabitant of New Holland, whose only
possessions are a spear, a fish-gig, and canoe, employs
some species of industry on the materials he receives
from Nature, and thus fits them to supply his wants
and gratify his desires.

Thirdly, labour produces wealth by increasing the
productions of the earth. When man, dissatisfied
with the precarious subsistence derived from the spontaneous gifts of Nature, begins to domesticate the
inferior animals, and to protect and rear them for his
use, the articles which supply his wants and gratify
his desires receive a considerable increase; but when

B

man, perpetually advancing from improvement to improvement, directs his attention to the cultivation of the earth, he produces a still greater accession to his wealth. Indeed, the advantages derived from the cultivation of the earth are so conspicuous, that many ingenious men have been led into the opinion that agriculture is the only source of wealth. But this opinion, first advanced by Mons. Quesnoi, and recently revived by Mr. Spence, is undoubtedly erroneous. A very slight inspection into the affairs of man is sufficient to convince us that there are other sources of wealth than agriculture; that the labour which appropriates and prepares the productions of the earth, is, as well as the labour that augments these productions, efficacious in giving existence to articles that gratify our desires and supply our wants. To illustrate what we here assert, let us suppose the existence of a country, similar, in some respects, to the islands of the Pacific Ocean. The earth produces nutritious plants, the waters abound with fish, the flax-plant grows wild, as in New Zealand. Is it not evident, that, in this country, the labour employed to appropriate and prepare the productions of the land and water would supply all our wants, and gratify many of our desires? Food, clothing, habitation, furniture—nay, many of the embellishments and luxuries of life, might exist in considerable abundance, though agriculture should be quite unknown. Agriculture, therefore, cannot be the only source of wealth. Indeed, it is to me a matter of surprise, that the idea of agriculture's being the only source of wealth should be entertained by men of acknowledged talents. Let us examine, as they are exhibited in a

recent publication, the arguments which support so
strange an opinion.

" That the examination" (says Mr. Spence) "into
" the truth of the opinion of the French economists,
" that agriculture is the only source of wealth, may
" be rendered as simple as possible, let us inquire
" what would take place in a country constituted
" much in the same way as this country is; where
" there should be a class of land proprietors, a class
" of farmers, and a class of manufacturers, but where
" there should exist no money of any kind, no gold,
" silver, or paper, in short, no circulating medium
" whatever. In such a society the land proprietor
" must receive his rent in kind, in corn, cattle, or
" whatever may be the produce of his land, and all
" transactions between man and man must be carried
" on by the medium of barter. However inconve-
" nient such a state of society might be, it may be
" very well conceived to exist, and has, indeed, ex-
" isted in a great degree, at one period, even in our
" own country. In a nation so circumstanced, though
" part of the subsistence of the manufacturing class
" would be drawn from the farmer, from the profit
" which would remain with him after the maintenance
" of his family and the rent of his landlord were
" deducted, yet by far the greatest portion of their
" subsistence, it is evident, must be drawn from the
" class of land proprietors; from that surplus pro-
" duce paid to them under the denomination of rent.
" It will, therefore, in a still greater degree, simplify
" our illustration, if we suppose, what will in no re-
" spect influence the accuracy of our reasoning, that
" the *whole* of the subsistence of the manufacturing

" class must be derived from the class of land pro-
" prietors.

"From this system" (continues Mr. Spence) "results
" such as the following would ensue ; the competition
" which would necessarily take place amongst the
" class of manufacturers, to dispose of their articles
" to the land proprietors, would restrict the price of
" these articles, as is the case at present, to a quan-
" tity of provisions barely necessary to replace the
" subsistence of the manufacturer whilst he had been
" employed on them. This being the case, all the
" articles which the manufacturer might fabricate in
" the course of a year, would, by the end of that
" year, be in possession of the land proprietors, in
" exchange for provisions."

Here Mr. Spence has fallen into an error. The
competition among the manufacturers, to dispose of
their articles to the land proprietors, would not restrict the price of these articles to a quantity of provisions, barely sufficient to replace the subsistence of
the manufacturer, whilst he was employed on them ;
all the articles which the manufacturer might fabricate
in the course of a year, would not, at the end of that
year, be in possession of the land proprietors in exchange for provisions. On the contrary, a *part* of the
manufacturer's articles would be found sufficient to
purchase a quantity of provisions equal to the subsistence he had consumed whilst employed on them ; the
other part would remain with him for his own consumption.

This is the case at present. The weaver, for instance, does not give the *whole* of his cloth in exchange
for provisions ; a part of it must remain with him to

clothe himself and his family. The fabricator of
household utensils cannot give the *whole* of these articles in payment for his food, because utensils of some
sort are necessary to his own existence. Now, every
article of wealth that remains with the manufacturer,
after he has given the land proprietor a just equivalent for the produce which he consumed whilst at
work, is an article of wealth created by manufactural labour. We concede to Mr. Spence that the
value of the agricultural produce which the manufacturers consumed during the year is to be deducted
from the value of the articles they fabricated; but,
this concession avails him little; the manufacturers,
besides replacing by a just equivalent the subsistence
which they drew from the land proprietor and farmer,
must have fabricated for themselves various articles of
furniture and clothing. Here, then, the manufacturer
has done more than "fix or transmute the value of a
"perishable article into one more durable." Besides
replacing the produce of the soil which he consumed
during the year with a just equivalent, he has created
wealth which did not before exist. But further, it
will be found, on an accurate investigation, that the
manufacturers, besides giving a just value for the
provisions they consume, and besides creating various
articles of furniture and clothing for their own consumption, pay, as well as the farmers, a surplus rent
to the land proprietor. In a state of society such as
Mr. Spence has supposed, where every transaction
between man and man is carried on by the medium
of barter, the manufacturer must fabricate articles
with which to purchase food, he must fabricate articles for his own consumption, and he must fabricate

articles to pay the land proprietor for the house in which he lives. Here, then, the manufacturer, out of the articles which he fabricates, " besides maintaining " his family, pays the owner of his [house] a net " surplus under the name of rent. This surplus must " be considered as clear profit, for it remains after " every expense attending [the fabrication of the arti- " cles] has been repaid," and though it is not what Mr. Spence has been pleased to call " a new creation " of matter which did not before exist," yet it is an evident " creation " of wealth.

Many other arguments occur to me, against the opi- nion of the economists, that agriculture is the only source of wealth, but I dismiss them as superfluous. It is not necessary that I should detain my readers with a laborious refutation of a theory which contra- dicts experience. As has been already hinted, agri- culture, instead of being the only, is, in fact, the last source from which man, in the progress of his im- provement, derives articles to supply his wants and gratify his desires. Long before he thinks of aug- menting the productions of the earth, he acquires wealth, by appropriating and preparing her sponta- neous gifts. A country circumstanced, in some re- spects, like the island of Otaheite, might possess all the necessaries, and many of the luxuries of life, though agriculture should be quite unknown. I trust sufficient has now been said to convince those who reflect on subjects of political economy, that the sources of wealth are, first, the land and the waters; secondly, labour, appropriating, preparing, and aug- menting their productions.

CHAPTER II.

In the last chapter we treated of the sources of wealth; we shall in this chapter consider the means by which it is augmented. Now, it is a self-evident proposition, that wealth cannot be augmented by any means different from those by which it is produced. Inquiring how our wealth may be augmented, is the same thing as inquiring how the sources of wealth may be rendered more productive. The first source of wealth is the earth; but, as we cannot enlarge the dimensions of our globe, we have no way of augmenting wealth except by rendering the second source of it more copious; that is, in other words, except by augmenting the productiveness of the labour which appropriates, prepares, and multiplies the articles of our use and desire.

The employment of capital is perhaps the first means by which man augments the productiveness of his labour. The inferior animals Nature has furnished with instruments by which they procure food, and perform the labour that is necessary to their existence. Man she sends into the world naked and unarmed, but has compensated those wants by enabling him to procure instruments for himself. The instruments which he thus procures to assist him in the performance of his labour are denominated " fixed capital." The employment of fixed capital is not confined to the cultivated periods of society. The most ignorant savage will avail himself of some rude instrument to abridge his labour, or to perform that which the naked human hand would be unable to perform. In the first stone he flings at the animal he pursues, in the

first stick he employs to strike down the fruit that
hangs above his reach, we see him augmenting the
productiveness of labour by means of capital; but as
society advances, the productiveness of human industry is augmented to an astonishing degree by the
extension of fixed capital, and by the improvements
that take place in all the tools and instruments of
which it is composed, till, in the application of wind,
water, and steam in our mechanical operations, we
press the powers of nature into our service, and "arm
" us with the force of all the elements." But it is
not necessary, for any purposes that I at present have
in view, to dwell longer on the advantages derived
from the employment of fixed capital. They who
wish to pursue this subject at greater length, will find
it ably unfolded in Lord Lauderdale's work on public
wealth. I proceed to point out another means by
which the productiveness of labour is increased.

In very early periods of society men must have
been prompted to exchange with each other the articles of their wealth. The hunter who had been fortunate enough to kill a large animal, having more flesh
than he could consume, would be willing to barter a
part of it with his neighbour who had chanced to discover a quantity of fruit. The man who had procured
a piece of wood capable of making *two* bows, would be
glad to exchange his superfluous bow with the man
who had a superfluity of arrows. Now, as soon as
this system of exchange became familiar to the minds
of men, it would naturally give rise to a division of
their labour. The man who happened to be slow of foot
would begin to perceive that, by gathering fruit and
preparing implements for the fleet-footed hunter, he

could obtain a greater quantity of the flesh of animals than if he had himself engaged in the labours of the chase; while the fleet-footed hunter would discover that, by pursuing wild animals, and exchanging them with the man, who, from nature or habit, was more expert at mounting trees, he could obtain a greater quantity of fruit, and a greater number of branches fit for bows and arrows, than by endeavouring to procure these articles by his own immediate labour. Hence mutual interest would establish a division.

As the division of labour augments in a very considerable degree the productiveness of human industry, and as I shall, in the course of this work, have frequent occasion to allude to the benefits it confers, the reader, I trust, will not deem me tedious if I here examine it at greater length.

Though the earth is the primary source of wealth, yet the immediate supply of our wants, or gratification of our desires, is procured from the second source of wealth; from labour appropriating, preparing, and augmenting the productions of the land and water. Now, as our wants and desires are very various, the labour which supplies and gratifies them must be very various also. Indeed it would be a task of some tediousness to enumerate the different kinds of industry which must be exerted before we can be supplied, moderately, with the conveniences of life. If each individual were to combine, in his own person, these different branches of industry, the mere business of shifting his tools and adjusting his materials would occupy half a day. This inconvenience is obviated by the division of labour. When each man confines himself to a particular branch of industry, he no longer wastes his time in shifting from employment to employment; and, in addition to this advantage, he acquires, from habit and experience, a degree of skill and dexterity in his particular calling, truly astonishing to those who have always lived in places where the division of labour is but imperfectly established.

The division of labour that we have been here considering I call the mechanical division of labour; another division of labour, which, for the sake of distinction, I shall denominate the territorial, remains to be considered.

Different soils and climates are adapted to the growth of different productions. One district abounds with luxuriant pasture, another is calculated for tillage; in one country the sheep have the finest fleeces, in another country, where these animals have but a coarse and scanty covering, the earth supplies abundant quantities of cotton. Now, in countries, the soil and climate of which are thus diversified, if the system of exchanging commodities has become familiar to the minds of the people, a territorial division of labour will be established. The proprietor of arable land will perceive that it is his interest to confine himself to tillage, and exchange his corn for the cattle of his neighbour who possesses pasture grounds. A similar perception of advantage will render the possessor of the pasture grounds desirous of the exchange. Each will co-operate with the agency of nature, and give his fields that peculiar cultivation which best suits the varieties of their soil. By this territorial division of labour, the productiveness of human industry will be greatly augmented; the things necessary

and desirable to man will receive a wonderful increase.

This view of the advantages resulting from the mechanical and territorial divisions of labour, enables us
to ascertain the nature of the benefits derived from
trade. When the proprietor of arable land gives the
proprietor of meadow grounds a quantity of corn, and
receives in return an equal value of the products of
grass, this act of exchange, considered in itself, has
made no addition to the public wealth. The corn of
the cultivator has passed into the hands of the grazier,
and the cattle of the grazier have become the property of the cultivator; but it is quite impossible that
this transfer of wealth, already in existence, should,
when considered in itself, create any new article of
human desire: however, if we consider trade as a
mere system of transfer, if we leave out the influence
which it exerts on production and on the division of
labour, then we take a most confined and inadequate
view of the subject.* When the proprietor of arable
land gives a quantity of corn for an equal value of
animal food, he does not, by this exchange, bring any
article of wealth into existence; but we must not
forget that it was the *prospect*, the *expectation* of this
exchange, that induced him to raise a greater quantity of corn than was necessary for his own consumption, that induced him, in fact, to establish a territorial
division of labour, and to cultivate his fields in such a
manner that nature herself co-operated with his exertions and augmented the productiveness of his industry.
Again, when the weaver gives twenty yards of cloth
for an equal value of household furniture, this transfer,

* See note A (at the end).

considered in itself, adds nothing to the nation's
wealth; but then, it was the expectation of this
transfer, that induced him to fabricate more cloth
than was sufficient for his own consumption; it was
the expectation of this transfer, in fact, that caused
him to establish a mechanical division of labour,
which, by saving time and giving skill and dexterity,
greatly augments the articles which supply our wants
and satisfy our desires. But in order to evince more
fully the beneficial operation of trade, in establishing
the mechanical and territorial divisions of labour, let
us examine, for a moment, the effects that would result
from a cessation of all interchanges between man and
man. The instant the articles of wealth became un-
transferable, the division of labour, with all its advantages, would be discontinued. The weaver would no
longer fabricate a greater quantity of cloth than he
thought necessary for his own consumption: he would
be obliged to supply all his wants, and to gratify all
his desires, by combining in his own person a great
variety of employments. Hence, half his time would
be consumed in shifting his tools and adjusting his
materials, and his attention, distracted with a multi-
plicity of occupations, he could become expert at
none. Again, the occupier of arable land, no longer
able to dispose of his surplus corn, would cultivate no
more than what he thought necessary for his own use.
Those fields, whose produce he formerly exchanged,
would now lie waste, or else be made to yield a scanty
supply of some article not congenial to their soil.
Similar interruptions would take place in the occupations of the grazier. We should see cattle feeding
in the neglected corn-field, and the moist meadow

ploughed up, in order that it might produce grain.
Men being no longer able to give their labour the
direction calculated to co-operate with the agency of
nature, the productiveness of their industry would
suffer a great diminution, the earth would not yield
half the riches which she is capable of yielding.

From what has been here advanced, we are enabled
to ascertain the way in which trade is a means of
augmenting wealth. The *act* of exchanging does not,
indeed, bring wealth into existence; but the *expectation* of exchanging gives rise to divisions of labour,
which multiply, to an immense extent, the articles
that supply our wants and gratify our desires. Prohibit trade, and the divisions of labour cease; restore
it, and the divisions of labour, with all their benefits,
return. Hence, whatever may be the benefits resulting from the divisions of labour, these benefits are to
be referred to trade, as to their original and proper
source.

Trade being, in this manner, a means of augmenting wealth, it follows, that everything which facilitates
the interchange of commodities must conduce to render
the divisions of labour more perfect, and be also a
means of augmenting our possessions. Thus improvements in roads, canals, and navigation, by facilitating
the intercourse between man and man, perfect the
divisions of labour, and consequently enrich a nation.
But the circumstances most efficacious in perfecting
the divisions of labour is the employment of stock, or
floating capital. By stock, or floating capital, ex-
pressions which I shall use synonymously, I mean all
those articles of wealth which are not intended for
immediate consumption. The manner in which these

facilitate the establishment of more perfect divisions
of labour may require some explanation.

We have seen that the expectation of being able to
exchange superfluous commodities gives rise to the
division of labour. Now, the division of labour,
though it so greatly augments the productiveness of
human industry, is yet liable to many inconveniences;
and these inconveniences may, on some occasions,
become so extensive, as to render it the interest of
the individual to discontinue the division of labour,
and to combine several occupations in his own person.
Supposing that, under the expectation of being able
to exchange my superfluous corn for clothing, I give
my exertions, exclusively, to the cultivation of the
earth. When I expose my produce to sale, there
may, already, be a sufficient supply of food to meet
the effectual demand; but, if my necessities are ur-
gent, if my children have not wherewithal to protect
them from the inclement season, then I must dispose
of my corn for what I can obtain; the market becomes overstocked, and the price of my produce sinks
so low that it will not recompense my toil. I find
that, if I had raised corn for myself and family only,
and had omployod tho romaindor of my timo in fabricating cloth, I should have possessed a greater quantity of the necessaries of life than I have now obtained
by an exclusive cultivation of the earth. The division of labour, instead of benefiting, injures me.
Whatever time it may save, whatever dexterity it
may give, yet, in consequence of the fluctuations of
the market, I find that I can best provide for my
family by combining many occupations in my own
person. Nor are the mischiefs resulting from the

markets being overstocked with any commodity confined to the persons whose exertions were exclusively
directed to its production.   Though there should not
be a greater quantity of corn in the country than is
necessary to subsist the inhabitants until the next
harvest, yet the farmers may be compelled, by their
necessities, to overstock the market, and thus to induce an artificial superfluity.   This, giving rise to a
less economical expenditure, may occasion a real deficiency.   Many may perish from want, though there
was originally food enough to last throughout the
year.   Now, these evils, incident to the division of
labour, are all obviated by the employment of stock.
Suppose, for example, that I live in the neighbourhood of a man who has accumulated a greater quantity of clothing, furniture, and other articles of wealth
than is necessary for his immediate consumption, and
who employs this stock in buying up corn when it is
cheap, for the purpose of selling it again when it becomes dear; it is evident, I think, that the factor, by
this operation of his stock, will correct those sudden
fluctuations of price which caused me to abandon the
division of labour, and will prevent the recurrence of
artificial superfluity and subsequent want.   Not compelled by his necessities to dispose of the corn he has
purchased for anything he can obtain, he will expose
it to market in such proportions only as are sufficient to
meet the effectual demand.   The market will no longer
be overstocked.   Agricultural produce kept up to its
level price, I shall begin to perceive that, by confining
myself to the cultivation of the earth, I can obtain a
greater quantity of the articles of my desire than if I
combined in my own person the occupations of the

farmer and manufacturer. The divisions of labour, with all their advantages, are again established.

The reasoning we have here employed on the corn trade is applicable to all others. In each the employment of stock, or floating capital, obviates the inconveniences which are incident to the divisions of labour, and would prevent their establishment. This conclusion is confirmed by experience. In countries where stock is deficient, each person is obliged to divide his attention among a variety of occupations; in countries where stock abounds, a more perfect division of labour obtains; each becomes dexterous in his appropriate calling, every field receives that peculiar cultivation which nature dictates, and the necessaries of life are multiplied a thousandfold.

But it must not be concealed that the good resulting from the employment of stock has also its attendant evils. As a deficiency of stock may occasion an artificial superfluity, so an excessive accumulation of stock in a few hands may induce an artificial scarcity. A great corn-dealer may sometimes have it in his power to withhold corn from the market until it rises far above that level price which is marked by the proportion that exists between the annual consumption and the annual supply; and thus, though there should be a sufficiency of food in the country to last until the next harvest, yet the labouring classes may be reduced to much distress. But the evils resulting from overgrown capitals are less grievous than the evils experienced in countries where floating capital is deficient, for the evils arising from an excessive accumulation of stock have limits which they soon attain, and which, if Government be but wise enough to withhold her pernicious interference, it is impossible they should ever pass. The things necessary to human sustenance are of a perishable nature, and if the factor should withhold them from market beyond a certain period they must perish on his hands. If, indeed, all the corn-factors agreed to make an equal distribution of their profits, it might become their interest to let a part of their corn perish (as the Dutch are said to have done with their spices), in order to enhance in a greater degree the value of what remained; but in an extensive and wealthy country it is quite impossible that the scattered and numerous factors should enter into so close a combination; each would be anxious to dispose of his corn before it perished on his hands. Their mutual competition would quickly remove the artificial scarcity their avarice had produced. One man's selfishness, acting as an antagonist muscle to the selfishness of his neighbour, things would not recede excessively from their natural position. But even though it were possible for the capitalists of such a country as England to combine, for the purpose of raising the markets, yet the evils attending such combination would admit of an easy and obvious remedy. *Leave trade free* and the race of forestallers will disappear. As water finds its level, as air rushes to occupy vacuity, so commodities have a tendency to flow from the quarter where they are cheap to the quarter where they are dear. If our capitalists were to buy up corn and withhold it from market the price of corn would rise. This rise of price would operate as a bounty on importation. Foreign merchants would pour in supplies, and the artificial scarcity quickly disappear. Corn,

which had experienced an unnatural rise, would now
experience an unnatural depreciation. Those who had
conceived the detestable idea of starving their fellow-
men, would receive, in the consequence of their own
devices, the punishment of their crime. When will
the rulers of the earth desist from the intolerable
arrogance of substituting their impotent regulations
for the regulations that grow out of the system of the
universe?

Having thus seen that the employment of stock is,
in consequence of its obviating the inconveniences
which retard a perfect establishment of the divisions
of labour, a means of augmenting wealth, we can
now ascertain the source from which the profits of
stock are derived.

It has sometimes been asserted, that the proprietor
of floating capital is an unproductive labourer, who,
without being himself instrumental in augmenting the
riches of the country, acquires, by means of barter
and sale, a property in the wealth which others have
created; but if there is any justness in the principles
I have endeavoured to establish, this assertion cannot
be conformable to truth. When the husbandman and
weaver confine themselves each to his proper calling,
they augment the productiveness of their industry, we
will suppose, one-fourth; but this beneficial division
of labour cannot be established unless there is, somewhere, a capital to *keep up* their cloth and corn, and
to expose them for sale in such proportions only as
are sufficient to meet the effectual demand. The capitalist, therefore, who employs his stock in purchasing
cloth and corn, is instrumental in adding one-fourth to
our supply of these necessary articles. A *part* of this

fourth, he, with justice, appropriates to himself, and calls it "the profits of his stock."

There are many occupations, in which the division of labour will augment the productiveness of industry in a ratio different from that which we have here supposed ; but this can in no ways invalidate our position. Whatever may be the amount of the benefit resulting from the division of labour, that benefit the capitalist was instrumental in securing, and he will consequently obtain a part of it as the profits of his stock.

A part of the benefit resulting from the division of labour will always belong to the capitalist. It is evident that the whole of it he never can appropriate to himself; for, if the labourer did not gain something by confining his attention to a particular occupation, the division of labour would quickly be destroyed. ...

But though the augmented wealth, arising from the division of labour, must always be divided amongst the capitalists and the labourers, yet it will, under varying circumstances, be divided amongst them in very different proportions. By the aid of a monopoly, the capitalist may draw to himself *almost* the *whole* of the benefits arising from the division of labour, and leave to the labourer a degree of advantage barely sufficient to induce him to confine himself to a particular employment. On the other hand, when trade is left free and capital very abundant, competition will lower the profits of stock, and the capitalist will obtain a portion of the benefits flowing from the division of labour barely sufficient to induce him to pursue his mercantile speculations.

The view of the subject which we have here taken,

enables us to point out the advantages that accrue to
a nation from the accumulation of floating capital.
Every increase of capital increases the competition
amongst the capitalists, and, consequently, diminishes
the profits of stock.   Now, as the profits of stock are
diminished, a greater proportion of the benefits conferred by the division of labour will remain with the
labourer; or, in other words, the wages of labour will
rise.   Thus capital, gradually accumulating, may advance the wages of labour until every labourer, by a
moderate degree of industry and frugality, has it in
his power to become himself a capitalist.   This is the
most consolatory prospect that political science can
present.   Let us suppose that, by a gradual increase
in the wages of labour, and in the frugality of the
people, every man in England has accumulated as
much of the necessaries of life as he can consume
within the twelvemonth; from such a state of things
we should have the following results:—The people, no
longer compelled by their necessities to work for any
pittance that might be offered, could, when they
thought proper, withhold their labour from the market.
Wages would become very high, the profits of stock
very low: this would produce a revolution in the
mode of carrying on trade; master tradesmen would
cease to exist.   The people would no longer be con-
gregated in manufactories, to the ruin of their health,
and the destruction of their morals.   Every man would
" work for himself and not for another." Possessed of
sufficient capital to purchase the raw material, to
subsist himself while preparing it, and to keep it up
when prepared, for the effectual demand, the manufacturer would obtain not only the wages of the labour,

but the profits of the stock that was employed in fabricating his commodities. The whole of the advantages resulting from the division of labour would remain with the labourer; leisure and independence would be the inheritance of all.*

There is another circumstance attending the accumulation of capital which it would be improper to overlook. Capital will always be transferred, from countries where the profits of stock are low, to countries where the profits of stock are high. If, in America, money bore an interest of six per cent., while, in England, it bore an interest of but three, then nothing short of a total prohibition of our exports could prevent British capital from flowing to America. The consideration of this principle ought to abate that commercial rivalship among nations which has so often deluged the earth with blood. When peace shall be concluded, if a great accumulation of capital takes place in France, a *part* of it will flow to England, and better the condition of our people; but, should the profits of stock be much lower in England than in France, then will the agency of British capital advance the wages of French labour. The human race constitute but a single family, and the prosperity of one nation leads to the prosperity of all.

CHAPTER III.

HAVING shown that trade is a means of augmenting wealth, I now intend to consider, distinctively, the different branches into which it is divided, and to

* See note B (at the end).

point out, as I proceed, whatever is peculiar to each.
I shall, in the first place, treat of the home trade, or,
in other words, of those exchanges which take place
between the individuals of the same community.

All the observations which occurred when we considered trade, in a general point of view, are applicable to that particular branch of it denominated
" the home trade." When the individuals of the
same community have become familiarized to the
exchanging of their superfluous commodities with
each other, the divisions of labour will be established.
One man will perceive, that, by confining his exertions to the fabrication of cloth, he can save time,
acquire expertness, and obtain, in exchange for his
surplus cloth, a much greater quantity of the articles
he desires, than if he combined, in his own person, a
variety of occupations. Another man will discover,
that by limiting his attention to tillage, and giving
his superfluous grain for the products of grass, he
can enjoy a greater quantity of animal food, than
if he refused to co-operate with the agency of nature,
and fed cattle in the fields which she intended for the
growth of corn. But, in order to render it still more
evident, that it is the home trade which occasions the
establishment of these home divisions of labour, let us
examine, for a moment, what would take place if the
home trade were abolished. Unable to dispose of his
superfluous articles, no man would be prompted to
produce a greater quantity of any particular commodity, than should be found necessary for his own
consumption. Each individual would be compelled
to fabricate for himself all the various articles of his
desire. To obtain bread, the grazier would be obliged

to plough up his meadow grounds; in order to gain animal food, the proprietor of arable land must convert his corn-fields into pastures. Now, restore the home trade, and the home divisions of labour, with all their advantages, will be re-established. Expecting a market for their goods, men will be prompted to produce greater quantities of cloth and corn than are necessary for their own consumption. The manufacturer will become expert in his proper calling; the farmer will give every field its proper cultivation. Thus we have the fullest possible proof, that the home divisions of labour, with all their advantages, are to be referred to the home trade, as to their proper source.

Again, that augmentation of wealth which is produced by the home division of labour, constitutes the fund from which those who carry on the home trade derive their profits. If the weaver confines his exertions to the fabrication of cloth, he must carry his cloth to a neighbouring farmer, in order to exchange it for corn. But this farmer may already have a sufficient quantity of cloth, and be unwilling to purchase more; the weaver is therefore obliged to traverse the country, in quest of some other farmer, who has not a sufficient supply of clothing. All this while, the farmer who has not a sufficient supply of clothing, is, perhaps, seeking a weaver who has not a sufficient supply of food. In this process much time and exertion may be wasted. It is therefore found highly convenient to establish a further division of labour, and to have a cloth-merchant, who shall confine his attention to the buying and selling of cloth; a corn-factor, who shall devote his exertions to the vending

of corn. By this further division of labour our wealth
is considerably augmented. In consequence of its
establishment, the weaver becomes secure of obtaining
a ready supply of food from the corn-dealer, and no
longer wastes his time in seeking out a customer
among the farmers; the farmers become satisfied
that they can always obtain clothing at the shop of
the cloth-merchant, and no longer suspend the cultivation of their fields, to search for weavers who
may have a demand for corn: a greater quantity
of industry is directed to the production of those
things which are useful and desirable to man. Now,
whatever may be the amount of the benefit, resulting
from this greater quantity of industry being directed
to the production of things useful and necessary to
man, a portion of that benefit will belong to the cloth-
merchant and the corn-dealer. They have performed
a species of labour, which, but for their intervention,
the weaver and farmer would have been obliged to
perform, and in a much greater degree; and the
wages of this labour the weaver and farmer must
pay, out of that additional wealth which they derive
from the more perfect division of their industry.
Here, then, we detect the error, which such political economists as Mr. Spence fall into, when they
class the merchant among unproductive labourers.
The occupation of the merchant is a branch of those
divisions of labour which are so efficacious in augmenting wealth. While he collects his commodities,
and brings them to market, the farmers and manufacturers, no longer wasting their time in seeking
customers, are enabled to bestow an undivided attention on their proper callings, and are rendering

the nation much richer than it could be without his
intervention.   An example will demonstrate this.
When a dealer in laces buys ten pounds worth of
lace, and sells it again for fifteen pounds, by this
transaction he becomes five pounds richer; but it
does not therefore follow that the consumer of the
lace becomes five pounds poorer : because, if it was
not for the intervention of the dealer, the manufacturer would waste his time in seeking customers, and
distract his attention by combining, in his own person,
occupations that are now distinct.   This would reduce
the productiveness of his industry ; the supply of lace
would be diminished, and, in consequence, its price
advanced.   The consumer would not be able to obtain, for his fifteen pounds, so large a quantity of this
article of decoration, as, by the instrumentality of the
dealer, he now obtains.   This reasoning applies to all
the other branches of the home trade.   In every
instance the dealer is, immediately, a productive labourer, and the wages of his labour are drawn, not
from the pockets of the consumer, but from that augmented wealth, which arises from each man's confining himself to a particular occupation.   But the
gains of the dealer will not be limited to the wages
of his labour.   In order to carry on his business, he
must be possessed of stock, and this stock will be
entitled to a profit.   But, if I have been at all successful in unfolding the principles of political economy,
it will be unnecessary for me to descend, in this place,
into the proof, that the consumer is not impoverished,
by the dealer's drawing to himself, as the profits of
his stock, a portion of the benefit arising from those
divisions of labour which his stock is instrumental in

establishing. I may pass on to make some observations on the advantages that are peculiar to the home trade.

In contemplating the home trade, the first circumstance that strikes us, is, its superior magnitude and importance. In this country, the far greater portion of our wealth is the produce of our own soil, appropriated and prepared by our own labour. Many of the articles we consume are, indeed, the growth of other lands, but almost the whole of the food, clothing, and furniture, used by the great body of the people, is produced at home. The home trade, therefore, is that which augments the productiveness of the industry that clothes and feeds the great mass of our population. Destroy the home trade, and the home divisions of labour will cease, and England be incapable of maintaining half the inhabitants which at present she maintains. Another advantage peculiar to the home trade is, that its benefits are two-fold. If I give my attention exclusively to the cultivation of the earth, while my neighbour devotes himself to the fabrication of cloth, the benefits resulting from this division of labour are shared between us and the trader, by the aid of whose capital the division of labour was established. But, if I give my attention, exclusively, to the cultivation of the earth, and exchange my produce with a foreign weaver, then the benefits resulting from this division of labour will be shared between me and the foreign weaver, between the British and foreign merchants, by the aid of whose capitals the division of labour was established. Thus in every exchange of the home trade, the *whole* of the benefit remains in the country;

in every exchange of the foreign trade a *part* of the
benefit goes to enrich foreigners.   When England
sends a thousand pounds' worth of woollen cloth
to Ireland, and receives, in return, a thousand
pounds' worth of linen, the United Kingdom receives
a greater accession of wealth, than when England
exports to France a like value of cloth, and brings
back an equivalent in lace.   In the first exchange,
the *whole* of the benefit resulting from the division
of labour remains in the United Kingdom ; in the
second, a *part* of the benefit rests with foreigners.
This shows us that calculating the amount of exports
and imports, is a most inadequate means of ascertaining a nation's wealth.   When a parish exchanges
with its neighbour parish, a thousand pounds' worth
of its produce, the country receives an accession to
its wealth, twice as great, perhaps, as that which
would accrue, from an exchange, to a similar amount,
with a foreign nation.

Permanence is another advantage peculiar to the
home trade.   Whatever may be the benefits of foreign
trade, these benefits are held by an uncertain tenure.
The caprice of strangers, the hostility of rivals, ignorant of the great truth, that the prosperity of one
nation is the prosperity of all, may deprive us of a
great portion of our commerce.   But the home trade
is all our own ; and, if our governors were sufficiently
enlightened to unite the whole population of the
empire in defence of common rights, the confederated
world could not interrupt it.

The last peculiarity of the home trade that I shall
notice is, that its extension is essential to the extension of the colonial and foreign trades.   The colonial

and foreign trades are carried on by means of those
articles, the produce of our land and labour, which
remain, after our own effectual demand is supplied,
and can be increased only by the increase of these
surplus articles. But, by increasing the home trade,
and, consequently, rendering the home divisions of
labour more perfect, we do increase these surplus
articles, and thus enlarge the fund that purchases
colonial and foreign produce.

Having considered so many advantages peculiar to
the home trade, the question naturally occurs, What
are the most effectual means of encouraging it? In
order to encourage the home trade, two important
duties devolve on governments. The first is, to
secure to every member of the community a perfect
empire over the produce of his industry. The way
to render men industrious is to convince them that
their earnings are their own, that they labour for
themselves "and not for another." The shortest,
and most effectual way of rendering them idle and
vicious, is, to deprive them, no matter by what
means, of the fruits of their exertions. The second
duty that devolves on those who administer the
affairs of nations is, to abstain from governing too
much. When we see ministers and kings interfering
with the natural order of events, and prescribing the
channels in which trade shall flow, we are reminded
of the beautiful fable, where Phaëton is represented
as presuming to guide the chariot of the sun. Miser-
able vanity! it would excite derision, did not its
mischievous consequences call forth our detestation.

CHAPTER IV.

On the Colonial Trade.

HAVING considered what seems important and peculiar in the home trade, I will proceed to examine the colonial trade. This, like every other branch of mercantile industry, gives occasion to divisions of employment, and thus heightens the productive powers of labour and capital. England, for example, abounds with land peculiarly adapted to the feeding of sheep; but as a part of such land is sufficient to supply us with all the mutton and wool we require, the remaining part of it must be employed in producing something else for which we have a demand. Let us suppose that our demand is for sugar; and then the remaining part of the land peculiarly adapted to the feeding of sheep, will be employed in the cultivation of saccharine plants. Neither the soil nor the climate of England, however, is congenial to plants abounding with saccharine matter; and were we to lay out our grounds in plantations of the beet or of the parsnip, we should obtain only a small supply of sugar at a great expense. But let a tropical island, in which the sugar-cane grows luxuriantly, be discovered and taken possession of, and the proprietor of the English beet plantation will immediately perceive, that by feeding sheep upon the grounds which nature adapted to pasture, and exchanging his wool for the sugar of the colonist, he can obtain a much more abundant supply of this article than by raising it at home. The colonist, too, in whose warmer climate nature has given the sheep a thin and scanty covering, will find it his interest to raise more sugar than he requires for his own consumption, and to send the surplus to England in exchange for clothing. Hence, between the mother country and the colony, a mutually beneficial territorial division of employment will be established; and the home and the colonial proprietor, in consequence of their co-operating with nature, will augment, in a very high degree, the productive powers of their respective industry.

Here, perhaps, it may be asked, — If it is by establishing divisions of employment that the colonial trade promotes the formation of wealth, what can be the utility of incurring the expense of maintaining colonial establishments? Might not the trade which is carried on between a mother country and her colonies be equally extensive and beneficial, though the connection between them were dissolved and the colonies acknowledged as independent states ?

One answer to these questions is, that the territories in which colonies are generally established are inhabited by tribes of savages, professing neither the inclination nor the skill to render their soil productive, and that before any beneficial divisions of employment can be established with such territories, they must be taken possession of by a civilized people.

This answer, however, applies only to the policy of sending out colonists in the first instance to cultivate tracts inhabited by savage tribes, and does not go to show that any increase of national wealth is derived from retaining sovereignty over colonies which have been once thoroughly established, or over nations already sufficiently industrious. The proper answers to these questions are the following :—

In the first place, the colonial resembles the home

trade, in the twofold benefit which it confers, and in the security and permanence which it possesses. When England trades with an independent island, a part of the wealth created by the consequent division of employment goes to enrich foreigners. But when England carries on traffic with Jamaica, the whole of the increased wealth brought into existence by the divisions of employment hereby established, is the property of British subjects, and adds to the strength and resources of the British empire. Besides, when we exchange our commodities with an independent state, the beneficial divisions of employment to which this traffic gives occasion, are liable to be suspended by a declaration of hostilities or by the enacting of those restrictions and prohibitions which commercial rivalry is perpetually suggesting. But when a mother country and her colonies, particularly if they possess a commanding marine, interchange their surplus products, nothing short of a dismemberment of the empire can suspend their intercourse, or interrupt those divisions of employment by which they are enabled to make the most of the natural peculiarities of their soil and of their acquired advantages in the application of labour.

In the second place, from the relative proportions according to which population and capital have, in all old countries, been hitherto found to increase, the supply of labour has such a tendency to exceed the demand for it, that the labouring classes, even when there is no extraordinary stagnation or revulsion in the channels of industry, are commonly reduced to a degree of distress and temptation, for which, in the actual state of knowledge and of morals, there is

no conceivable remedy except in a system of colonization, sufficiently extensive to relieve the mother
country from superfluous numbers.   The question
of colonization, however, with respect to its influence
in mitigating the evils of excessive population, will
fall more properly under our consideration when we
come to examine the several circumstances which
regulate wages and affect the interests of the labouring classes.   It is alluded to in this place merely for
the purpose of exhibiting, in a strong light, the futility
of the objections which have sometimes been urged
against the extension of the colonial system.

It is extremely improbable that the objections
against colonial establishments, even were they as
valid as in reality they are futile, should ever have
the effect of inducing princes and sovereign states
voluntarily to resign such dependencies.   A question
of much greater practical importance presents itself
for our consideration ;—namely, can any accession of
wealth be derived from those restrictions which, in
modern times, parent states have almost uniformly
imposed upon the commerce of their colonies?   Such
restrictions have generally had for their object, either
to grant to particular companies and particular ports,
an exclusive privilege to trade with the colonies, or,
to compel the colonies to make the mother country
the mart, or *entrepôt*, for effecting all their transactions
with foreign countries, or to secure to the domestic
producer the monopoly of the colonial market.   I
shall examine the effects of these restrictions in the
order in which I have enumerated them.

When a particular company, or a particular town,
obtains the exclusive privilege of trading with the

colonies, home-made goods become dearer in the
colonial market, and colonial goods dearer in the
home market than they would be if the law of competition were allowed to operate unchecked. It is only
by being able to dispose of their commodities at
prices above the level which would be determined by
free competition, that the merchants of a particular
company or town can receive any benefit from the
exclusive privilege of trading with the colonies.

But raising the price of home-made goods in the
colonial market, and of colonial goods in the home
market, above the level of free competition, brings no
additional wealth into existence, but merely enhances
the profits of the merchant at the expense of the
consumer. Nay, this mode of raising prices, and of
enhancing the profits of the privileged merchant,
instead of increasing the general mass of wealth, will
tend to diminish it. Enjoying considerable profits by
the aid of their exclusive privilege, the merchants
trading between the mother country and the colonies
will not be compelled to shut out competitors by
taxing their ingenuity to the utmost in order to
discover the cheapest and most expeditious modes of
conducting their business. A greater quantity than
would otherwise be necessary of the labour and
capital of the country will, therefore, be employed
in exchanging commodities, and consequently a less
quantity will remain to be employed in directly
producing them. But this is not all. Many of those
articles which the mother country sends to the
colonies, and which the colonies send to the mother
country, will consist of the necessaries of life, or of
the articles expended in raising and fabricating the

D

necessaries of life. But whatever increases the expense of bringing such articles to market, lowers the return upon capital throughout all the departments of industry, sets narrower limits to the extension and improvement of tillage, and diminishes the quantity of food and of raw material which can be obtained for manufactures. Granting, therefore, to particular companies, or even to particular towns, the exclusive privilege of trading with the colonies, not only enriches the favoured individuals at the expense of the home and colonial consumers, but at one and the same time checks the prosperity both of the colonies and of the mother country.

The effect is different with respect to those restrictions on the colonial trade which have for their object to render the mother country the mart, or *entrepôt*, for conducting the commercial intercourse between the colonies and foreign countries. These increase the wealth of the mother country by diminishing that of the colonies. If we suppose that the British colonies consume a quantity of Russian linens, while Russia, in return, takes a quantity of their sugars, then it will be the clear and obvious interest, both of the colonies and of Russia, that their respective commodities should be carried and exchanged with the smallest possible expense. But, if England restricts her colonies from holding a direct commerce with foreign countries, and if, in consequence, the sugars and the linens must be first consigned to the port of London, and thence reshipped for their final destination, then the London merchants to whom the consignments are made, and by whom the reshipments are effected, will charge their commission upon these transactions, and this commission, paid by the Russian and colonial consumers in the increased price of their goods, will be a clear addition to the wealth of England, obtained by the restrictive system imposed upon the colonies.

It may, perhaps, be objected, that if the British colonies were permitted to hold a direct traffic with Russia, the London merchants to whom the consignments were made, and by whom the reshipments were effected, would employ their capitals in some other direction, and, by making the customary rate of profit, would effect the same addition to the national wealth as before. We answer, that mercantile capital consists, first and mainly, of the commodities which are circulated; and, secondly, of the vessels, docks, wharfs, and warehouses, by means of which their circulation is effected. If the restrictive system were abolished and a direct trade permitted between our colonies and Russia, all that portion of mercantile capital consisting of the sugar to be consumed in Russia, and the linen to be used in the colonies, which was consigned to the London merchant and upon which he obtained a commission, would disappear altogether from the port of London, and no longer pay England a per centage. Besides, that portion of mercantile capital which consisted of docks, wharfs, and warehouses, though it remained in the country, yet could not be transferred to agriculture or manufactures, and when London ceased to be the *entrepôt* between the colonies and Russia, the dues, profits, and rents paid for the use of these things by the colonial and Russian consumers, would be so much net revenue which England would lose by the abolition of the restrictive system.

Those restrictions which have for their object to secure to the productions of the mother country a monopoly in the colonial market, may also have the effect of enriching the mother country at the expense of the colonies. Supposing that Scotch and Irish linens cannot be sold with an adequate profit at so low a price as those of Germany, and that England, by protecting duties and prohibitions, compels her West India Islands to purchase the more costly articles,—it will be evident that the wealth of these colonies must be diminished by the amount of the difference between the price which they pay for British, and that at which, under a free trade, they might obtain German linens. A little consideration will also render it evident that this loss sustained by the colonies will be a source of gain to the mother country. Under the circumstances supposed, if it were not for the artificial protection afforded to them, Scotch and Irish linens could not be manufactured for the colonial market, and the manufacturers would be compelled to transfer their capital to the production of other articles with which to purchase the colonial produce required for the home market. But why, in the first instance, was colonial produce purchased with linens instead of with the other articles now fabricated for that purpose? For no other reason, assuredly, but because the merchant found that linens, when sold in the colonies at the prices secured by the restrictive system, enabled him to bring back a more valuable return in colonial goods than he could have purchased with any other article produced at home by an equal expenditure of labour and capital. Had there been any article, obtained at home at the same expense, which could have purchased in the colonies a greater, or even an equal quantity of their produce, this article it would have been the interest of the merchant to have exported. The fact of his having preferred the exportation of linen proves that this article, when protected against foreign competition, will purchase in the colonies a greater quantity of their produce than any other obtained at an equal expense. The restrictive system, therefore, which prevents foreign from beating home-made linens out of the colonial market, enables the mother country to purchase her colonial produce with a less sacrifice of labour and capital than she otherwise could do. While the colonies would be impoverished by giving a greater quantity of the produce of their labour and capital for the linens they required, the mother country would be enriched by giving a less quantity of her products for the sugar and rum which she consumed.

While the restrictions on the colonial trade which give the products of domestic industry a monopoly in the colonial market, increase the wealth of the mother country at the expense of the colonies, those restrictions which secure to colonial productions an exclusive privilege in the home market, enrich the colonies at the expense of the mother country. When England imposes an unequal duty upon the sugars of the East Indies, in order to encourage the trade with the West India islands, she renders herself tributary to her own colonies, and makes a voluntary sacrifice of wealth to

the amount of the difference between the quantity of
her products which she gives for her supply of West
India sugars, and the quantity for which she might
obtain an equal supply of sugars from the East.
Again: when the Legislature recently laid heavy
duties on the importation of Norwegian timber, in
order to force the people of England to purchase the
dear and inferior timber of Canada, the interests of
England were blindly sacrificed to those of Canada,
and the wealth of the country diminished by the difference between the price we are forced to pay for
American timber, and the price for which we might
obtain the article from the north of Europe. But this
is not the worst; with the single exception, perhaps,
of iron, timber is the most serviceable article in aiding
human labour. It enters, more or less, into every
portion of capital employed in production. Now, increasing the difficulty of obtaining the ingredients of
capital, and thereby raising their exchangeable value
with respect to other things, necessarily reduces the
rate of profit. Hence, the monopoly which England
has granted to Canada in the timber trade, not only
compels her to sacrifice a greater portion of her
wealth in exchange for the timber she requires, but
tends to lower the return upon capital throughout all
the departments of her industry. By the duties on
Norwegian timber, the mother country loses incal-
culably more than the colonies can gain.

In concluding this chapter on the colonial trade, it
may be expedient to show, that the principle, that
restrictions may benefit the mother country by
injuring the colonies, or enrich the colonies by impoverishing the mother country, is in no way incon-

sistent with the doctrine established in the preceding
chapter, that the utmost freedom of internal intercourse promotes the wealth of a country. When a
mother country and her colonies are regarded as one
empire, there can be no doubt that the aggregate
wealth of this empire will be increased by establishing
an entire freedom of trade between all the countries
composing it; in the same way as the aggregate
wealth of a country is increased by permitting unrestricted intercourse between its several provinces.
But, as in any country a monopoly, or exclusive
privilege, in favour of a particular set of persons, or of
a particular town, might enrich those persons, or that
town, at the expense of the community; so, in an extensive empire, commercial regulations may be devised
which will have the effect of rendering one country
tributary to another. In revising our colonial system,
if the object of the Legislature should be to increase
the wealth of the British dominions, the utmost
freedom should be extended to the trade between the
several countries of which these dominions are composed. But, should the object be to cause the greatest
possible portion of the general wealth to centre in the
United Kingdom, as a compensation for the expense of
protection; then restrictions should be imposed, rendering the mother country the *entrepôt* for the foreign
transactions of the colonies, and securing to her productions a monopoly in their markets. We cannot
conceive, that it is ever the real object of legislators
to enrich a colony by impoverishing the parent state;
because this would be to counteract the only end for
which colonial possessions are maintained; and therefore regulations, similar in principle to those under

which England imports her timber from Canada, must have their origin either in ignorance, or in a corrupt compliance, in return for parliamentary support, with the wishes of some powerful junta of shipowners and merchants, whose private interest is opposed to that of the public.

CHAPTER V.

WE come now to treat of foreign trade, or commerce. As this branch of our subject has been much obscured, by the inadequate manner in which Mr. Spence has considered it, it becomes necessary, in order that we may arrive at greater clearness in our conclusions, to recapitulate some of the principles formerly advanced.

The *expectation* of being able to exchange the articles which they do not want, for other articles that they stand in need of, induces men to divide their labour. The divisions of labour augment, to an astonishing degree, the productiveness of industry. By the mechanical division, each acquires, in his calling, an expertness and skill which he could not otherwise acquire; by the territorial division, cultivation is made to co-operate with the process of nature, and the productions of the earth are multiplied. Now, these beneficial divisions of labour may be established between the individuals of different nations, as well as between the individuals of the same nation. If the people of England have acquired greater dexterity than their neighbours in preparing wool, while the people of France excel in preparing silk, then, between the two nations, a mechanical division of labour, mutually advantageous, may be established: England confining herself to the manufacturing of woollens, France to the manufacturing of silks, these articles of clothing will be produced in greater abundance, than if each country wasted its capital and its labour in endeavouring to acquire dexterity in the occupation of the other. Again, if the sheep fed on the pastures of England have richer fleeces than the sheep fed on the pastures of France, while the vine of France grows more luxuriantly than the vine that is planted in England, then, between the two countries, a territorial division of labour, mutually beneficial, may be established: the English feeding sheep on their pasture-grounds, and exchanging wool for the produce of the Frenchman's vineyard, will obtain greater quantities of wine than if they cultured the grape at home beneath an uncongenial sky; the Frenchman, co-operating with Nature, and exchanging wine for the produce of the English pastures, will obtain the materials of clothing in greater quantities, than if he fed sheep in districts in which the food or the climate was injurious to their fleeces. Now, as it is the home trade that gives rise to the home division of labour, so it is foreign trade or commerce that gives rise to the foreign divisions of labour. Prohibit foreign trade, and the foreign divisions of labour, both mechanical and territorial, must be discontinued; restore it, and these divisions of labour will be re-established, and all their benefits return.

If this view of the subject is correct, the opinion of Mr. Spence, that " commerce adds nothing to national wealth," has received a sufficient refutation. But a

particular examination of the arguments by which his
opinion is supported, may tend to elucidate the principles of political economy which I have endeavoured
to establish.

" As all commerce" (says Mr. Spence) "naturally
" divides itself into commerce of import and export, I
" shall, in the first place, endeavour to prove, that no
" riches, no increase of national wealth, can in any
" case be derived from commerce of import:" and in
order to prove this, he goes on, in the next page—
" Every one must allow, that for whatever a nation
" purchases in a foreign market, it gives an adequate
" value, either in money or in other goods; so far
" then, certainly, it gains no profit nor addition to its
" wealth. It has changed one sort of wealth for
" another, but it has not increased the amount it was
" before possessed of." Here, as before, we find Mr.
Spence taking a narrow and inadequate view of his
subject, confining himself to the mere *act* of exchange,
and leaving out of the account the influence which
the *expectation* of an exchange has in establishing a
division of labour, and, consequently, in augmenting
production. Waving, at present, the discussion of
equivalents, and admitting that " for whatever a nation
" purchases in a foreign market, it gives an adequate
" value, either in money or in other goods," still it can
be demonstrated that commerce is instrumental in
augmenting wealth. "Thus, when the English East
" India Company has exchanged a quantity of [tin]
" with the Chinese for tea," I will not say " that this
" mere exchange is any increase of national wealth."
But I will say, that it was the *expectation* of this exchange which occasioned the English to work their tin

mines to a greater extent than was necessary to meet the home demand; and I will say that, by raising a surplus quantity of tin, and giving it to the Chinese for tea, they supply themselves more abundantly with this article of wealth than if, inverting the order of nature, they endeavoured to culture it at home. I feel that in making these assertions, I am not exposed to the hazard of refutation. Men never waste their labour and capital in the production of articles which they believe will lie useless on their hands. Demand must ever regulate supply. Take away the foreign demand for tin, and not a pound of it, beyond what is necessary to supply home consumption, will be raised from the mine. Here it may be asked, "cannot the " labour and capital, which are thus withdrawn from " the production of tin, for the foreign market, be " directed to the production of some other article of " equal value ?" This question, which seems to involve the great leading argument of those who deny that commerce adds to a nation's wealth, admits of an easy and an obvious answer. The labour and capital withdrawn from the production of articles for the foreign market must, if employed at all, be directed either to the production of articles adapted to our soil and climate, or to the production of articles which are not so adapted. But we find that our effectual demand for articles congenial to our soil and climate is already sufficiently supplied. A greater quantity of these cannot, therefore, be produced. It follows that the labour and capital withdrawn from the supplying of the foreign market, must be directed to the production of articles which are not adapted to our soil and climate. Here, then, instead of seconding, we should counterwork the operations of Nature; consequently, the labour and capital withdrawn from the production of articles for the foreign market could not be directed to the production of other articles of equal value. I must own that this reasoning is, to me, self-evident in all its steps. We cannot produce a greater quantity of the articles adapted to our soil and climate than is necessary to meet our effectual demand. When this demand is once supplied, our surplus labour and capital will be employed, either directly or indirectly, in supplying articles adapted to the soil and climate of foreign countries. But when our surplus labour and capital are employed to supply, indirectly, the articles adapted to the soil and climate of other countries, we obtain such articles in greater abundance than if our labour and capital were employed to supply them directly. When we dig from our mines more tin than we can consume, and exchange it for tea, we have more tea than if we cultured it in England. And in like manner every other branch of industry is rendered more productive by the establishment of a foreign territorial division of labour. But commerce is the instrument by which the national divisions of labour are established; consequently commerce is a means of augmenting wealth.

The example here employed to illustrate my position, varies a little from that employed by Mr. Spence. Tin is substituted for bullion. " But this can in no " respect influence the accuracy of our reasoning." When England, after having supplied her home demand for the articles adapted to her climate, employs her labour and capital in the production of surplus woollens, exchanges these for bullion, and then sends

out the bullion in order to purchase tea, the process is
a little more complex than if she had obtained the tea,
by a direct exchange for something, the produce of
her own soil, but the result is precisely similar. For,
whether we suppose the exchanges of commerce direct
or indirect, they equally give rise to the foreign divisions of labour, equally augment the articles which
supply our wants, or gratify our desires.

Having thus demonstrated, as I think, that commerce, by establishing divisions of labour between the
individuals of different nations, is a means of augmenting wealth, I now proceed to make some observations
relating, in a more peculiar manner, to this branch of
trade.

It has been supposed that the wealth which one
nation gains by commerce, some other nation must
lose. But if there is anything of truth in the principles endeavoured to be established in this work, the
supposition that a nation is impoverished by any particular branch of her commerce is perfectly absurd.
When England manufactures a surplus quantity of
cloth, and exchanges it with France for wine, she
obtains more wine than she could have obtained by
cultivating the grape at home. But in this transaction the gain of England is not the loss of France.
On the contrary, France has made an accession to her
wealth. In exchange for her wine, she has acquired a
greater quantity of cloth than she could have acquired
by converting her vineyards into sheep-walks and
manufacturing wool at home. She has obtained her
full proportion of the benefit resulting from that
foreign division of labour which enables each nation
to co-operate with the processes of nature. As, in the

home trade, the advantage is always twofold, so, in foreign trade, it is always reciprocal.

But though the advantages of commerce are reciprocal, yet it does not follow that they should be equal. When countries exchange their commodities, each may be benefited, but each in a different degree. When England gives Spain a thousand pounds' worth of hardware for an equal value of wine and fruit, the wealth she receives perishes the instant it is enjoyed; the wealth she bestowes is durable, and may continue for years to supply the wants, and to gratify the desires of the Spanish people. Thus this exchange is more beneficial to Spain than it is to England. But the degree of advantage which commerce confers on one nation, more than on another, does not always depend on the different degrees of durability which belong to the exchanged commodities. We give France a thousand pounds' worth of coarse woollens, and receive, in return, a thousand pounds' worth of lace. By this exchange we obtain a greater quantity of lace than if we manufactured it at home; France obtains a greater quantity of woollens than if she fabricated them for herself. So far the advantage is mutual. But the additional lace which we obtain by this national division of labour is expended on the headdress of *one* lady of quality; the additional woollen cloth obtained by France protects a *hundred* of her people from the inclemencies of the season. Here, then, though the value and durability of the articles exchanged should be equal, yet the benefits resulting from the exchange would be widely different. On one side, the desire of a single individual would be gratified; on the other, the wants of many would be supplied. Hence we learn, that the nation which imports necessaries is more interested in extending her commerce, than the nation which imports luxuries. This consideration is calculated to give a swell of exultation to every British heart. The humiliating opinion has prevailed, that France is independent of foreign trade, while England leans on commerce for existence. But the reverse of this opinion is nearer to the truth. We can subsist much better without French lace and French cambrics than France without our hardware and our woollens. He who will carefully estimate the productions proper to our soil, as well as the direction which our industry has assumed, will unhesitatingly pronounce, that if there is, in the world, a country that can enjoy all the necessaries and all the comforts of life, independently of commerce, that country is England. When the powers of the Continent shut their ports against our trade, they injure themselves much more than they can injure us.

I shall now endeavour to estimate the extent of the benefit which foreign trade confers. It was long the custom to estimate the benefit conferred by commerce, by the degree in which our reports exceeded our imports. Nothing could have been more erroneous or absurd. If England sends a thousand pounds' worth of broad cloth to Spain, and receives in return nine hundred pounds' worth of fruit and wine, it is evident that, instead of gaining an accession of wealth by this excess of export, she is a hundred pounds poorer than if Spain had given her the full value of her cloth. Here it may be said that Spain will pay the deficiency in the precious metals, and thus give us the full value of our cloth. Let it be so; but if England receives,

for a thousand pounds' worth of cloth, nine hundred
pounds in fruit and wine, and one hundred in gold
and silver, then are her imports exactly equal to her
exports, and the whole theory of the balance of trade
is absurd.   In vain do the advocates for this theory
contend, that when we receive part of our returns in
the precious metals, money becomes more plenty, and,
consequently, the nation richer.   For, as the individual who possesses a thousand pounds' worth of cloth
is just as rich as the individual who has a thousand
pounds in money, so the nation that possesses a thousand pounds' worth of cloth, beyond her effectual demand for clothing, has as much disposable wealth as
the nation that possesses a thousand pounds' worth of
gold or silver, beyond what supplies her effectual
demand for plate, and a circulating medium.   But
even conceding (what indeed we are not called upon
to concede) that the precious metals are to be preferred
before all other articles, which supply want or gratify
desire, still, nothing but narrow views of the subject
could have suggested the idea, that the amount of the
benefit conferred by commerce is to be estimated by
the balance received in gold and silver : for when we
take an enlarged survey of the topics of political
economy, we discover that a nation cannot, for any
length of time, receive such balance.   Gold and silver
are not perishable commodities requiring to be periodically supplied.   The country that imports them
quickly fills up the measure of her effectual demand,
and when this has been filled up they must overflow
the market and run out in foreign channels.   Thus,
if a regulation existed, requiring that all the gold and
silver which we receive from Spain should remain in

the country, these articles would quickly overstock
the market, and consequently fall in price. But as
bullion fell in price, individuals would be impelled to
export it, and no possible vigilance on the part of
Government could give effect to the laws and prevent
it from flowing out of the country. Our demand for
the precious metals is soon supplied. After it has
been supplied we cannot import more bullion than we
export. It is grossly absurd to say that the amount
of the benefit conferred by trade is to be measured by
the balance we receive in money.

The only way, therefore, of ascertaining the amount
of the benefit derived from commerce, is to ascertain
the degree in which the foreign divisions of labour augment the productiveness of human industry. Thus, if I
wish to know the extent of the advantage which arises
to England, from her giving France a hundred pounds'
worth of broad cloth, in exchange for a hundred
pounds' worth of lace, I take the quantity of lace which
England has acquired by this transaction, and com-
pare it with the quantity which she might, at the same
expense of labour and capital, have acquired by
manufacturing it at home. The lace that remains,
beyond what the labour and capital employed on
the cloth might have fabricated at home, is the
amount of the advantage which England derives from
the exchange.

It would be difficult, indeed I think impossible, to
ascertain, with exactness, the amount of the benefit
which nations derive from each particular branch of
their commerce. In some occupations, foreign trade,
and its sequence, the foreign divisions of labour, will
augment the productiveness of industry more than in

E

others. When England gives France thick broad
cloth, in exchange for broad cloth of a lighter texture,
the benefit derived from the foreign divisions of employment which this intercourse establishes is very
trivial. For, in these divisions of employment, the
direction of capital and the habits of the workmen
are so similar, that, without much loss or inconvenience, they may be transferred from the one to
the other. The capital and labour which we employ
in manufacturing thick broad cloth might, with ease,
be directed to the fabricating of light cloth ; with
equal facility, the labour and capital that France
employs on light cloth might be directed to the
production of a cloth more substantial. If the foreign
division of labour, established by this exchange of
woollens, augments the productiveness of industry by
three per cent., it is, I think, as much as it possibly
can do. But of far greater magnitude is the benefit
derived from some other branches of our foreign
trade. When England works a thousand pounds'
worth of tin beyond what is necessary for her own
consumption, and gives it in exchange for wine, she
obtains a greater quantity of wine by a hundred per
cent. than if she employed the labour and capital
which procured the tin to cultivate the grape at
home. Every branch of commerce which thus enables us to establish the foreign territorial division
of labour, and to co-operate with the processes of
nature, is not, indeed, so greatly beneficial as that
which we have mentioned. And as the habits of
workmen are more mutable than the operations of
nature, the commerce which establishes the foreign
mechanical division of labour is not so advantageous

as that which establishes the territorial. Taking,
therefore, one branch of commerce with another, I
think that in those divisions of labour which it
enables us to establish, it cannot add much more
than twenty per cent. to the productiveness of industry. Let us, then, in order to form some rude
estimate of the benefit which England derives from
foreign trade, assume that by her foreign divisions of
labour she gains twenty per cent.

In the most favourable years, England exchanges
with foreign nations articles to the amount of fifty
millions. If on these exchanges she makes, in consequence of the divisions of labour which they
enable her to establish, twenty per cent., then, in the
most favourable years, she will derive from her
commerce an accession of wealth amounting to ten
millions. This is, indeed, a considerable sum. But
as Mr. Spence justly observes, when compared with
the public and private revenue of the country, it will
appear perfectly insignificant, and the trade from
which it springs in no degree entitled to rank as the
chief source of our wealth. For as this island contains twelve millions of inhabitants, and as each
person, on the average, consumes food to the amount
of at least ten pounds, we must derive from the
soil, in the mere article of provisions, a gross yearly
revenue of one hundred and twenty millions. Again,
as each inhabitant of this island must, on the average,
consume annually, clothing, furniture, &c., &c., to the
amount of at least ten pounds, we must, from some
source or other, derive, in these articles, another
yearly revenue of one hundred and twenty millions.
But again, there is, in this island, a vast floating

capital, or articles of wealth which are not consumed within the year. There is also a vast fixed capital vested in the various contrivances by which we abridge our labour. These capitals we may safely estimate at sixty millions. Thus we see that the wealth of England, in food and manufactured articles annually consumed, in capital floating and fixed, amounts, in any given year, to three hundred millions. Of this enormous sum ten millions are derived from commerce. Of that wealth, which renders us the wonder and the envy of the world, one-thirtieth part arises from sources which the caprice or enmity of strangers can destroy. However I may differ with Mr. Spence and Mr. Cobbett * on subjects of political economy, yet I honour them for being the foremost to controvert the degrading opinion that England's greatness depends on anything which foreigners can grant or take away. The dignified and independent way of thinking which they have contributed to diffuse, cannot fail of producing beneficial consequences.

But though it is highly desirable that the people should, at the present momentous crisis, have a just confidence in the strength and innate resources of this great empire, yet to inflate them with false hopes might produce the most fatal effects : for disappointed hope conducts us to despair, and they who have been unduly sanguine are the most likely to despond. It must not be concealed, that the evils arising from an interruption of commerce might extend beyond the destruction of the wealth which that commerce be-

* See Note c (at the end).

stowed. Mr. Arthur Young, in a letter published
in Mr. Cobbett's ' Political Register' of the 20th of
February, gives an alarming picture of the pressure
which, in the American war, accompanied an interruption of our commerce. I shall here endeavour to
trace the manner in which a diminution of our exports
produces, in addition to the loss occasioned by the
interruption of the foreign divisions of labour, that
indirect embarrassment which Mr. Young has described.

Let us suppose a country, the population of which
consists of a class of land proprietors, a class of merchants, a class of manufacturers, and a class of farmers.
In this state of society the land proprietor, when he
has obtained a sufficiency of home productions, would
give his surplus rent to the merchant, in exchange for
foreign articles; this surplus rent the merchant would
give to the manufacturer, who prepared the commodities which purchased the foreign articles; the manufacturer would exchange it with the farmer for provisions, and the farmer would again pay it to the
land proprietor. Thus wealth would circulate freely,
and animate every member of the community. Now,
if any circumstance occurred to prevent the merchant's
obtaining foreign articles, it is plain that he could no
longer draw to himself any portion of the land proprietor's rent, and no longer be able to take off from
the manufacturer the commodities which were formerly exported. The manufacturer, being thus
thrown out of employ, would cease to have so large
an effectual demand for provisions; and this diminution of demand would reduce the value of the farmer's

produce; he would no longer be able to pay his rent
to the land proprietor.   An universal stagnation would
take place similar to that which Mr. Young describes.
In vain, then, may Mr. Spence, as a remedy for the
evils arising from an interruption of trade, exhort the
land proprietors to expend, in home-made luxuries,
that income which they formerly expended in foreign
luxuries.   For while the land proprietor is acquiring
new wants, and the manufacturer learning to supply
them, a diminution takes place in the effectual demand for provisions; the value of the farmer's produce
is reduced, and the income that should purchase the
home-made luxuries ceases to exist.   However, it
appears to me that the evils which arise, indirectly,
from the interruption of foreign trade, may be re-
medied in a very considerable degree.   We have
seen that it is the diminution which takes place in
the value of the farmer's produce that reduces the
land proprietor's income, and prevents his having an
effectual demand for home-made luxuries, instead of
the foreign ones which he formerly enjoyed.   If,
therefore, the value of the farmer's produce could,
for a little time, be kept up, the land proprietor's
income suffering no diminution, he would soon acquire new desires and give employment to the manufacturer; and the manufacturer, again rendered an
effectual demander of provisions, would enable the
farmer to pay his accustomed rent.   No stagnation
or distress would be felt, except what might arise
from the loss of the wealth which was formerly
created by the foreign divisions of labour.   Now
there are two circumstances which may keep up the

value of the farmer's produce, namely, the accumulation of capital and the interference of the Government. Before I conclude this chapter, I will notice, briefly, the way in which these two circumstances produce the effect I have mentioned.

If the farmers and factors could, in consequence of their great accumulation of floating capital, keep up the produce of the earth, and diminish the supply in proportion to the diminution which took place in the effectual demand, then it is obvious that produce would suffer no depreciation; the farmer's corn possessing the same exchangeable value as formerly, he could pay the same rent to the land proprietor; while the land proprietor, receiving the same income, could spend on home-made luxuries all that he before expended on foreign ones: thus the manufacturers, again employed, would again become effectual demanders of provisions, and carry off the produce which the diminished consumption had left on the farmers' hands. Everything would go on in its proper train. It must be confessed, however, that the operation of floating capital here described, implies an understanding and intimate combination amongst the capitalists which, in countries where trade is left free, can scarcely ever take place; and even should the necessary combination take place, though an effectual, yet would it prove a severe and violent remedy: for by keeping up the price of subsistence, at a time when the price of labour was reduced, it would, for the moment, add to the manufacturer's distress. But, fortunately, there is another operation of floating capital equally efficacious in obviating the embarrassment incident to the interruption of commerce, and, at the same time, more

certain and less violent.   When the farmers have accumulated considerable capitals, they are not dependent
on the sale of a single crop for the means of paying
their rent; consequently, the interruption of commerce
which reduces the price of their produce, cannot effect
any immediate diminution in the revenue of the land
proprietor.   But if the revenue of the land proprietor
suffers no immediate diminution, the sums which he
formerly laid out on foreign commodities will not lie
idle in his coffers.   The love of distinction and display,
which, before the interruption of commerce, prompted
him to cover his table with costly wines, will now
prompt him to some other mode of expenditure.   The
unemployed manufacturers will soon be called upon,
either to fabricate new articles of decoration or to
give superior beauty to the old.   They will again become effectual demanders of provisions; the farmer's
produce will recover its value, and the land proprietor's
revenue, not having suffered on the first check given
to industry, will no longer be in danger of diminution.
The only injury inflicted by a loss of commerce will
be, our possessing a smaller quantity of those articles
which are augmented by the foreign divisions of labour.
Thus we see the great advantage that arises to a
nation from her farmers being opulent.*   During the
last twenty years the farmers of England have accumulated considerable capitals.   From this circumstance
I think we may predict, that the present interruption
of our commerce will not produce so much distress as
was produced during the American war, by an interruption less expensive.

* See Appendix.

But an abundance of capital is not the only means by which the price of provisions may be kept up. Knowledge is power. This maxim is applicable to the science of human nature, as well as to the science that relates to the material world. In each, when we have ascertained the chain of causes and effects, we can, to a certain degree, regulate the succession of events. In countries where the important truths of political economy are understood, Government may, in a great measure, obviate the indirect distress which an interruption of commerce occasions. For, by affording a regulated and temporary relief to the unemployed manufacturer, it may render him an effectual demander of provision, and thus prevent the diminution of the revenue of the land proprietor, until he acquires new desires, the gratification of which shall create a new demand for labour. As soon as the new demand for labour has been created, things go on in their proper train, and the interference of Government should be withdrawn, because it is no longer useful.*

These considerations suggest an observation on the poor-laws. The poor-laws check individual exertion, and thus create the distress they are established to relieve. Perhaps their chief advantage is the following: On sudden interruptions of trade, by affording relief to the manufacturer, they keep up, in a great degree, the effectual demand for the farmer's produce, and thus render temporary that want of employment which, if the land proprietor's revenue suffered diminution, must necessarily be lasting.

* See Note D (at the end).

But Government may exert its influence in a manner more beneficial than that which has been here described. If there are any restraints on agriculture, any restraints that retard a more perfect establishment of the domestic and colonial divisions of labour, the abolition of these would perhaps augment our wealth in a greater proportion than a total interruption of foreign trade could diminish it.

APPENDIX:

ON THE

POLICY OF PROHIBITING CORN

IN THE

DISTILLERIES.

IT appears to the writer of the foregoing inquiry, that the observations which it contains, respecting the benefit resulting to a nation from the opulence of her farmers, are calculated to draw a lively and general attention 'to every measure in which the farmers' interest is involved. He, therefore, proceeds to examine the propriety of a legislative interference with the consumption of corn in the distilleries.

If there is, in the science of political economy, any general principle to which every mind that reflects upon the subject is compelled to assent, it is—that demand regulates supply. But, though demand always regulates supply, yet it does not, in every instance, regulate it with the same exactness. Thus, while our coal and tin mines continue unexhausted, the supply of coal and of tin will be measured, with considerable accuracy, by the effectual demand. In particular districts, indeed, the quantity of these articles brought to market may, for a time, be diminished, in consequence of damaged roads, or of winds unfavourable to the coasting trade. But no general deficiency, no general superfluity can obtain ; supply will neither sink much below, nor rise much above, the effectual demand. With respect to other articles of our wealth, however, the case is widely different. Though the *demand* for corn should remain unaltered, yet, in the *supply*, great and general fluctuations may obtain ; in one year the farmer's produce may lie upon his hands unsold, and, in the next year, the country may be on the verge of famine.

The reason why demand does not regulate the supply of corn as accurately as it regulates the supply of the articles which we mentioned above, is very obvious. In obtaining tin and coals, the whole of the labour is performed by men, and men regulate their labour by the demand that rewards it ; but, in the production of corn, *nature* performs a part of the process, and, over this part, demand has no control. Though the demand for corn should remain the same, and though the farmer should, in consequence, bestow the same cultivation on his fields, yet a variety of circumstances which he cannot foresee, may, in one year, render his crop abundant, and, in another year, deficient.

The fluctuation which the varieties of season thus induce in the supply of corn, suggests one of the most interesting questions that occur in the science of political economy. The farmer will not cultivate to such an extent, that, in years of deficient crop, the supply will equal the demand ; for, if he did, then in abundant, and even in average years, the supply would exceed the demand, and the surplus perish on his hands. All that can be expected from him is, that he will regulate his cultivation by average years.

Now, if the farmers cultivate to such an extent, that, in average years, the supply will equal the demand, then in abundant years, the supply will exceed the demand, and, in deficient years, fall short of it. This being the case, to what cause is it owing that modern nations are, in a great degree, exempt from those alternate visitations of superfluity and famine which were incident to the earlier periods of the world? I will endeavour to give a solution of this highly-important question.

I believe it has been a generally-received opinion that commerce corrects the irregularity which fluctuating seasons occasion in the supply of food, and obviates, in modern nations, the alternate recurrence of superfluity and famine. When an abundant harvest has given any nation a supply of corn, more than sufficient to meet the home demand, the price becomes low, and individuals find an interest in carrying the superfluity to foreign markets. On the other hand, when a deficient crop has rendered the supply of corn inadequate to meet the wants of the inhabitants, the superfluity of other countries flows in and occupies the vacuity. To deny, therefore, that foreign trade has a tendency to correct the evils that arise from the irregular manner in which nature furnishes subsistence, would be to the last degree absurd. However, there are several considerations which induce me to believe that commerce is not the only, or even the chief, means of preventing in modern times the alternate visitation of superfluity and famine. For, in the first place, commerce can never strike at the root of the evil. As in England, there may this year be an abundant harvest, and next

year a deficient one; so, in the whole of Europe, the
quantity of corn produced in one season may be
greater or less than the quantity produced in another.
Nay, the quantity of human sustenance which can be
obtained from the habitable globe itself will fluctuate
from year to year. Now this is an evil which no
operation of commerce can correct. When one nation
has a superfluity of that which in another nation
is deficient, then commerce may remove the excess
of the former and supply the want of the latter.
But when the earth produces a greater quantity of
food than is necessary to meet the demands of her
population, commerce cannot convey the surplus to
" that undiscovered country from whose bourn no
" traveller returns." In years when the earth does
not yield a supply equal to meet the demand of her
inhabitance, commerce cannot voyage through the
attenuated ether and waft abundance from another
planet. Under these circumstances, therefore, all
that foreign trade can perform, though left perfectly
free, is to equalize the evil arising from irregularity
in the supply of food, and to prevent one nation from
suffering more severely than another. Here another
consideration suggests itself. Commerce has never
yet been left perfectly free. There is a perpetual
tendency on the part of governments to turn trade
aside from her natural channels. Therefore, whatever
advantage she bestows, this advantage must be precarious. The hostility of enemies, the schemes of
rivals, the errors of domestic legislation, may prevent
us, in years of abundance, from exporting our superfluity, and, in years of deficiency, from *importing* the
superfluity of other countries. To some cause, then,

more efficacious, more permanent in its operation than commerce, modern nations must be indebted for the prevention of that alternate recurrence of super-abundance and famine which was found so destructive in earlier periods. Distilleries, breweries, all things in fact which create a demand for corn beyond what is necessary to preserve us in a state of healthful existence, constitute this cause. Let us trace out the manner in which it produces its effects.

In countries which have no foreign trade, the farmers will cultivate to such an extent that, in average years, the supply of corn will equal the demand. Now if the people of these countries have a demand for corn-spirit, beer, and the refinements of cookery, then the farmer will cultivate to such an extent, that, in average years, the supply of corn will be more than sufficient to preserve them in a state of healthful existence. This being the case, a year of deficient crop may come without producing famine ; the corn which was raised to be consumed in the stilleries and breweries will flow in the bakers' shop and supply the wants of the people. The deficient crop will raise the price of bread, of corn-spirit, and of beer, but it will not raise the price of these commodities in the same proportion ; for, when the supply of any two articles is diminished, that which is most necessary will experience the greatest rise. The sensations of hunger being more powerful than the sensations which prompt us to use strong drink, the people, in a time of scarcity, will cease to consume strong drink in order that they may obtain a sufficient supply of food. For example, if each man in the community, after obtaining the necessary supply of

habitation .and clothing, has, on the average, ten
pounds to lay out on food and five pounds to expend
on corn-spirit and beer, then it is evident that a
deficient crop, which obliges him to give twelve
pounds for his food, will leave him but three pounds
to expend on drink. Thus every diminution in the
supply of corn must produce a diminution in the
demand for corn-spirit and for beer. But as the
demand for these articles is diminished, they will
cease to be prepared; when corn brings a higher
price in the form of bread than in the form of in-
toxicating liquors, it will flow from the stilleries and
breweries into the bakers' shop. Thus we see that
nations which have a large demand for the products
of malt, are far removed from the miseries of famine.
A much greater quantity of corn being raised than is
necessary to preserve the people in heathful existence,
a great quantity may, in years of deficient harvest, be
taken away without exposing them to absolute want.

The view of the subject which we have here taken
is calculated to make us view, with no common
anxiety and alarm, any tendency on the part of
Government to interfere with the distilleries. Even
in a period of absolute scarcity the utility of such
interference would be doubtful. For, in the first
place, it would, as to removing the scarcity, be
nearly nugatory. When the deficient supply of corn
obliged the people to appropriate a greater portion of
their incomes to the purchase of bread, they would
have less to expend on spirit. The demand for spirit
being thus diminished, corn would, without any
interference on the part of Government, cease, in a
great degree, to be consumed in the still. All, there-

fore, that the interference of Government could effect, would be to restrict the opulent who might still possess the means of purchasing corn-spirit form consuming in their drink the materials of human sustenance. But corn-spirit is rarely the beverage of the opulent, and even some of these who now use it would, from motives of humanity, renounce it in a year of scarcity. In a year of deficient harvest, the saving in the consumption of corn, which a legislative inference with the distilleries could effect, would be of very small amount; Government, therefore, may safely leave the distilleries to themselves. But the objections that may be urged against Government's interfering, even in times of scarcity, with the con-sumption of corn in the distilleries, are not all of this negative nature. For though such interference can compass little good, it may yet be efficacious in pro-ducing mischief. In years of scarcity the high price of bread imposes on the people the necessity of economical expenditure, and of a system of substitu-tion. This economical expenditure and system of substitution diminishes consumption and assists in enabling the supply to last throughout the year. Thus we see, that in years of actual scarcity, the consequent high price of corn corrects, to a certain extent, the evils of a deficient crop, limits the ex-penditure in such a manner as to prevent the supply from being prematurely consumed, and produces effects exactly similar to those which arise from the crew of a ship being, during a deficiency of provisions, put on a reduced allowance. From this it follows that anything which, in a year of scarcity, reduces the price of corn without effecting at the same time

F

a proportioned increase in the supply, must be productive of extensive mischief, must obviate the necessity of economy and substitution, and render the deficiency more alarming. It is to be apprehended that a restriction on the distilleries, if it had any effect, would reduce the price of corn without increasing the supply in the same proportion. Though the scarcity should have compelled the people to pay more for their bread, and left them less to bestow on drink, yet let us suppose that there is still a portion of corn consumed in the distilleries and that Government interferes to prevent its being so consumed. By this interference the corn which was kept up for the purpose of being converted into spirit will be thrown suddenly on the market. Some reduction in the price of corn will consequently take place; and this, by obviating to a certain extent the necessity of economy and substitution, will increase consumption. Now, by the supposition no supply of corn has been brought into the country to support this increased consumption. The increased consumption is supported by the corn which was before kept up for the purpose of being used in the stilleries, but a part of which, if increasing scarcity compelled the people to give still more for their food and left themselves still less to bestow on drink, would have assumed the form of bread, and perhaps have averted famine. Thus we see, that, throwing on the market a quantity of corn which was kept up to be used in the stilleries, has a very different effect from throwing on the markets an equal quantity of foreign corn. In the latter case, the increased supply of corn in the country would support the increased consumption consequent to the diminished price that would necessarily take place, and the relief enjoyed by the people would not be purchased at the risk of greater future evil But, in the former case, there is no increased quantity of corn in the country to support the increased consumption consequent to diminished price ; the temporary relief enjoyed by the people is obtained by breaking up the reserve against increasing want. But a legislative restriction on the stilleries, besides breaking up the reserve against increasing scarcity, might, perhaps, have a pernicious influence on future production; and thus render permanent the evil which it was intended to correct. Demand regulates supply, but does not, in every instance, regulate it with the same exactness. Though the demand for corn should remain the same for several years, and the farmer, consequently, bestow the same degree of tillage on his fields, yet his crop may be abundant in one year and deficient in another. However, these irregularities in the operations of nature have limits which they seldom pass. The farmer is able to calculate with considerable exactness the average favourableness of season, and so to proportion his cultivation that, one year with another, the price of corn will be sufficient to insure him an adequate reward. Now this being the case, will not a tendency on the part of Government to interfere, in any way, with the consumption of the farmers' produce, give rise to pernicious consequences? The farmer can, indeed, calculate with considerable exactness, the average fluctuations of *supply* arising from irregularity in the operations of nature, and measure his cultivation accordingly. But how can he, from any past experience, ascertain the fluctuations in *demand*, occasioned by the profligacy or the folly which may, from time to time, preside over the councils of the nation? How can he adjust his proceedings by the varying caprice of those who delight to "govern too much?" When he sees his profits interfered with by the state quackery of the ministers, is it to be expected that he will cultivate with the same ardour and perseverance as if his produce were left to find its level price?

Now, if prohibiting the distillation of corn, would, even in years of actual scarcity, be a measure of such doubtful utility, what opinion are we to form of the political wisdom of those who would prohibit its distillation in an average year? If in average years there is not a greater quantity of corn produced than is necessary to preserve the people in healthful existence, then it is evident that, in deficient years, the country will be exposed to the miseries of famine; but there is no possible means of inducing the farmers to produce a greater quantity of corn than is necessary to healthful existence, except by creating a demand for superfluity. Breweries, stilleries, and the refinements of cookery, create this demand. Prohibit corn in the breweries and stilleries, enact sumptuary laws to prevent its consumption in the shop of the pastrycook, and the farmer will have no inducement to produce, in average years, a greater quantity of corn than is necessary to subsist the people. Every year of deficient crop will, therefore, be a year of famine. The diminution in the supply will, indeed, compel the people to give more for their food, and leave them less to bestow on drink; but this diminished demand for drink will not, as formerly, disengage a quantity of corn, and cause it to assume the form of bread. The greatest advantage which modern nations have obtained over those of antiquity will thus be done away; we shall be visited, alternately, by the extremes of superfluity and famine.

Hitherto we have considered this important question in a general point of view; it remains to be ascertained, whether the general principles which we have endeavoured to unfold are applicable to the particular case, of a nation permanently importing corn, and then having that importation suddenly interrupted. ·

A country that in average years imports a part of her corn, in the event of this importation being suddenly cut off, may, if the people have a considerable demand for corn-spirit and for beer, make up the deficiency, by prohibiting corn in the stilleries and breweries. Thus supposing that, in average years, England imports 770,000 quarters of grain; it is evident, that in consequence of her large demand for the products of malt, she could, on the interruption of the foreign supply, make up the deficiency in the market by disengaging 770,000 quarters from the brewhouse and the still. Now whether she disengages 770,000 from the brewhouse and the still, or imports it from a foreign country, it is self-evident that the same proportion must exist between the demand and the supply, and, consequently, the price of corn remain unchanged. But if the price of corn remain unchanged, the people will be able to obtain the same quantity of bread as formerly. Let years of average crop continue, and the 770,000 quarters disengaged from the brewhouse and the still will occupy, pre-

cisely, the place of 770,000 quarters no longer imported: from interrupted importation no inconvenience can arise.   But, unfortunately, average years
cannot continue always.   Nature is, to a certain
degree, irregular in her operations; seasons of deficient crop will come.   In these seasons it will be
ascertained, that the general principles which we
have endeavoured to unfold, respecting the prohibition of corn in the stilleries and breweries apply,
with the greatest accuracy, to the particular case
of an importing nation having her importation suddenly suspended.   The deficient crop would raise
the price of bread, and, consequently, leave the
people less to bestow on drink.   But this diminished
demand for drink cannot, as formerly, throw a quantity of corn into the market, and cause it to be
converted into food.   For the reserve against want
will already have been trenched upon.   There will
no longer be a demand for a supply of corn beyond
what is necessary to preserve the people in healthful
existence.   Every deficient crop must, therefore,
produce famine.

The miseries which, on the recurrence of a deficient
year must result, necessarily, from our having supplied the loss of importation by disengaging corn from
the brewhouse and the still, demonstrate the necessity
of an extended cultivation.   To avoid famine in deficient years, it is necessary, that, in average years,
a greater quantity of corn should be procured than is
necessary to subsist the people.   A nation accustomed to procure a part of this quantity from foreign
countries, and having the foreign supply cut off, can
avoid the recurrence of famine only by extending her

cultivation, until, in average years, she raises, from
her own soil, more food than is necessary to subsist
her population. Now the interruption of the foreign
supply of corn has a tendency to extend cultivation
at home. A diminution of supply increases price,
and, as the price of corn increases, farming becomes a
more profitable concern. Now capital and labour
always seek the most profitable employment. As
the produce of the earth acquires additional value,
new lands will be enclosed, and superior cultivation
given to the old, until the deficiency, occasioned by
the interruption of the foreign supply, is replaced.
Thus we see, that the high price of corn arising from
suspended importation, is the cause that stimulates
to increased agricultural exertion, and renders a
nation independent of foreign supplies. If we take
away the cause, we take away the effect also. If, on
the interruption of our accustomed imports, we prevent the price of corn from rising, by disengaging it
from the brewhouse and the still, then the farmer will
have no motive for extended cultivation; in average
years we shall have no supply of corn beyond what is
necessary to subsist the population, and, in deficient
years, we shall be visited by famine. Thus do we
again arrive at our former conclusion, and ascertain,
that the general reasoning, which we employed on
the prohibition of corn in the stilleries, is strictly
applicable to the particular case, of a country accustomed to import a part of her corn and having
that importation interrupted. If a country accustomed to import a part of her corn should have that
importation interrupted during a year of deficient
crop, then the prohibiting of corn in the stilleries

and breweries would scarcely produce a perceptible
effect. For, in such circumstances, the deficiency
would be alarming; the people would be obliged
to give so much for their food, that they would have
little to bestow on drink; and thus the demand for
the products of malt ceasing almost entirely, nearly
the whole of the corn in the country would, without
any interference on the part of Government, assume
the form of food. But if an interruption of foreign
supply should take place in an abundant, or in an
average year, then the prohibiting of corn in the
stilleries and breweries would be productive of widely-
extensive consequences. In an average year, a restriction on the stilleries and breweries would throw
upon the market a supply of corn, equal to that which
an interruption of import would withhold. This
would prevent corn from experiencing a rise of price,
and take away the great motive that prompts to extended cultivation. Now as we have already seen,
if a nation acccustomed to import corn does not, on
the interruption of that import, extend her cultivation
until, in average years, she raises from her own soil a
greater quantity of food than is necessary to subsist
her population, then, on the recurrence of a deficient
harvest, she will be exposed to the miseries of want.
Thus, from whatever point we set out, we arrive at
the same conclusion, and discover, that when the
foreign supply of corn is cut off in an average year,
a restriction on the stillery and brewery, instead of
being a wise precaution against famine, checks extended cultivation, and renders the country unable
to feed her population in a year of deficient crop.

Having thus shown that our general reasonings,

on the subject of prohibiting the use of corn in the stilleries and breweries, are strictly applicable to the particular situation of a country, accustomed to import a part of her corn, and having that importation suddenly interrupted, it now remains that we obviate some popular objections.

It may be urged, " if it is necessary, in order to " avoid the miseries of casual scarcity, that a nation " should, in average years, raise a certain quantity " of corn to be consumed in superfluities, or, in other " words, to be thrown away, then it is full as well to " throw away sugar as corn." This objection would be of weight, if the sugar consumed in superfluities, or " thrown away," could, in a year of scarcity, be converted into food. But sugar, whatever nutritious properties it may possess, cannot be substituted for bread. If it were consumed in the stilleries instead of corn, the people would still be obliged, in a scarce year, to give more for their food, and less for their drink; but this diminished demand for drink could not, as formerly, disengage subsistence, and mitigate the general distress. The objection is sufficiently answered.

Again, " if there were 300,000 quarters of corn in " the West Indies, no one would object to their being " brought to England, in order to make up, in part, " the deficiency occasioned by the loss of the foreign " supply: but it is the same thing whether we import " 300,000 quarters of corn from the West Indies, or " bring thence a quantity of sugar, which will save " the consumption of 300,000 quarters. It is there- " fore inconsistent to object to the use of sugar in the " stilleries." This objection is no better than the

former. It is *not* the same thing whether we import
300,000 quarters of corn from the West Indies, or
bring thence a quantity of sugar which will save
300,000 quarters consumed in superfluities. In the
first case, if a scanty crop should increase the price of
necessaries, and diminish the demand for superfluities,
corn would be disengaged, and assume the form of
bread. In the second case, the diminished demand
for spirituous liquors, consequent to scarce years, will
disengage sugar, not corn, and, consequently, add
nothing to the supply of bread. With perfect con-
sistency, a man may acquiesce in the importation of
300,000 quarters of corn from the colonies, and yet
be hostile to any measure that would import a quantity of sugar, and substitute it for 300,000 quarters of
corn consumed in superfluities.

  " Whether we throw 300,000 quarters of corn on
" the market by disengaging it from the still, or by
" extending cultivation, the depression in its price
" must be the same; but if, in each circumstance, the
" price of corn be equally depressed, then, under each
" circumstance, the farmer will sustain the same in-
" jury; consequently, he who objects to the disen-
" gaging corn from the still, would, if he were con-
" sistent, object to extended cultivation." In this
objection there is some truth mixed with some error.
It is indisputable, that whether we throw 300,000
quarters of corn upon the market by disengaging it
from the stilleries, or by extending cultivation, the
depression in its price must be the same; but it by
no means follows that, in each case, the farmer would
sustain the same injury; for though in each, the *rate*
of profit on agricultural capital must be the same, yet

when 300,000 quarters of corn are obtained by extending cultivation, a greater capital is vested in agriculture, and the profit on this greater capital goes into the pocket of the farmer, and compensates, in part at least, for the diminished value of his produce : but when 300,000 quarters are obtained by restricting distillation, there is no increased capital employed, the profits of which may compensate for diminished price. This distinction deserves to be maturely weighed. Though the *rate* of profit on agricultural capital should remain the same, yet in one period the farmers may be distressed, and in another acquire fortunes. If the demand for corn be such, that every farmer in the country can on an average obtain 20 per cent. on a capital of 500*l.*, then every farmer may have an income of 100*l.* a-year; but if the demand for corn should become such that every farmer can on the average obtain 20 per cent. on a capital of 1500*l.*, then, though the rate of profit would be the same, yet the income of the farmer would be trebled. Thus we see, that in order to ascertain the effect of any measure, either in depressing or encouraging the farmer, we must estimate not only the rate of profit which it enables him to obtain, but the quantity of capital which it enables him to invest beneficially in agricultural pursuits. The retail dealer of an obscure village obtains a higher profit on the capital he employs than the merchant of the metropolis who embarks 100,000*l.* in commercial speculation, yet the dealer is in narrower circumstances, while the merchant enjoys all the refinements of European luxury. The friend to the agricultural interests will be more solicitous to increase the amount of the capital that may be bene-

ficially invested in cultivation, than to augment the
profits of that which is already so invested. An
increase in the value of produce, whether it arises
from an augmentation in the home demand, or from
an interruption of the foreign supply, is indeed that
which induces men to invest larger capitals in
agricultural pursuits. When these larger capitals
invested in agricultural pursuits, have increased the
supply until it meets the augmented demand, or
makes up the deficiency occasioned by interrupted
importation, then the value of produce will necessarily
sink to what it was before. But to say that this
reduction in the value of produce, occasioned by the
farmer's being able to invest, beneficially, a greater
capital in agricultural pursuits, can in any way be
injurious to the agricultural interests, is to assert a
contradiction. But even if it could be demonstrated
that obtaining 300,000 quarters of corn from extended
cultivation would be as injurious to the agricultural
interests as disengaging 300,000 quarters from the
still, yet it by no means follows that he who disap-
proves of a restriction on distillation, must, in order to
be consistent, disapprove likewise of extended cultivation. For though these two modes of lowering the
price of corn should inflict equal injury on the farmer,
yet they would not be equally injurious to the public.
Extended cultivation would leave our resources unimpaired ; but a restriction on the distillation of corn
breaks up one of the granaries which secure modern
nations against the alternate visitations of superfluity
and famine.

In a popular journal, Mr. Arthur Young and other
friends of agriculture, have been represented as hold-

ing opinions inconsistent and contradictory, because
at one time they expressed alarm at the foreign supply
of corn being cut off, and afterwards opposed the substitution of sugar in the stilleries. Juster views of
the science of political economy would have taught
the journalists alluded to, that the opinions of these
gentlemen, instead of being inconsistent and contradictory, have a necessary connexion with each other,
and are, in fact, parts of the same consentaneous
system. The alarm expressed by Mr. Arthur Young
and others at the prospect of our being suddenly deprived of the foreign supply of grain, was undoubtedly
well founded. Great Britain has imported annually
770,000 quarters of corn. The interruption of this
importation cannot, indeed, in an average year, be productive of any very serious distress. We have so large
a demand for spirits, beer, and other articles no ways
necessary to healthful existence, that the supply of
corn may be reduced 770,000 quarters without inducing want. This reduction in the supply would
indeed increase the price of food, and thus occasion
some inconvenience to the people; but, on the other
hand, the increased price of food would diminish the
demand for superfluities, would cause the corn to flow
from the brewhouse and the still, and prevent an
alarming deficiency of bread. Very different would
be the situation of the country if a deficient crop
should succeed the interruption of the foreign supply.
In this case, it is to be feared, that the deficiency
would be so great, that no quantity of corn which
could be withdrawn from superfluities, would be adequate to avert the miseries of famine. Hence every
enlightened friend of this country must participate in

Mr. Young's anxiety to have the agriculture of the United Kingdom extended, until we become, even in years of deficient crop, independent of supplies of foreign grain. But it is demonstrable, that to diminish the demand for corn, by preventing it from being consumed in the distilleries, is to discourage extended cultivation. If the interruption of the foreign supply should take place in an average year, and Government proceed to correct the deficiency by disengaging corn from the still, then the price of corn would not rise so high as it otherwise would rise, and the people would be relieved from a part of their embarrassment. But this relief would be obtained by " heaping up " wrath against the day of wrath:" for by keeping down the price of corn, Government would have taken from the inducement to extended cultivation. The diminution in the demand for the farmer's produce would prevent the agriculture of the country from being so improved as to replace the deficiency occasioned by the loss of the foreign supply. We snould be unprepared against the event of a deficient crop. Hence, he who is anxious that we should, even in deficient years, obtain from our own soil a sufficient quantity of food to subsist our population, will, if we understand the science of political economy, concur with Mr. Arthur Young in condemning any measure that diminishes the demand for corn.

In concluding this Appendix, it may not be improper to remark, that the accuracy of our conclusions can in no respect be influenced by our having, in some of our reasonings, treated the stilleries in conjunction with the breweries. For the general principle, respecting the advantage which a country derives from consuming in average years a greater quantity of corn than is necesssary to the healthful existence of her population, is equally applicable to both. In average years, it is necessary that we should have a demand for corn, in the form of drink, in order that we may in deficient years, have a sufficient quantity for bread. Every *increase* in the demand for corn beyond what is necessary to support life removes us, in years of deficient crop, a stage further from absolute want; every *diminution* in the demand for superfluous corn, whether occasioned by a restriction on the still or by a restriction on brewery, leaves us more at the mercy of the unequal seasons, and destroys a part of that resource which obviates, in modern nations, the frequent succession of superfluity and famine.

NOTES.

(A) While perusing the pamphlet, entitled, "Britain Independent of Commerce," I was more forcibly struck, than I ever before had been, with the truth of an observation of the celebrated Professor Stewart—that all the pursuits of life, whether they terminate in speculation or action, are connected with that general science which has the human mind for its object. Political economy is, in fact, a branch of the sciences of human nature; it is conversant with the *motives* which prompt men to the production, the accumulation, and the transfer of the articles which supply want and gratify desire. He who, in treating any of the topics it includes, confines himself to calculations on the value of exchanged commodities, may be a very correct arithmetician, but never can become a successful expounder of the theory of wealth. The "Wealth of Nations" was given to the world by the author of "The Theory of Moral Sentiments."

(B) To the disciples of Mr. Malthus, the picture which we have attempted to draw of the benefits to be derived from the accumulation of capital will appear too highly coloured. At present let it suffice to remark, that the conclusions contained in "The Essay on Population," are not conformable to experience. In Ireland, where the people are wretchedly poor, marriages are more frequent, and more early than in England, where the labouring classes enjoy such superior accommodation. Consequently, population has no necessary tendency to increase, in proportion to the increase which may be induced in the comforts and necessaries of life.

(c) In Mr. Cobbett's writings, we often meet with an uncommon sagacity and justness of remark. But it appears to this writer, that his mind is deficient in that enlarged comprehension which seizes a general principle, and traces it through a variety of inferences. Hence, his inconsistencies and want of system, and hence, we find him earnestly contending for contradictory conclusions. In his " Political Register," he frequently represents the taxes as being derived from the labour of the people. This is a position which it is impossible to refute. Let us mark the inferences to which it leads. If the taxes are derived from the labour of the people, then labour is a source of wealth. Now, if labour is a source of wealth, everything that adds to the productiveness of labour must be a means of augmenting wealth. But trade and commerce, by establishing divisions of labour, add to the productiveness of industry. Consequently, it is demonstrable, from Mr. Cobbett's own principle, that trade, both foreign and domestic, is a means of augmenting the wealth of a nation.

(D) The temporary interference here recommended, is essentially different from those permanent regulations which we have deprecated throughout this work. When Government exerts her authority on particular emergencies, she moves in her proper sphere ; when she attempts to disturb, by permanent institutions, the order of events which grows out of the system of the universe, perhaps it will be found that, in every conceivable instance, she produces mischief.

LONDON: PRINTED BY W. CLOWES AND SONS, STAMFORD STREET AND CHARING CROSS.